D1001186

AFRICAN HISTORICAL DICTIONARIES
Edited by Jon Woronoff

Historical Dictionary

of

SWAZILAND

by

John J. Grotpeter

African Historical Dictionaries, No. 3

The Scarecrow Press, Inc.

Metuchen, N. J.   1975

Library of Congress Cataloging in Publication Data

Grotpeter, John J
  Historical dictionary of Swaziland.

  (African historical dictionaries ; no. 3)
  Bibliography: p.
  1. Swaziland—Dictionaries and encyclopedias.
I. Title. ~~II. Series.~~
DT971.2.G76   968'.3'003   75-4734
ISBN 0-8108-0805-6

Manufactured in the United States of America

To the people of Swaziland, may this volume be of service.

To the writers on Swaziland who have preceded me and whose work has been of great assistance to me, especially, to J. S. M. Matsebula, The Hon. S. S. Nxumalo, Christian Potholm, and Hilda Kuper.

To my parents, Aurelia and Isadore John Grotpeter.
It is not possible to thank them enough.

EDITOR'S FOREWORD

The third volume in this series of African Historical Dictionaries is devoted to one of Africa's smaller countries, the Kingdom of Swaziland. But, rather than diminishing its importance, this "dictionary" shows the real value of the series. It not only has the most up-to-date information on Swaziland, it is also one of very few works about a country that was all too often lumped together in writings on the three High Commission Territories or inserted somewhere in volumes on its huge neighbor, South Africa. Here then, in one book, is a major compilation of facts on leading persons, places and events and, in the bibliography, pointers on where to find more.

Far from being an appendage to any other entity, Swaziland is a distinct state and, unlike many other emerging countries, a nation in its own right. Its history goes back well beyond the days when Europeans drew the boundaries and decided what its name should be. This is clearly shown in entries that trace this history as far back as records (sometimes oral tradition) permit, while also carrying it forward to the present day, one of crisis and change. Although the influences of the outside world, especially of Great Britain and South Africa, are clearly shown, they are seen primarily in their effects on Swaziland, while the more specifically Swazi elements are highlighted.

Of particular importance in this dictionary is that, as with its predecessors, it has been possible to bring together a vast collection of reference works in a bibliography such as has perhaps never before been compiled on Swaziland. This, we hope, will be one of its major aids to the student, the teacher, and the librarian, for whom this series was designed.

The author of this volume, Dr. John J. Grotpeter, is presently Professor of Political Science and Director of the Liberal Arts Division at the St. Louis College of Pharmacy and Lecturer in African Politics at St. Louis University.

v

Dr. Grotpeter's doctoral dissertation was directed to Political Leadership and Political Development in the High Commission Territories, which he visited in 1965 in order to interview many of the people mentioned in this book. These countries were also prominent in his more recent book, The Politics of African Decolonization: A New Interpretation. This dictionary illustrates his knowledge of one of them, Swaziland, as well as--and this can be sensed from the coherent and lively presentation--his attachment to this part of Africa.

Jon Woronoff,
Series Editor

CONTENTS

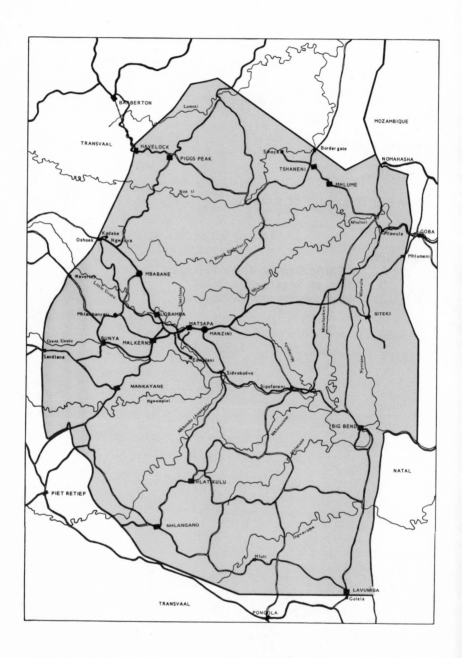

INTRODUCTION

Swaziland, a pleasant country with considerable future potential, presents to the observer an interesting study of contrasts. For example, it is one of the newest of the African states to emerge from colonial rule, yet it is currently governed by the longest reigning monarch in Africa, King Sobhuza II. Most of the inhabitants live a simple, agriculture-based life, yet the country is in the middle of an economic boom that promises to doom unemployment and the need to export labor to South Africa. It is a haven for South African liberals who feel the need for more freedom, yet the conservative ruling family will not tolerate anti-South African political activity. Rightfully proud of their traditional folklore, dancing and religious customs, especially the annual Ncwala ritual, the Swazis--and the numerous Whites living there-- also manage to patronize productions of old operettas such as The White Horse Inn or oratorios by Handel.

For five years the practitioners of British-style democracy, the Swazis, led by the elderly but vigorous Sobhuza II, cancelled the old Constitution in 1973 and appointed a Royal Constitutional Commission to develop a new one which would restore traditional leadership to its rightful place in the formal political structure of the country. Meanwhile, in contrast to the numerous African countries which have experienced military takeovers in recent years, the army-less Swaziland called upon a traditional means of providing a militia for the King, the emabutfo system, in order to lessen the possibility of disorder during this constitutional crisis.

Swaziland is not a very large country. Its area of 6,705 square miles makes it larger than Kuwait, smaller than the American state of Massachusetts, and about the same size as Wales. Its maximum length from north to south is 120 miles, and its maximum width from east to west is 90 miles. It is almost completely surrounded by two South African provinces, Transvaal and Natal, and at its nearest point is about 230 miles from Johannesburg. Sixty miles of its eastern border adjoins the Portuguese territory of Mozambique, and it is less than 100 miles from the attractive port city, Lourenço Marques. Several points of this oval-shaped country are within forty miles of the Indian Ocean.

The population of Swaziland is rapidly approaching half a million, of which about thirty thousand are not members of the Swazi nation. Over half of these are non-Swazi Africans (Zulu, Tonga, Shangaan); and there are about eight thousand people of European descent and about four thousand Eurafricans. Many of the non-Swazis consider themselves to be true citizens of the country, based on both long residency and identification with the people and the national leadership.

While a number of Bushmen, Nguni, and Sotho peoples have moved through parts of Swaziland in the course of centuries, the story of the country is primarily that of the Dlamini clan of the Nguni people. This clan, led by its founder, Dlamini, moved into southern Africa during the last part of the sixteenth century, settling south and west of what is now Delagoa Bay in Mozambique, east of Swaziland. They remained there almost two hundred years, until their leader, Ngwane III, brought them across the Lubombo Mountains into what is now Swaziland. Starting with Ngwane III in about 1750, the Swazis were fortunate to be led by four outstanding Ngwenyamas (Kings) in succession. Ngwane III died in 1780. His son, Ndvungunye, died in 1815. Ndvungunye's son, Sobhuza I, died in 1836. And Sobhuza's son, Mswati II, died in 1868.

This period of over a century of outstanding military and diplomatic leaders saw the Swazi nation become a major unit in southeastern Africa, dominating and controlling an area much larger than the territory of Swaziland today. Numerous clans and tribes, some of Sotho origin as well as other Nguni clans, were absorbed into the Swazi nation, some by conquest, some by coercion, and some by diplomacy and impressive leadership. This unification and expansion of the Swazi nation occurred partly in spite of and partly because of the military threats of such neighbors as the Zulus, the Ndwandwes, the Ndebeles, and the Bapedis. While the Swazi people still refer to themselves as Bantu baka Ngwane (the people of Ngwane) because of Ngwane III; the more common name, Swazi, is derived from the name of Mswati II.

The movement of people of European-descent into the territory of the Swazis began as early as the 1830's, but the

Swazis did not lose their first land to Europeans[1] until 1846
when some of the Afrikaners claimed that they had a treaty
with Mswati II which ceded them a large portion of the eastern Transvaal. Swazi denials were futile. Similar losses of
areas known as New Scotland and the Little Free State also
occurred. The most far-reaching losses of the Swazis occurred during the 1870's and the 1880's, however, during the
reign of a young king, Mbandzeni. The land problems of the
Swazis had three separate origins: 1) the expansion attempts
of the South African Republic (Transvaal) and its Afrikaner
farmers; 2) the discovery of gold in Swaziland and the search
for other valuable minerals; and 3) the inexperience of the
young Mbandzeni and his inability to handle the Europeans who
were flocking into the territory and who were often coming into conflict with each other. As a result, the King sold for
minimal payment land and mineral concessions to numerous
Europeans, thereby alienating the major portion of what is
today Swaziland. The Swazis claim that Mbandzeni made it
clear that he was only granting use of the territory, as he
could not, by Swazi custom, sell his people's land. Regardless, that was not the Europeans' interpretation of the transactions, and even today large portions of Swaziland are owned
by Europeans. Diplomatic negotiations and agreements among
the Portuguese, the British, and the South African Republic
during the 1860's, 1870's, and 1880's set the boundaries of
the territories adjacent to Swaziland, limiting its area even
more.

Despite British guarantees of Swazi independence, a
series of agreements between Great Britain and the South
African Republic in the 1890's resulted in the Swazi nation
falling under the civil administration of the Transvaal in 1895.
The beginning of the Anglo-Boer War several years later put
a quick end to that, but in 1903 Britain formally announced
that it was taking over the administration of Swaziland. In
1906 Swaziland was officially placed under the British High
Commissioner for South Africa, with a Resident Commissioner
located in Swaziland.

The next several years saw a continuing controversy
over the question of the ownership of the land of the Swazis.
The Land Partition Proclamation of 1907, an attempt by

---

1. The term European designates those people who are generally accepted to have stemmed ultimately from European ancestors, even if they have no current ties in Europe.

Britain to straighten out the confused land question, triggered
a series of Swazi protests that led ultimately to the Privy
Council in London in 1926. Dispossessed of 60 per cent of
their land by the 1907 Proclamation, the Swazis, led by their
young King, Sobhuza II, protested that their land had never
been transferred by acquiescence, annexation, force or cession to Britain, and thus Britain had no legal right to dis-
pose of it. Again, however, the British Government rejected
the Swazi plea.

Great Britain, once gaining a dominant position in
Swaziland, displayed a remarkable reluctance to perform more
than minimal administrative or economic functions there.
Authoritative native administration, court, and treasury proclamations were not promulgated until 1950. Some of Britain's
reluctance was due to the long-standing dispute over whether
or not Swaziland, Basutoland and Bechuanaland should be
transferred to the control of the Union of South Africa, which
had been attempting to get them for forty years. South African Government policy toward its own Africans confirmed
Britain's second thoughts, and the rise of the Nationalist
Party to power in 1948 with its apartheid policy convinced
Britain that transfer was not the answer.

In 1960 the first movements toward the reemergence
of Swazi independence began. Both King Sobhuza II and the
European Advisory Council made suggestions to Britain that
steps toward a modern self-government system should be
taken. The formation of the Swaziland Progressive Party
that same year was another sign of a Swazi political awaken-
ing. The next eight years saw a series of competitions for
influence among Swazi traditionalists, the European community in Swaziland, and the Swazi political parties. An early
coalition between the first two put the political parties at a
disadvantage, but the coalition broke up when the Swazi traditionalists created their own political party, the Imbokodvo
National Movement, and found that they needed no help from
anyone else.

Swaziland thus regained her independence on September
6, 1968. The country functioned under a Parliamentary system led by Prince Makhosini Dlamini, leader of the Imbokodvo National Movement. A former teacher, he is a member
of the royal clan of Swaziland and a nephew of King Sobhuza
II. Imbokodvo had remarkable success in the elections of
1964 and 1967, losing no seats in Parliament to Swazi political parties. In 1972, however, one tri-member constituency

sent three members of the Ngwane National Liberatory Congress, including its leader, Dr. Ambrose Zwane, to Parliament. This precipitated a series of reactions by both the Imbokodvo leaders and the King himself, especially concerning the eligibility of one of the three, B. T. Ngwenya, to run for office. When the courts ruled consistently against the Government's actions, King Sobhuza, in April 1973, suspended the Constitution, declaring it unsuitable. Later in the year he appointed a Royal Constitutional Commission which was to hear opinions around the nation and make recommendations for a new Constitution for the country, presumably (judging from the appointees) one that would be more responsive to the Swazi traditional leaders while retaining some aspects of modern political systems. Prince Makhosini has continued as leader of the Government during the interim, with decrees being issued by the King-in-Council. An interesting aspect of this constitutional crisis is that the King alerted the Swazi emabutfo to be prepared for military action in case violence should erupt during the period of constitutional crisis. This was to avoid the need for turning to Britain for troops, which would have been a considerable embarrassment. With the principal leader of the opposition, Dr. Zwane, under detention by the Government, however, no threats of organized disturbances have occurred.

   The economy of Swaziland has certainly been the most encouraging aspect of its development. Where gold was the first impetus to the country's development, its role is now minimal. The development of an iron ore industry in the 1960's brought the building of a railway that now cuts through Mozambique to the Indian Ocean. Iron exports now double asbestos exports in producing revenue for the country. The timber industry is also highly profitable, as are numerous agricultural schemes which produce major exports of cotton, sugar, and pineapples, among other items. If there is a real growth industry, however, it is the tourist industry. Numerous hotels have sprouted throughout the country and others are on the planning boards. It appears that Swaziland will continue to attract large numbers of southern Africans to its pleasant hills and valleys, adorned as they now are by casinos, swimming pools, night spots, health spas and even game reserves. All of this has freed the country and its leaders from dependence on Great Britain and, to some extent, from South Africa. Jobs for Swazis are developing and the country is in the middle of a program to diversify industry and employment even more.

The one thing Swaziland desperately wants to avoid is to antagonize the South African Government to the point where it might take actions which would damage Swaziland's economy. The story is told by a prominent observer of Southern Africa that he was conversing with King Sobhuza in the middle 1960's about the problem of South African political refugees and even guerrilla fighters using Swaziland as a base for operations. While Swaziland was not allowing this, there was considerable pressure from members of the Organization of African Unity that it should. Sobhuza, an aging but very astute politician, commented, "I feel like a man sitting in my home facing a poised snake. I am trying to be very calm and avoid sudden movement. Meanwhile my friends outside the door are throwing rocks at the snake. I am the one endangered, not they."

A special reason for the Swazis to want normal relations to continue with South Africa involves South Africa's own special problem of Bantustans or native homelands. Several times in recent years there have been indications that South Africa might allow parts of South African territory with large numbers of Swazi inhabitants to become part of Swaziland. Likewise, Swazis are enthusiastic about the emerging status of the kwaZulu homeland under Chief Gatsha Buthelezi potentially providing another outlet to the Ocean. These considerations among others have encouraged the Swazis to be very circumspect about their relations with South Africa.

ABERCORN. A Swazi community on the eastern border with
Mozambique at the gorge where the Usutu River cuts
through the Lubombo mountains. It was named after
the Duke of Abercorn who became Chairman of the British South Africa Company upon its foundation in 1888.

AERS, IAN. Speaker of the Swaziland House of Assembly until 1973. He was born in India, attended Dulwich College in England, and was commissioned from Sandhurst.
After service in World War II, he joined the Tanganyika
Administrative Service, where he served from 1948 to
1963. In 1964 he became Clerk to the first Legislative
Council in Swaziland and in 1965 served as Acting
Speaker. That same year he was appointed Director
of Broadcasting, which he then began in Swaziland.
He continued in that post when he was elected Speaker
of the House in 1968.

AFRICAN LABOUR PROCLAMATION. A law of Swaziland
strictly regulating the recruiting of laborers for work
outside the country. Contracts may not exceed one
year (with a nine-month renewal), and normally range
from three to nine months. The Proclamation also re-
stricts the number of recruiting licenses issued and
such licenses are issued only when the Government is
satisfied that employment conditions are satisfactory.

AFRICAN METHODIST EPISCOPAL CHURCH (AME). Founded in the United States by its first bishop, Richard Allen, this church has numerous adherents throughout
Africa, thousands in Swaziland. It first began work in
Swaziland in 1894, and one source reports that by 1938
it had 215 ordained non-European ministers, 279 places
of worship, and thirty-five thousand members. It also
sponsors educational institutions. The Swaziland AME
is amalgamated with the AME in the United States. Its
doctrine is not much different from that of any other
Methodist church.

AFRICAN NATIONAL CONGRESS (ANC). A political organization founded in 1912 by South African Blacks. It became especially active in the decade or more after the
Second World War, until the organization was banned
in 1960. Swazis became active in the ANC while living
or working in South Africa and turned their political
knowledge against the colonial rule of Great Britain.
Some members of the Swaziland Progressive Party had
especially close ties with the ANC. After the shooting
at Sharpeville, South Africa, in March, 1960, quite a
number of ANC refugees came to Swaziland to stay for
varying periods. They included Jordan Ngubane, Macdonald Maseko, Dennis Brutus, Peter Yenga, Dr. Con-
co, and many others.

AFRIKAANS. One of the two official languages of South
Africa and originally the language developed by the
South Africans of Dutch ancestry. Since many of the
early white settlers in Swaziland spoke Afrikaans, and
because of its importance in South Africa, many Swazis
have learned the language at least to some extent. The
most prominent of Swazi place names in Afrikaans was
Bremersdorp, the old name for Manzini.

AGE GROUPINGS. The Swazi distinguish eight different
stages in the life of an individual from birth to "almost
an ancestor." A separate term fits each stage. Nevertheless, the phrase "age groupings" would normally
have more significance in reference to the regimental
age classes, the emabutfo (singular: libutfo, q.v.).

ALLEYNE COMMISSION. A three-man Royal Commission
appointed early in 1880 by Sir Garnet Wolseley to decide on the boundaries between Swazi territory and the
Transvaal. Led by Major James Alleyne, it also included Gerhardus Rudolph and Lieutenant Rudolph Little-
dale. When their report was finished and approved at
the end of March, 1880, large areas of Swazi territory
were lost, including areas around Komatipoort, Carolina, and Barberton, and the whole Mbhuleni valley.

ALLIANCE OF POLITICAL ORGANIZATIONS (also CONSTI-
TUTIONAL ALLIANCE OF SWAZILAND POLITICAL
ORGANIZATIONS). An ad hoc arrangement between
some of the participants in the London Constitutional
Conference of 1963. It was formed on January 5 at
the conference by Simon Nxumalo of the SDP and Dr.

A. Zwane of the SPP as a result of Nxumalo's appeal
for unity of the party leaders against the traditionalist
and European forces. J. J. Nquku failed to join, but
Dr. Msibi of the Mbandzeni National Convention Party,
A. Sellstroom of the Eurafrican Welfare Association,
and Dr. David Hynd, an independent delegate, joined at
least in spirit, along with Dr. Allen Nxumalo (later of
the SDP) who defected from the traditionalists at the
conference. This alliance rejected the proposals of the
traditionalists and the Europeans, proposing instead a
one-man, one-vote franchise, non-racial, with the
Ngwenyama to be a constitutional monarch. It wanted
him as Head of State, relatively detached from politics.
This Alliance, led by Simon Nxumalo, convinced the
British that there was a hopeless deadlock among the
Swazis. The British eventually imposed their own constitutional plan. The Alliance fell apart when the
party leaders returned home, despite superficial
attempts to keep it alive as an "Alliance of Swaziland
Progressive Parties" during the 1964 elections which
they contested against one another. Eventually it developed into the Joint Council of Swaziland Political
Parties (q. v.) under Obed Mabuza.

ALLISON, REV. JAMES. The founder and leader of a Wesleyan Church mission at Mahamba. It began when a
Wesleyan missionary conference at Grahamstown, South
Africa, accepted King Mswati's request in 1844 to send
missionaries to Swaziland. Rev. Allison and Rev.
Richard Giddy were sent with two Basotho evangelists
from a mission near the Caledon River considerably to
the West. The two missionaries returned to the Caledon
River mission briefly and Rev. Allison returned in 1845
with his wife and Rev. John Bertram and twelve evangelists. The Mission at Mahamba was successful until
an attack on it due to an internal Swazi argument. (See
MALAMBULE.) The attackers specifically spared the
missionaries. Nevertheless, Rev. Allison, his co-
workers, and about 800 Swazi fled the country. They
moved to the Pietermaritzburg area where he founded
the Edendale Mission.

AMANGWANE. Like Amaswazi, a term used to describe the
entire Swazi nation.

AMERY, RT. HON. L. S. Great Britain's Colonial Secretary
from November, 1924, and also Secretary of State for

Dominion Affairs from July, 1925, until leaving both posts in June, 1929. One of the few London administrators to take an active interest in Swaziland, his visit in 1927 spurred the development of the country with British aid. While official policy was still that the High Commission Territories would eventually be transferred to South Africa, with Swaziland probably the first, Amery wanted to discourage General Hertzog from applying for any of them. Along with Capt. Clifford, Amery felt that an infusion of money into Swaziland would be very beneficial, regardless of its future. He regretted that they had been treated as "museum pieces" by Britain until then. He also hoped that Britons could be encouraged to settle in Swaziland to make it "effectively British" before transfer to South Africa occurred. Amery's visit with Hertzog in South Africa in 1927 resulted in postponing the possible transfer for at least five years, as Amery feared Afrikaner nationalism and its possible effect on Swaziland. Among other good effects of Amery's visit were: the institution in 1928 of parliamentary grants-in-aid to cover budget deficits, the establishment of a Land and Agricultural Loan Fund in 1929, and an inquiry into the financial and economic situation of Swaziland by Sir Alan Pim in 1931.

AMSTERDAM. A town of about 2,500 inhabitants in the eastern Transvaal, twelve miles west of the Swaziland border at Sandlane. The area attracts some Swazi workers. The town was founded in 1867 as Roburnia (after Robert Burns) by Alexander McCorkindale who hoped to attract Scots to settle in this "New Scotland" area. The scheme failed.

ANGLICAN CHURCH. One of the significant religious denominations in Swaziland, with a membership of 5,200 in 1962. Of these, 3,600 were Africans, 1,300 Europeans, and 300 Eurafricans. It sponsors some educational institutions in Swaziland, including St. Christopher's High School.

ANGLO-AMERICAN CORPORATION OF SOUTH AFRICA. The South African mining corporation established by Sir Ernest Oppenheimer in 1917. Its principal project at present in Swaziland is the production of iron at Ngwenya through its subsidiary, the Swaziland Iron Ore Development Co. Ltd. It has other investments as well, including coal mining. A non-profit one was the

purchase and donations of 350 acres to extend the
Milwane Game Sanctuary.

ANGLO-BOER WAR (also: SOUTH AFRICAN WAR). A war
between the two major European groups in South Africa,
it began on October 11, 1899, and finally was termi-
nated on May 31, 1902. The immediate effect of the
War on Swaziland was that most Europeans left the
country, leaving government again in the hands of the
Swazi King. Very little of the war occurred within
Swaziland and the Swazis did not take sides. A successful attempt to blow up the bridge at Komatipoort
brought fame to Ludwig Steinacher working for the British. This led to some combat with Boer troops at
Bremersdorp and the destruction of that city by fire.
Another incident near the end of the War involved a
small force under long-time inhabitant, David Forbes,
which captured a commando of Boers stationed in southern Swaziland. Perhaps most important, the British
victory in the War meant that Swaziland did not return
to Boer rule and, over sixty years later, won its independence from Britain.

ARDEN-CLARKE, SIR CHARLES. British civil servant who
served as Resident Commissioner in Bechuanaland from
1936 to 1942, when he became Resident Commissioner
in Basutoland. In September, 1961, Sir Charles was
sent by the British Secretary of State for the Colonies,
Reginald Maudling, to assist the committee in Swaziland
charged with the duty of framing constitutional proposals.
The committee's report displayed none of the experience
or advice of Sir Charles, however, and in fact he submitted his own report to London separately.

ASBESTOS. One of the major exports of the country, asbestos exports totaled 6, 046, 000 Rand in 1968. The
main producer is the Havelock Asbestos Mine. From
1939 to about 1960 this was almost the only major industry of the country. While asbestos was first noticed
along the banks of Dudusi Creek in the beginning of the
20th century, its modern exploitation began only after
Mr. I. Holthausen of Barberton rediscovered the deposit
in 1918.

ASSEGAI. The word for "spear" among several Southern
African ethnic groups. There are two kinds, the throwing assegai, and the newer type, a stabbing assegai re-

portedly developed by the great Zulu leader Chaka. The
business end of the Swazi assegai sometimes had a
broader but shorter head than those of most other
groups.

ASSEGAI RIVER. Another name for the Mkhondo River.

ATHLONE, EARL OF (ALEXANDER A. F. CAMBRIDGE).
Governor-General of South Africa and High Commissioner from January 21, 1924, to December 21, 1930.
Upholding the British position while High Commissioner,
he insisted that the three territories would not be transferred to South Africa without their approval and firm
guarantees of their future rights. Athlone agreed with
L. S. Amery that some settlement of British people in
Swaziland might be desirable.

ATTORNEY-GENERAL. The principal legal adviser to the
Government under the 1967 and Independence Constitutions. He was also an ex-officio member of the House
of Assembly. He had responsibility for handling all
criminal proceedings in the courts of Swaziland for the
Government, and had to intervene in private prosecu-
tions. His duties also included establishment of pro-
cedures for judging the right to be a Member of Parliament or a presiding officer of either House. The
Attorney-General was appointed by the Judicial Service
Commission and must have been either qualified to be
appointed a judge of the High Court or have practiced
law in Swaziland for at least ten years.

-B-

BADEN-POWELL, LORD ROBERT STEPHENSON SMYTH.
British soldier born in England, February 22, 1857. He
was a member of the Joint Commission (q. v.) appointed
by Great Britain and the South African Republic to visit
Swaziland in 1889. During his visit he made a study of
the Swazi emabutfo, and he is said to have used this as
the basis on which his Boy Scout movement was founded
in 1908. He died in 1941.

BALEGANE. A community in north-central Swaziland, just
south of the Komati River. It is in a good cotton-producing area.

BANTFANENKOSI.   Variant spelling of Bantfwabenkosi.
(plural of Mtfanenkosi, q. v.)

BANTU.   A broad classification of African peoples based on
some common linguistic patterns.   The classification
includes the Swazis along with the vast majority of the
peoples of central and southern Africa, excluding especially the Bushmen, Hottentots, and Bergdama.   There
are well over two hundred different Bantu languages, but
there are enough internal similarities to cause anthro-
pologists to link the users of the languages in a
"family. "   The word "Bantu" or a variation of it means
"man" in many of the languages.   Bantu is also a preferred word by the Government of the Republic of South
Africa to generalize about the indigenous inhabitants.

BANTU BAKA NGWANE.   Variant spelling of Bantfu Ba Kwa
Ngwane and Ebantfu Ba Kwa Ngwane.   "People of
Ngwane, " a term used by Swazis to refer to all Swazis ·
collectively.   It contributes to the sense of national
unity and distinguishes them from other southeastern
African national groups.   Ngwane in this context refers
specifically to Ngwane II, the first king commemorated
in current Swazi ritual.

BAPEDI (also: PEDI).   A Sotho group living in the northern
and eastern Transvaal.   There are about 750, 000 in the
Republic of South Africa today.   Under Sekwate they re-
covered from near devastation at the hands of Mzilikazi,
the Ndebele leader.   However, Sekwate and his people
were constantly embattled by Swazi King Mswati's forces.
Eventually, Sekwate was forced to acknowledge Mswati's
leadership.   The Bapedi continued to resist, however,
and Swazi raids were required as well as outposts north
and west of today's Swaziland.   However, the Swazi
under Mbandzeni were defeated by the Bapedi under
Sekhukhune at Mosega Kop.   They got revenge in 1879
when the British administrators Sir Evelyn Wood and
Sir Garnet Wolseley persuaded King Mbandzeni to form
an impi to join the British against Sekhukhune.   In the
battle that followed, Sekhukhune was defeated and captured but the Swazi suffered 500 casualties.   The Bapedi
cattle were given to the Swazis by Wolseley.

BARBERTON.   A South African town of over twelve thousand
located about twelve miles north of Havelock, Swaziland.
It is linked with the Havelock Asbestos Mine by a

cableway that carries asbestos down from the mountains. Barberton became important during the 1880's
as a center of the De Kaap gold fields. The bubble
burst quickly. Today it is an agricultural center. The
land in the Barberton area formerly belonged to the
Swazis. It was the location of several outposts put up
by Mswati II in his conflicts with the Bapedi.

BARCLAY'S BANK. One of the three main banking institutions in Swaziland, it is incorporated in the United Kingdom but has branches throughout many of the former
British territories. In Swaziland it has branches at
Mbabane, Manzini, Nhlangano, Big Bend, Tshaneni and
Havelock, and it has over ten agencies in other parts
of the country.

BARING, SIR EVELYN (LORD HOWICK OF GLENDALE).
British administrator who served from October 27,
1944, to October 1, 1951, as High Commissioner for
the United Kingdom in South Africa and Administrator
of the High Commission Territories. While High Commissioner he steadfastly opposed the transfer of the
High Commission Territories to South Africa, which, he
felt, would "sacrifice the true interests of the Africans. " On the other hand, Britain could only justify
retention of the three Territories if it would greatly
improve agricultural, health, and educational services.
He served from 1961 until June 30, 1972, as Chairman
of the Colonial (Commonwealth) Development Corporation. He died in March, 1973.

BASUTO. Also known as the Southern Sotho (or Sutu), this
nation of about one million dwells for the most part in
the southern African country called Lesotho (or Basutoland before independence). The Basuto became a unit
as a result of the leadership of their first paramount
chief, Moshoeshoe (variant spelling of Moshesh), who
unified many thousands of people, especially from the
Koena clan of Sutu. They were all fleeing from Chaka
and the Zulus in the 1820's. This unit grew in number, went through numerous military and diplomatic in-
teractions with both Boer and Britain before Basutoland
became, along with Swaziland and Bechuanaland, one of
the High Commission Territories. Early in the history
of the Swazis, there was considerable interaction with
Sutu people, some of whom became the Bapedi and some
undoubtedly became part of the Basuto. Some of the

first Christian evangelists in Swaziland were Basuto,
coming with Rev. James Allison.

BATSAKATSI (Plural of UMSTAKATSI, q. v.).

BATTLE AT ANZIO. World War II battle in which the
    Swazis led the landing on the beach on January 21, 1944.
    Their job was to throw smokescreens to provide cover
    for the landing of the Allied Forces. Thus this group
    of Swazi soldiers, the "91" company (actually, 1991),
    was nicknamed the "Smoke Company. " Its leaders were
    Mfundza Sukati, who was appointed senior indvuna of the
    impi, Prince Dabede, and Joseph Mkhwanazi.

BATTLE OF LUBUYA. A battle against a Zulu impi sent out
    by Zulu King Mpande in 1854. Not far from Hlatikulu
    is a small river, the Lubuya. The Zulu and Swazi
    impis clashed here, the Zulus under Masiphula Sibiya
    and the Swazis led by Mngayi Fakudze. The battle
    lasted the entire day and casualties were heavy on both
    sides. The next morning the Zulu impi was gone. This
    was the last battle the Swazis fought inside their
    country.

BATTLE OF MOSEGA KOP. Of uncertain date but prior to
    1875, this battle was against the Bapedi of Sekhukhune
    (q. v.). A Swazi impi tried to follow a number of Swazi
    refugees who had sought asylum under Sekhukhune earl-
    ier. The Swazi impi got as far as Mosega Kop in the
    Transvaal where they were soundly defeated. A num-
    ber of Swazi princes died during this battle, but Matsa-
    feni Mdluli, who was feared lost, returned home six
    months later.

BATTLE AT SEKHUKHUNE'S STRONGHOLD. On the request
    of Sir Evelyn Wood and Sir Garnet Wolseley, the Swazis
    supplied an impi of eight thousand men to fight the
    Bapedi under Chief Sekhukhune in November, 1879. They
    attacked Sekhukhune's stronghold at dawn on the morn-
    ing of November 28. A main column of several thou-
    sand Europeans and about the same number of Africans
    attacked from the front, while the Swazis plus less than
    a thousand Europeans and other Africans attacked from
    the rear (actually, from high up the mountain). The
    Swazi impi was under the command of Mbovane Fakudze
    (q. v.) and consisted of King Mbandzeni's libutfo plus
    several complementary regiments. Most of the battle

was over that day, with about five hundred Swazis and
forty-two Europeans dead or wounded.   Sekhukhune himself got away but he was quickly hunted down and captured.   This was on December 2, 1879.   As a reward
for the aid of the Swazis, Sir Garnet Wolseley awarded
Mbandzeni most of the captured cattle and promised
that the independence of the Swazis would be assured
forever!

BAYETHE (variant spelling of BYETA).   A Swazi Royal
        salute; a word used in a variety of contexts, but always
        as a way of addressing with honor the King.   Roughly
        translated as "Hail."

"BEEHIVE" HUTS.   The traditional homes of the Swazi which
        resemble somewhat the shape of a beehive.   It is said
        that over a thousand saplings had to be bent to con-
        struct the walls and curved roof.   The scarcity of such
        young trees today has made this kind of hut relatively
        rare.

BEETHAM, E. B.   British civil servant who was Resident
        Commissioner in Swaziland from 1946 until 1950.   He
        is given credit for having persuaded the High Commis-
        sioner to accept certain changes in the Native Adminis-
        tration Proclamation of 1944 which would make it satis-
        factory to the Swazis.   These entailed especially
        greater recognition of the Swazi King-in-Council.   This
        agreement led to the Native Administration Proclamation
        of 1950, the Native Courts Proclamation of 1950, and
        the National Treasury Proclamation of 1950 (see each).
        Thus, by breaking the deadlock between the British and
        the Swazis, Beetham was responsible for three very
        significant administrative advances.

BEMANTI.   Literally: "People of the water".   A Siswati
        term which, along with Belwandle (literally: "People of
        the sea"), is applied to the national priests who control
        the annual Incwala ritual.   The term refers to their
        duty to fetch river and sea water to strengthen the king,
        the beginning of the ritual.   Throughout the several
        days they also have other distinct duties.   There might
        be about twenty bemanti for a specific Incwala.

BEMBO-NGUNI (variant spelling of EMBO-NGUNI). Northern
        Nguni, to differentiate from some of the Nguni dwelling
        further south, such as the Zulu.   The Bembo Nguni

spent several centuries in the area between Delagoa Bay
and the Lubombo Mountains, where the Dutch encountered them in the eighteenth century. The Swazis are
of Bembo-Nguni origin since Dlamini, the founder of the
Swazi royal clan, had been a leader of the Bembo-Nguni.

BEMDZABUKO (variant spelling of BOMDZABUKO). True
    Swazis, those who originated at Shiselweni. The clans
    of Swaziland are divided into three groups (see also
    EMAKHAND ZAMBILI and EMAFIK'EM UVA), the senior
    group being those clans which can trace their member-
    ship in the Swazi nation to Shiselweni. That is the
    village of Sobhuza I, the grandson of Ngwane III, who
    is recognized as the first of the great "modern" Swazi
    kings. As loyal followers of the ruling Dlamini clan,
    the "true Swazi" perform special duties relating to the
    ruling clan and the King himself. Among the clans
    classified as Bemdzabuko are: Mhlanga, Madonsela,
    Mavuso, Fakude, Hlophe, Mabuza, Simelane, Matsebula,
    Twala, Ngwenya, Sihlongonyane, Nkonyane, and Manana.

BERLIN ACT (1885). An international agreement that culmi-
    nated a conference called by French Premier Jules
    Ferry and German Chancellor Otto von Bismarck. The
    conference lasted from November 15, 1884, to February
    26, 1885. While none of the provisions specifically
    applied to Swaziland, the attitude of Great Britain seemed
    to change after 1885 and it began to lay the groundwork
    for further acquisitions, in contrast to its previous
    guarantees of Swazi independence.

BHUNU, KING (variant spelling of BUNU; also: Ngwane V,
    Mahlokohla, and Hhili). Son of King Mbandzeni, who
    died in October, 1889, Bhunu became King of Swaziland
    and remained so until his death on December 10, 1899.
    He was only 23 years old at the time of his death. Dur-
    ing most of this time effective government was in the
    hands of his mother, Queen Mother and Regent Gwamile
    Mdluli (q. v.), also called Labotsibeni. Most of the sig-
    nificant political activities, domestic and especially in-
    ternational, were of her making, not Bhunu's. On
    September 3, 1890, he was officially "shown" to his
    people as heir, but he had little effect for some time.
    His capital was at Zombodze, his mother's home, but
    he later set up his own royal village at Ezabeni for ad-
    ministrative purposes. Bhunu was, from several re-
    ports, a rather ill-tempered youth, and not as well-liked

as other future kings.   Yet one incident rallied the nation around him.   On the night of April 9, 1898, an
important indvuna, Mbhabha Sibandze (q. v.), was killed
at Zombodze, the capital, reportedly at the orders of
Bhunu.   The Government of the South African Republic,
pretending to rule Swaziland, commanded that he be
brought to trial.   When he arrived at the court of Commissioner Krogh, he was accompanied by a large force
of singing warriors.   Their war-like appearance pan-
icked the town of Bremersdorp and a force of about two
thousand Boers and troops was organized in reaction.
The Swazis, not wishing their King to be treated as a
commoner, were ready to go to war.   On the advice of
his elders, Bhunu avoided confrontation by escaping
with a small band of men to British officials in Zululand.   The British argued with the Boers that the Republic had no right to try the King.   The Republic
officials insisted but agreed to a token trial.   After a
guarantee of Bhunu's safety, he returned to Swaziland
on August 19, 1898.   A two-week trial at Bremersdorp
began September 5 and he was eventually found guilty of
allowing public violence without trying to prevent it and
was fined.   An important added result was the Protocol
of 1898, an Anglo-Boer agreement that, in effect, reduced the Swazi King to a Paramount Chief subject to
European control.   In April, 1899, Bhunu was invited
by President Kruger to visit him in Pretoria.   Bhunu
went, accompanied by one thousand warriors.   Later
that year, in October, the Boer War began and many
Europeans left Swaziland.   On December 10, however,
Bhunu died.   He was buried near his father on Mdimba
Mountain.   His four-month-old son, Mona (later Sobhuza II), was declared heir.   Queen Mother Gwamile
Mdluli again became Queen Regent, assisted by her son,
Bhunu's younger brother Malunge.

BHUNYA (variant spelling of BUNYA).   A community in the
west-central part of Swaziland, about 14 miles east of
the border.   It is the site of the Usutu Pulp Mill and
has a population over 1600 people.   It is in the midst
of the Usutu Forests.

BIG BEND.   One of the principal towns in the Lubombo District in the eastern section of Swaziland, with a population of about 3000, mostly Swazi.   It is on a bend in
the Great Usutu River, and is a center for the sugar
industry in the southern Lowveld.   Sugar production is

helped greatly by the Big Bend Irrigation Scheme, which
uses the Usutu River as its source. The Ubombo
Ranches, Ltd. has a large mill and refinery there.

BILHARZIA. Also called Schistosomiasis, it is a chronic in-
fection that affects as many as 25 percent of all Africans, and an estimated 30 percent in Swaziland. Infec-
tion occurs during immersion in fresh water containing
the larval forms.

BLACK UMBELUZI RIVER.   The northern one of the two
main branches of the Umbeluzi River.   It starts near
the South African border southwest of Forbes Reef, dips
south near Mbabane, then undulates across most of
Swaziland before joining the White Umbeluzi fifteen miles
west of the Mozambique border.

BOMVU RIDGE. A geological formation just inside the western border of Swaziland, north of the main highway from
Oshoek to Mbabane. It contains 30 million tons of high
grade iron ore. While evidence exists that Stone Age
men first worked this deposit in the Ngwenya Mountains
as early as 25,000 B.C., the first modern report on
the ore and the potential of the area did not come until
1955. (See NGWENYA, and IRON ORE.)

BORDER CAVE. A cave in the Ngwavuma district of South
Africa near the southeastern border of Swaziland. Ex-
cavations there provide evidence through skeletal remains of some of the earliest known relatives of modern
man. They indicate that Swaziland was occupied by
early man in the Middle Stone Age.

BORDERGATE. A small Swazi community in northeastern
Swaziland. Located at the border with the Transvaal,
and alongside the Komati River, it is the principal exit
point for anyone wishing to go to Komatipoort, forty-
three miles away.

BOTHA, GENERAL LOUIS. South African soldier and statesman. Born in Natal in 1862, he eventually made the
Transvaal his home. In May, 1896, he was appointed
by the South African Republic to be Swaziland's native
commissioner and resident justice of the peace in Mbabane, where he stayed only until November. He eventually became Commandant-General of the Transvaal
forces in the Boer War. After the war he was more

active politically and later became the first Premier of
the Union of South Africa. He signed for South Africa
at the Versailles Peace Conference in 1919 and died on
August 28 of the same year in Pretoria. Throughout
his terms of executive office, Botha was very firm that
the High Commission Territories and Southern Rhodesia
must be incorporated into South Africa. Botha especially pushed the Governor General, Lord Gladstone to
transfer Swaziland to South Africa in 1911. He argued
that many Transvaal citizens spent much of their time
in Swaziland and that there were numerous white residents there. British Colonial Secretary Harcourt resisted.

BOTSWANA.   About 350 miles west of Swaziland, it was formerly the British protectorate called Bechuanaland until Independence Day, September 30, 1966. The Tswana people
who make up the largest part of the population are divided
into eight separate "tribes, " most of whom are related to
the Sotho people of other parts of southern Africa. Sharing
a common past with Swaziland as one of the three former
High Commission Territories, there is a certain amount
of interaction with Swaziland, especially through membership in the South African Customs Union, and as partners
in the University of Botswana, Lesotho, and Swaziland, as
well as membership in the Commonwealth.

BRAUN, PETER J.   A Swaziland attorney and a Senator in
the first Parliament of independent Swaziland. Born in
Johannesburg in 1923, he served in the South African
Artillery in World War II. Because of his family's
citrus holdings in the Malkerns Valley, he has served
on the Board of the Citrus Co-operative. He became
active politically at the time of the first Legislative
Council elections when he helped form the Swaziland
Independent Front (SIF), which he served as secretary.
He and other "moderate" whites continued to oppose the
United Swaziland Association (USA) by forming the
Committee of Twelve (q. v.) in 1965. After the 1967
elections, the House of Assembly selected him as one
of its five choices for the Senate. In June, 1973, he
was appointed to the newly created Civil Service Board.

BREMERSDORP.   Now Manzini (q. v.), the town of Bremersdorp was named after Albert Bremer who opened a
store there in 1887. When the provisional government
committee was established in 1890 and used it as its

headquarters, Bremersdorp became the country's first
administrative capital. It continued as the base of administration when the South African Republic took over
the country from 1895 to 1899. The town was partly
destroyed by a Boer commando raid during the Anglo-
Boer War. It lost its status as administrative center
when the British took control of Swaziland in 1902 and
sent a Special Commissioner to Mbabane. Bremersdorp
was renamed Manzini, after a local chief, in 1960.

BRUTON, C. L.   British civil servant who was Resident
   Commissioner in Swaziland from 1937 to 1942. During
   much of this time Great Britain was distracted by war;
   thus it was a fairly uneventful period in colonial administration.

BRUTUS, DENNIS.   A South African refugee who took political asylum in Swaziland in 1963. Formerly the secretary of the non-racial South Africa Sports Association,
   he was to have appeared in a South African court under
   the Suppression of Communism Act. Refused a residence permit in Swaziland, he applied for political
   asylum and it was granted. He tried to leave Swaziland
   with a valid British passport, accompanied by Dr.
   George Msibi (q. v.), but was arrested by Portuguese
   authorities at the Mozambique border despite the valid
   visa. He was turned over to the South African authorities instead of Swazi authorities and in September,
   1963, was seriously wounded in Johannesburg by South
   African police. This incident raised the question of the
   status of refugees in Swaziland. He now lives in the U.S.A.

BRYANT, REV. A. T.   A Catholic missionary who became
   a scholar and historian of the Nguni people, especially
   the Zulu, but also the Swazi. His book Olden Times
   in Zululand and Natal contains interesting material regarding the beginnings of the Swazi nation.

BULUNGUPOORT.   A gorge (poort) cut through by the Great
   Usutu River south of Sidvokodvo. There is a magnificent waterfall there.

BURGERS, THOMAS F.   President of the South African Republic from 1873 until it was temporarily taken over for
   the British Crown in 1877. His main effort (other than
   battling the Bapedi) was to build a railway across Swaziland to Delagoa Bay, claiming a strip of land one mile

wide on each side of the Great Usutu River. He arranged a loan in the Netherlands and got equipment to
Lourenço Marques where it rusted. Born in South
Africa in 1834, he became a minister before being
asked to enter Government. He died in 1881.

BUSHMEN. Inhabitants of southern Africa of unique charac-
teristics and unknown origin. Seemingly the original
inhabitants of the area, yet of physical and linguistic
types far different from the Bantu near whom they now
live. They are small in stature and not pigmented the
same as the Bantu, and they are nomadic peoples, primarily living by hunting and gathering. Today they live
mostly in the Kalahari Desert of Botswana and Namibia.
Among the contributions of the Bushmen to Swaziland
are the "clicks" (or unique consonant sounds) from their
language and their remarkable rock paintings (q. v.).

BUXTON, LORD (SYDNEY CHARLES BUXTON). Second Governor-General of the Union of South Africa and therefore the Second High Commissioner for Swaziland,
Basutoland, and Bechuanaland. He served in the dual
capacities from September 8, 1914 to July 17, 1920.
As High Commissioner he was closer to the Swazi than
many others in his position. He visited Mbandzeni's
widow, the old Queen Regent, in her home at Lobamba.
When South Africa wanted to place poor white farmers
in Swaziland, he tried to forestall this by advocating
sale of land to British farmers. Buxton tried to dis-
suade Jan Smuts from trying to incorporate Swaziland
into South Africa, unless the Swazis themselves were
at least somewhat in agreement.

-C-

THE CABINET. The King's Cabinet under the 1967 and Independence Constitutions consisted of a Prime Minister,
a Deputy Prime Minister and six other Ministers. Later
a seventh ministry was added. It was the job of the
Cabinet to propose legislation and guide it through the
legislative process, as well as to handle the administrative matters that were part of the duties of each individual member of the Cabinet.

CECE. A leader of the Maseko peoples living near Mankayane during the reign of Sobhuza I. Sobhuza and his

followers were taken by Cece and his people to the foot
of the Mdimba Mountains, the area now of the royal
villages and royal graves. Sobhuza then took over the
rule of the many clans he found there.

THE CENSUS OF BEADS. The first census conducted by the
   British in Swaziland (the South African Republic conducted one in 1898), it took place in 1904. The head
   of each homestead had to thread black and yellow beads,
   large and small, on a string to be collected by officials.
   They represented male and female, adults and youths.
   A counting of the beads indicated 36, 851 males and
   47, 678 females, for a total Swazi population of 84, 529.
   There were also 890 Europeans and 72 other non-Africans.

CHAKA. Variant spellings are Chaga, Shaka, Tshaka. King
   and first great leader of the Zulu nation. Born in 1787,
   his ascent to leadership in 1818 was due in part to his
   great display of courage and skill, especially in battle.
   As King of the Zulu he revolutionized warfare with new
   weapons and means of attack. Soon he had almost complete control of the present region of Natal. His impis
   (q. v.) scourged neighboring peoples, especially Africans,
   who were to be either enemies or vassals, never allies
   and equals. The result was a "crushing of peoples"
   ("Mfecane" to the Nguni, and "Difaqane" to the Sutu)
   and a scattering of tribes and groups to escape the fury
   of the Zulu under Chaka. Finally Chaka was killed by
   his half-brother Dingane (Dingaan) and a group of con-
   spirators in 1828. While the Zulu did not clash with
   the Swazis (under Sobhuza I) during Chaka's lifetime,
   partly due to the discretion of the Swazis who moved
   their peoples to the northern-most part of their land,
   the Swazis were affected by the Mfecane. It became
   necessary either to assist or to absorb some of the
   refugees from Chaka's wars. As a sign of friendship,
   King Sobhuza sent Chaka a number of Swazi girls, including princesses of the royal clan. Chaka ordered
   some of them killed when they became pregnant because
   he feared a male heir would be a potential source of
   alternate allegiance for his detractors among the Zulu.
   Sobhuza I visited Chaka about 1825.

CHIEF JUSTICE. Until independence came to the High Commission Territories, they shared a Chief Justice among
   them. Under Swaziland's Independence Constitution,
   however, the country has a Chief Justice who, in addi-

tion to being head of the Judiciary and presiding officer
of the High Court, is also Chairman of the Judicial
Service Commission. He is appointed by the King on
the advice of the Judicial Service Commission.

CHURCHILL, WINSTON. The renowned British statesman
served as under-secretary in the Colonial Office early in
the 20th century, and became Colonial Secretary on February 14, 1921. As Chancellor of the Exchequer seven
years later, he authorized funds as loans to settlers in
Swaziland to help in the development of the Territory. During his term as Prime Minister in the 1950's, he adamantly
refused any consideration of the transfer of the High Commission Territories to the Republic of South Africa.

CILONGO. A brass military trumpet, probably introduced to
Swaziland near the turn of the century by the British army.

CLAN see SIBONGO

CLARK, SIR WILLIAM H. High Commissioner for Basutoland, Bechuanaland and Swaziland, and Commissioner
for the United Kingdom in South Africa from January 7,
1935 until January 3, 1940. Born in England in 1876,
he had over thirty years administrative experience in
India and as High Commissioner in Canada before coming to South Africa. When he left office in South Africa
in 1940 he doubted whether any agreement between South
Africa and Great Britain over transfer of the High Commission Territories would be possible. The only way
out, he suggested, was for Swaziland to receive and
accept some fantastic offer from South Africa, thus
allowing Swaziland to serve as a test case. He died in
England in November, 1952.

CLIFFORD, CAPT. BEDE. Imperial secretary and representative of the British government in South Africa,
1924-31. Between January and March, 1931, he was
Acting High Commissioner. He strongly favored active
British interest in the High Commission Territories.
He felt development loans to the settlers in Swaziland
would produce quick results. Even if the Territories
were eventually given to South Africa, the pattern would
be set for South Africa to continue. Also the good-will
and confidence of the Africans should be nurtured as
they were some of the firmest allies of Britain in
southern Africa.

COAL MINING. An industry with tremendous potential for
    Swaziland, but presently a limited amount of production.
    With an estimated 220 million tons in the Lubombo Dis-
    trict alone, coal could become a major export and a
    source of thermal power exportable to South Africa.
    Present production is by the Anglo-American Corpora-
    tion at their mine at Mpaka, twelve miles east of Siteki.
    Mining at Mpaka began in 1964 with the idea of supply-
    ing the new Swaziland Railway.

COHEN, DAVID. Appointed Attorney-General of Swaziland in
    1972. Born in South Africa's Cape Province, Novem-
    ber 1, 1905, he was educated at the University of Cape
    Town. An Advocate of the Supreme Court in South
    Africa, he was an Advocate and an Attorney in Kimber-
    ley for many years. In 1967 he came to Swaziland as
    Senior Crown Council, but soon became Solicitor-Gen-
    eral of Swaziland. As Attorney-General he has served
    the Government through the Ngwenya (q. v.) affair and
    during the 1973 Constitutional change. In the latter, he
    was made Professional Advisor to the Constitutional
    Commission.

COLLEGE OF TECHNOLOGY see SWAZILAND INDUSTRIAL
    TRAINING INSTITUTE

COLONIAL DEVELOPMENT AND WELFARE ACTS. A series
    of acts passed by the British Parliament which provided
    for the expenditure of funds for approved development
    projects in the Colonies and High Commission Terri-
    tories. The Colonial Development Act of 1929 provided
    up to one million pounds for that purpose. The Colo-
    nial Development and Welfare Act of 1940 broadened the
    range of expenditures and increased the amount up to
    five million pounds a year during the next ten years.
    The Colonial Development and Welfare Act of 1945
    raised expenditures to 120 million pounds for the years
    1946 to 1956. A 1950 Act increased that figure to 140
    million pounds. After the Pim Report (q. v.) of 1932,
    some small grants-in-aid and development funds trickled
    into Swaziland for such purposes as improving the
    water supply of Bremersdorp and building a butter fac-
    tory (creamery) there. The 1940 Act allowed about half
    a million pounds that had been loaned to Swaziland to
    be converted to grants-in-aid. It also allowed money
    for transfer of Crown Lands and purchase of other lands
    for Land Settlement Schemes (q. v.) for the Swazis. The

1940 and 1945 Acts both allowed for expansion of social
services, especially used in the fields of education (e.
g. the Swaziland Teacher Training College and expansion
of the Swazi National School at Matsapa) and health (for
expansion of two Government Hospitals). In addition,
the Commonwealth Development Corporation (q. v.)--
originally the Colonial Development Corporation--was
created by the British government to implement the 1945
Act. Its activities especially stressed major economic
development projects.

COLOURED. A term used especially by white South Africans
to indicate people of mixed racial parentage. The term
Eurafrican is preferred in Swaziland, if at least one of
the direct ancestors was European and one African.

THE COMMITTEE OF TWELVE. An informal political grouping put together in 1965 by former members of the
Swaziland Independent Front. It consisted, among
others, of Leo Lovell, Peter Braun, and Frank Corbett. It rejected the United Swaziland Association view
that there should be reserved seats for Europeans in a
new Parliament, and hoped aloud that the Ngwenyama
would appoint some non-Swazis to Parliament on a
merit basis. While ridiculed by the USA as the
"Twelve Apostles, " the Committee of Twelve proved
accurate in gauging the future.

THE COMMONWEALTH. An international association or
grouping of states with a common link: all were part
of the old British Empire, mostly in Asia or Africa.
There were twenty-seven other member states when
Swaziland became independent and joined in 1968. In
addition to their former imperial bond, the countries
cooperate in certain economic and trade measures, and
political and economic subjects dominate the regular
meetings of Commonwealth prime ministers, foreign
ministers, or whatever.

COMMONWEALTH DEVELOPMENT CORPORATION (CDC).
Created as the Colonial Development Corporation to implement the Colonial Development and Welfare Act of
1945, it began a series of technical studies and economic surveys as early as 1948. In the intervening
twenty-five years it has invested about $60 million of
British government funds in Swaziland. It was given
the present name in 1963. In addition to financing or

aiding such programs as developing the road network, creating hydroelectric facilities and underwriting part of the cost of the Swaziland Railway, it has been heavily involved in irrigation schemes, mining ventures, and plantation projects. A partial listing of the projects for which it is either wholly or heavily responsible is: Vuvulane Irrigated Farms, Swaziland Irrigation Scheme, Swaziland Railway, Mhlume Sugar Co. Ltd., Usutu Pulp Co. Ltd., Libby Swaziland Ltd., Swaziland Development Corp. Ltd., Swaziland Iron Ore Development Co. Ltd., Neopac Swaziland Ltd., and Shiselwini Forestry Co. Ltd. Its phenomenal impact on the economy and future of Swaziland cannot be overestimated.

CONCESSION COURT. Set up after the recommendations of the Joint Commission (q. v.) in 1890, this three-judge court had the duty of ruling on the validity of disputed concessions. While the British and South Africans accepted the judgments of this court, the Swazis did not recognize it as having any validity. Later British-South African agreements voided the court.

CONCESSIONS PARTITIONS PROCLAMATION OF 1907. Coming as the result of a concessions commission appointed by Sir Alfred Milner (q. v.) in 1904 and which finished its work in 1907, High Commissioner Selborne issued this proclamation which divided the country into three land categories: European farms, Crown Lands, and Swazi areas. While the British saw this as a fair way of returning to the Swazis some of the land that had been bought by unscrupulous concession-hunters, the Swazis saw it is a land steal since, they claimed, no concessions were ever meant to grant permanent ownership to Whites, which this proclamation now granted. It specifically provided that one-third of all land and grazing concessions would be returned to Swazi use or, in some instances, made Crown Land, according to a division to be set up by a special commissioner (to be George Grey). Swazis living on "European land" would be protected for five years, but then must move or accept the conditions of the European, if permission to stay were granted. This proclamation was disputed by the Swazis, who sent to London a Deputation of 1907 (q. v.).

CONNAUGHT, PRINCE ARTHUR OF. The third High Commissioner for South Africa and Governor General of the

Union of South Africa, he served from November 20, 1920, until December 5, 1923.

CONVENTION OF 1881 (also: PRETORIA CONVENTION OF 1881). A document signed in Pretoria by the British and Transvaal governments on August 3, 1881. In addition to returning the Transvaal to Boer rule, the Convention set the boundaries between the Transvaal and Swazi territory. More important, article twenty-four read: "The independence of the Swazis within the boundary line of Swaziland ... will be fully recognized." It thus became an internationally recognized State. The next month, Sir Evelyn Wood went to Swaziland and explained the Convention and its effects to the King-in-council.

CONVENTION OF 1884 (also: LONDON CONVENTION OF 1884). An agreement between the British and Transvaal governments that was signed in London; it amplified and amended the Convention of 1881. It not only repeated the statement regarding Swaziland's independence, but also committed the South African Republic to doing its utmost to prevent its citizens from encroaching illegally on Swazi territory.

CONVENTION OF 1890 see FIRST SWAZILAND CONVENTION, 1890

CONVENTION OF 1893 see SECOND SWAZILAND CONVENTION, 1893

CONVENTION OF 1894 see THIRD SWAZILAND CONVENTION, 1894

COOPERATIVE SOCIETIES. Organizations set up to utilize cooperation among small-scale producers for the purpose of mutual gain. Among the oldest of these is the Swaziland Tobacco Cooperative Company in Nhlangano and the Swaziland Cooperative Rice Company which is managed from Manzini. Peasant farmers did not take to this kind of organization until 1966, however. The Cooperative Department has noted a steady growth in the trend since then, with over sixty of them belonging to the Central Cooperative Union of Swaziland at the end of 1972.

CORBETT, FRANK. A farmer from the Manzini area, and

a member of the Reconstituted European Advisory
Council at the time of the first constitutional proposals
in the early 1960's.   He resisted the leadership of Carl
Todd (q. v.) and rejected any future ties of Swaziland to
South Africa.   He wanted an orderly transition to African majority rule without political parties, if possible.
When Todd formed the United Swaziland Association in
1964, however, Corbett and others founded the more
moderate Swaziland Independent Front in April, 1964,
and he became chairman of its Steering Committee.   In
1965 he and other SIF members formed the Committee
of Twelve (q. v.).

CORYNDON, SIR ROBERT THORNE.   Born in South Africa
in 1870 but educated partly in England, he became Resident Commissioner of Swaziland from October, 1907,
until 1916.   He later served in Rhodesia and Basutoland, then as Governor of Uganda and finally as Governor of Kenya.   His service in Swaziland included the
very hectic period during which the concessions controversy was first being thrashed out.

COTTON.   Grown in Swaziland since the 1920's, it has
emerged since the mid-1950's as a major crop for the
country.   Peasant farmers have successfully adopted it,
partly as a result of a research program developed by
the government along with the Empire Cotton Growing
Corporation (now the Cotton Research Corporation).
Record harvests have made it a successful export item,
especially since a ginnery at Matsapha processes the
seed cotton.

COURT OF APPEAL.   The highest appeals court in the
country, it is presided over by a Judge President and
includes three Justices of Appeal appointed by the King
on the advice of the Judge President.

COWEN, PROF. DENIS V.   Prominent South African lawyer
and Professor of Comparative Law at Cape Town University who became a constitutional adviser to the
Basuto nation in the mid 1950's, and later, in 1961, to
the Swaziland Progressive Party and the Eurafrican
Welfare Association.   He was hired by the SPP to pre-
pare a proposal for constitutional reform after the SPP
felt that the Constitutional Committee was stacked
against it by the traditionalists.   His report was rejected by many at the time (except for the various po-

litical parties who used it for their platforms), but it
eventually proved to be very much the basis for the
1967 Constitution.   Professor Cowen's attachment to
African interests in southern Africa was shared by his
brother-in-law, Patrick Duncan (q. v.), editor of the
Liberal paper, Contact.

CREWE, LORD.   British Colonial Secretary, 1908-1910.   It
was his decision and his policy that prevented transfer
of the High Commission Territories to South Africa
early in the century.   Among the principles he insisted
on were: 1) immediate transfer was out of the question; 2) ultimately, they would be included in the Union
of South Africa; 3) but Britain insists on insertion in
the constitution of specific safeguards for the Africans
without which the House of Commons would not grant
approval.   Thus an elaborate Schedule providing a number of specific conditions was appended to the Act of
Union.

CROCODILE RIVER.   A west-east river in the Transvaal,
some fifty to one hundred miles north and west of the
Swazi border.   Boers claimed that Swazi King Mswati
granted all land between the Crocodile and Olifants
Rivers to the Lydenburg Republic of the Boers in 1846.
Swaziland would be much larger today with that land.
The area where the Komati and Crocodile Rivers meet
was not officially taken from the Swazis until the
Alleyne Commission (q. v.) finished its work in 1880.

CROWN LAND.   Land in Swaziland was divided into three
categories: private European Land, Swazi National Land,
and Crown Land, as a result of the Concessions Partition Proclamation of 1907.   One-third of the land previously granted to concession holders was to be returned
to Swazi control, but still under Crown title.   Special
Commissioner George Grey was to decide how the land
would be divided.   If he chose more than one-third of
a specific concession, the owner would be compensated;
if he chose less than one-third for Swazi use, the dif-
ference became Crown Land.   This third kind totalled
63, 549 hectares.   The Swaziland Crown Lands and Minerals Order-in-Council of 1908 added more to the
Crown Lands through the process of reversion of rights.
The Swazis became very angry when some of the Crown
Lands were sold to Europeans instead of being given to
the Swazis.   This was reversed in part in the 1940's.

As independence neared, Crown Lands were being converted either to Swazi use or, as in the case of the
Ngwenya iron area, sold for the benefit of Swaziland's
economy.

-D-

DABEDE, PRINCE. Appointed by the Ngwenyama, Sobhuza
    II, as his personal representative in the Swazi contin-
    gent that fought in World War II. He also served in a
    liaison capacity between the Swazi soldiers and the
    European commanders of the force.

DAGGA. Marijuana. This is one of several terms used in
    southern Africa to describe this drug. It is often
    smoked in a special dagga pipe. While it has been
    legislated against in both South Africa and Swaziland,
    there are numerous arrests and convictions for illegal
    possession and use of marijuana. See INSANGU.

DE KAAP GOLD FIELD. A center of excitement in the
    1880's, this field did not last long but attracted num-
    erous prospectors to the Eastern Transvaal-Swaziland
    area. Located near Barberton, just to the northwest
    of Swaziland, it produced several millions' worth of
    gold. There is little production there today.

DELAGOA BAY. An important Indian Ocean port at which
    grew the city of Lourenço Marques in Portuguese Mo-
    zambique. The British had also claimed the Bay, but
    under binding arbitration President MacMahon of France
    awarded it to Portugal in 1875. Delagoa Bay is a na-
    tural port for Swaziland, less than fifty miles away.
    Several groups planned to build a railway from the
    Transvaal through Swaziland to the Bay: the first was
    led by Alexander McCorkindale (q. v.) in the 1870's;
    later, in the 1920's, South African Prime Minister Jan
    Smuts (q. v.) had a similar idea. Finally the Swaziland
    Railway was built in the 1960's; it ends in Lourenco
    Marques.

DEPUTATION OF 1894. A delegation of Swazis sent to Lon-
    don by the Regent in October, 1894, to request of
    Queen Victoria that she establish a protectorate over
    Swaziland. They protested recent British-South African
    agreements which were turning the Swazis over to the

Transvaal Government. They were unsuccessful. The deputation consisted of Prince Longcanga (a half-brother of Mbandzeni), Mnkonkoni Kunene, Mabovu Nkosi, Mhlonishwa Nkosi, Zibokwana Nkosi, Cleopas Kunene, plus an interpreter James Stuart and the Chief Secretary to the Swazi Nation, George Hulett. They left London in November, 1894.

DEPUTATION OF 1907. A deputation sent by the Swazi Regent to London in 1907 to protest the British action on concessions in the several years previous, but especially the Concessions Partition Proclamation of 1907 (q. v.). It consisted of Prince Malunge, Prince Logcogco, Josiah Vilakazi, Nehemia Vilakazi, Manikiniki Nkambule, and an interpreter, A. G. Marwick. They were there for three months, beginning in November, 1907, and met the Secretary of State Lord Elgin on November 21. They especially pleaded that King Mbandzeni had specifically told the concessionaires that ownership was not being granted, and even if that was ignored, the Swazis should receive far more than the one-third of the land that the Proclamation provided. A reply by Lord Elgin giving them some feeling of satisfaction was either changed, ignored, or false, leading to further Swazi anger. In any event, the deputation was unsuccessful.

DEVONSHIRE, 9th DUKE OF. British Colonial Secretary, 1922-1924. This was an important period during which King Sobhuza II traveled to London and the Swazis were constantly pushing the British for recognition of Swazi land rights.

DE VRIES, VAN WYK. South African lawyer (and later a judge) who advised King Sobhuza II in the early 1960's concerning political maneuvers vis-a-vis Great Britain. His advice, later published in the Rand Daily Mail, was to hold out for complete recognition as King and holder of all land and mineral rights. If this was unobtainable, Sobhuza should accept the new constitution under protest and then form a political party centered around himself and the Swazi National Council. All this occurred just as de Vries outlined it. De Vries belonged to the National Party and, reportedly, to the Broederbond.

DHLAMINI. A variant spelling of the sibongo of the royal clan, Dlamini, (q. v.).

DICKIE, JAMES J.   Born in New Zealand in 1919, he at-
tended universities there and later joined Her Majesty's
Colonial Legal Service.   He was appointed Swaziland's
Attorney General in 1963 and served until his death on
March 13, 1967.   He also served on the 1966 constitu-
tional committee.

DICKSON, T. A.   Resident Commissioner in Swaziland from
1928 to 1935.   In this capacity he encouraged and helped
in the founding of the Swaziland Progressive Association
(q. v.) in January, 1929.   The SPA eventually nurtured
the Swaziland Progressive Party in 1960.

DIFAQANE.   A word used by the Sutu meaning a crushing of
peoples.   It, like its Nguni equivalent, Mfecane, refers
to the period in the 1820's and later when African
peoples throughout southeastern Africa fled from the
wrath of the Zulus, especially when under their great
leader Chaka.

DINGANE (variant: DINGAAN).   Zulu King, half-brother and
assassin of Chaka.   Dingane came into conflict with the
Swazi during the late 1830's when some Swazis raided
northern Zululand and captured some cattle.   Dingane
sent his soldiers to attack the raiding Swazis and get
back the cattle.   With the aid of the rifle fire of about
thirty European allies, Dingane's men were successful.
In 1838 Dingane and his followers tricked Piet Retief
and a number of Voortrekkers and killed them.   Diffi-
culties with other Voortrekkers caused the Zulus to
flee, however.   Dingane's manner of death and its exact
date are in doubt, but after his defeat at Blood River
in December, 1838, he became a fugitive.   He died
probably in 1843, somewhere in the southeast corner
of Swaziland.

DISTRICT COMMISSIONER.   The title of the chief administrative officer of each of the four districts of Swaziland: Shiselweni, Lubombo, Manzini, and Hhohho.
Among his major functions is to coordiante and promote
development.   In this he works with the Minister of
Local Administration and with technical experts.

DLAMINI I.   The founder of the royal clan of Swaziland, the
Nkosi Dlamini (q. v.).   A leader of the Bembo-Nguni
(q. v.) people.   He probably lived during the fifteenth
century, generally south and east of the Limpopo River.

More warlike than any of his predecessors as leader of
the Bembo-Nguni (among whom was Ngwane I), he conquered and absorbed a number of other clans near the
Lubombo Mountains.   He died of smallpox and was
buried at the southern end of the Lubombo range, in
the Nyawo area.   He was also called Matalatala.

DLAMINI II.   An early leader of the Bembo-Nguni group that
was later to be called the Swazi.   According to one
semi-official genealogical table, he was preceded by
Ngwane II and succeeded by Nkosi II.   This might have
been in the early seventeenth century or so.

DLAMINI III.   A leader of the Swazi people in the first half
of the eighteenth century, immediately preceding the
dynamic Ngwane III.   Dlamini III was not the rightful
heir to the throne of his father Ludvonga I.   His half-
brother, Hlubi (q. v.), should have been the successor
but was eliminated because Swazi custom does not allow
an heir to have full brothers, as Hlubi did.

DLAMINI IV.   The official title of the nineteenth century
Ngwenyama who is more popularly known as Mbandzeni
(q. v.).

DLAMINI, CLEMENT DUMISA.   Usually noted as Dumisa.
One of the ablest yet the most erratic of the Swazi political activists in the pre-independence period.   A
nephew of the King, he studied one year at Pius XII
College in Basutoland, but returned to Swaziland a con-
vert to activist politics.   A stirring speech in Mbabane
in December, 1960 won him election the next month as
President of the Youth League of the Swaziland Progressive Party.   In this capacity he traveled throughout
Africa to Pan-African conferences.   A protege of Dr.
Zwane, Dlamini broke from Nquku's SPP with Zwane
and eventually became Secretary-General of Zwane's
NNLC.   His brilliant ability to speak and lead put him
at the heart of almost all the labor unrest of 1963 as
well as demonstrations and marches throughout Mbabane.
He received a six-month sentence for disturbing the
public order and inciting to violence.   This was not his
only time in jail, as he had both previous and subsequent arrests for civil offenses unrelated to politics. In
March, 1965 he jumped bail and fled the country after
involvement in an assault case.   He spent some time in
Dar es Salaam and working with the Organization of

African Unity Liberation Committee. He returned home
in 1966 and was sentenced to nine months in jail. After
his release on November 15, 1966, he publicly stated
that he was no longer associated with the NNLC and
that he saw a need for Swazi political unity, something
that could be achieved only by support of King Sobhuza
and of the Imbokodvo Party. He saw Imbokodvo as
greatly changed in its methods and goals since the time
when he was actively opposing it.

DLAMINI, HENRY D. A co-founder of Swaziland's first
trade union, the Swaziland Pulp Timber Workers Union,
March 30, 1962, he led a strike four days later. Although short-lived, the strike was the first of a series
of strikes throughout the country that year. He and
the other leaders called for improved wages and better
working conditions. Charges against him of inciting
public violence were dropped but he was given a suspended sentence after being found guilty of inciting to
strike.

DLAMINI, (PRINCE) MAKHOSINI. Prime Minister of Swaziland from 1967 to the present and President of the
Imbokodvo National Movement. A great-grandson of
King Sobhuza I, he was born in 1914 at the Enhletsheni
Swazi Royal Residence near Hlatikulu. Educated at
Franson Christian School and the Swazi National School,
he trained as a teacher from 1938 to 1940 at the
Umphulo Training Institute in Natal, South Africa. While
a teacher he served as secretary-general and chairman
of the Swaziland Teachers Association. In 1946 he was
appointed principal of the Swazi National High School at
Lobamba, but resigned the next year after conflict with
the Education Secretary of the Government. He became
a member of the Swazi National Council in 1949. From
1949 to 1962 he was a rural development officer and a
member of the Central Rural Development Board. In
1959 he studied public administration in England on a
scholarship. From 1960 through 1968, he was a member of every constitutional commission or conference,
going to London on a number of occasions to negotiate
or protest. In mid-1964 King Sobhuza II announced the
formation of the Imbokodvo National Movement and that
Prince Makhosini would be its leader. As President
and parliamentary leader he successfully led the party
through the elections of 1964, 1967 and 1972, and has
been Prime Minister of Swaziland since 1967. His

contacts with other African heads of government helped
legitimize the Imbokodvo in Pan-African circles despite
its conservative approach.

DLAMINI, (PRINCE) MASITSELA.　A son of King Sobhuza,
he has been an active member of the Government
for ten years and is now Minister of Local Administration.　Born in December, 1930 at Lobamba, he re-
ceived education through high school at Swazi schools.
He became clerk of the Swazi National Higher Court of
Appeal, but in 1963 he was appointed Representative of
Labor Affairs by the King in Council.　He is a member
of the Swazi National Council.　He was elected to the
Legislative Council in 1964 as a member of Imbokodvo,
and also to the House of Assembly in 1967 and 1972.
He also served on the 1966 constitutional committee.
In 1967 he became Assistant Minister in the Deputy
Prime Minister's Office.　In 1972 he was named Minis-
ter of Local Administration.

DLAMINI, (PRINCE) MFANASIBILI GILBERT.　Active in the
Government of Swaziland for ten years despite his
youth, he is one of the youngest leaders of the Imbokodvo Party.　Born in 1939 in the Manzini District, he
was educated at the Swazi National School and at the
University of Sussex.　Elected to the 1964 Legislative
Council, he was appointed in 1966 to the new constitutional committee.　Meanwhile, in 1963 he became a
member of the Swazi National Council, and he is now a
member of its Standing Committee.　In 1967 he was
elected to Parliament and then was appointed Minister
for Local Administration.　In 1972 he failed to get reelected by less than seventy-five votes, losing to the
NNLC candidates.　He was then appointed to the Senate
by King Sobhuza and was appointed Minister of Commerce and Cooperatives.

DLAMINI, (PRINCE) MSUNDVUKA (variant: SUDUKA
DLAMINI).　A prince from the village of Emvembili
who was quite elderly when he accompanied Sobhuza II
as a counselor on Sobhuza's trip to England in 1922-23.

DLAMINI, NIMROD.　Chairman of the Ngwane National Liberatory Congress Youth League for a time in the early
1960's, he was arrested in 1963 for participation in
strikes and public disturbances.　He was finally acquitted in 1964.　He was assistant Secretary-General of the

NNLC and its Secretary for Pan-African Affairs when
he was stabbed to death in a non-political incident on
September 24, 1966.

DLAMINI, DR. PERCY PYM.   Minister of Health and Education in Swaziland since June, 1972.   He was educated
in Mbabane and also received a B. S. degree at Fort
Hare College.   After teaching in Swaziland for several
years, he went to Edinburgh University for a degree in
dentistry.   He then became a Government dentist in
Swaziland until King Sobhuza II nominated him to Parliament, at which time he was immediately made Minister of Health and Education.

DLAMINI, POLYCARP KA-LAZARUS.   Except for King Sobhuza II, perhaps the most influential man in contemporary
Swaziland.   Born July 1, 1918, at Pigg's Peak, he attended the Swazi National High School and read for a
Social Science degree at the Natal (South Africa) University College from 1947 to 1951 while working as a social welfare and probation officer.   King Sobhuza requested his return in 1952 to serve as Secretary to the
Swazi National Council, a post he held until 1964.   He
received a B. A. in Social Science from the University
of South Africa in 1957.   He became the King's main
representative on constitutional matters beginning in 1960
when he was appointed to the constitutional committee.
He attended a London meeting with Colonial Secretary
Maudling in December, 1961, and was a member of the
Swazi National Council delegation to the 1963 London
constitutional talks, where he bitterly opposed the position of the political parties.   He was chosen to the 1964
Legislative Council for the "traditional" seats (not by
election), and was appointed to the Executive Council
with attention to Education and Health.   He was responsible for education until 1967 when the King appointed him to the new Senate.   He was then appointed
Minister for Works, Power, and Communications, a
post he held until July, 1971, when he was appointed
Minister for Justice.   Reappointed to the Senate in 1972,
he has continued in the Justice Ministry.   In September,
1973, he was appointed chairman of the very important
Royal Constitutional Commission.

DLAMINI CLAN see NKOSI DLAMINI

DLANGENI.   Also called Makhosini.   It is a village located

in the Dlangeni Hills about five miles east of Mbabane
at which there are located a number of royal graves
under the care of the Gama chief.   Thus, this village,
mostly composed of members of the Gama clan, is the
site of occasional ritual observances.

DOMINIONS DEPARTMENT.   In 1907 the responsibility for
administration of the High Commission Territories was
placed in the Dominions Department of the Colonial
Office.   This department was transformed into the Dominions Office at the end of 1925, and it was renamed
the Commonwealth Relations Office in 1947.   For almost half a century the administrators of this office felt
that Swaziland would eventually become part of South
Africa, yet most of them fought to prevent it until such
a union would be both desirable for the Swazis and desired by the Swazis.

DONGA.   Gullies, found frequently throughout Swaziland, usually as a result of simple erosion.   They are often
the result of long-used paths and cattle trails causing
ruts which wash out further with rainfall.   They then
sometimes become borders delineating political regions.

DRAKENSBERG MOUNTAINS.   The highest reaches of the
great southern African plateau, this range extends from
the Natal-Lesotho border north to include also the Highveld of Swaziland.   Called the Quathlamba or Kahlamba
Mountains by some Africans, they reach high points of
over eleven thousand feet.   Especially impressive are
the sheer walls of the escarpment as seen from Natal
looking toward Lesotho.

DUMISA.   An area in north-central Swaziland along the
northern bank of the Black Umbeluzi River.   It is the
site of a major irrigation scheme.   Dumisa is also a
name given to an area in eastern Swaziland, about five
miles south of Big Bend.

DUNCAN, PATRICK BAKER.   Publisher and editor of Con-
tact, a Southern African Liberal fortnightly newspaper,
Duncan did much to publicize the early political parties
of Swaziland during his editorship from 1958 to 1963.
Born in Johannesburg in June, 1918, he was the son of
Sir Patrick Duncan, Governor-General of South Africa
from 1937 to 1943.   A member of the South African
Liberal Party, he was active in the Defiance Campaign

and was both jailed and, eventually, banned. He served
several years in the Colonial Service in Basutoland.
Part of his interest in Swaziland came when his brother-
in-law, Denis Cowen (q.v.), became constitutional advisor to the Swaziland Progressive Party. Duncan, the
only White admitted to membership in South Africa's
Pan African Congress (q.v.), was eventually prohibited
from re-entering Southern Africa and died abroad.

DUTCH REFORMED CHURCH. The Church to which most
Afrikaners belong. There are three DRC churches in
Swaziland. Of the 1,900 Dutch Reformed Church mem-
bers in Swaziland in 1962, 1,700 were Europeans.

DZAMBILE, PRINCESS. A sister of King Mbandzeni who
was sent by the Swazis in the late nineteenth century to
become the wife of the ruler of the Tembe peoples.
Until that time, intermarriage between the ruling clans
of the Tembe and the Swazis had been prohibited by
custom.

-E-

ECKSTEIN, HERMAN. A German, born in Stuttgart in 1849,
he became a diamond and gold mining pioneer and mag-
nate in Southern Africa as of 1882. Before King
Mbandzeni died, he granted Eckstein a concession that
has been described as effectively surrendering control
over the foreign policy of Swaziland. Eckstein, a friend
of Paul Kruger (q.v.), died in Germany in 1893.

ECONOMIC SURVEY MISSION. Appointed by the High Commissioner, Sir John Maud, in July, 1959, this mission
of five experts, chaired by Professor Chandler Morse,
visited each of the High Commission Territories in the
period from September 12 to December 17, 1959.
Among its tasks, in addition to surveying the state of
development in each territory, was to discover development projects which could result in economic viability
for the Territories. While generally conservative in its
recommendations, the Mission's report, submitted
March 1, 1960, resulted in a small increase in British
funding for Swaziland, and a minimal amount for Basutoland and Bechuanaland. The Mission also recommended increased political development, especially
seeming to advocate some kind of multi-racial advisory

council or legislature.

EDEN, ANTHONY. British Secretary of State for Dominion
Affairs from September 3, 1939 to May 10, 1940 (and
later Prime Minister of England from April, 1955 to
January, 1957). During his period in the Dominions
Office, he resisted attempts by Gen. J. C. Smuts to
get immediate transfer of the High Commission Territories (and especially Swaziland) to South Africa. He
made his position clear to Smuts' representative, Col.
Deneys Reitz, in a discussion on October 23, 1939.

EDWALENI POWER STATION. About six miles south of
Manzini at Edwaleni, this is the country's main power
station. Begun in the mid-1960's, by 1969 its capacity
was 28.5 megawatts, 21.5 being hydro-electric and 7
diesel.

EHLANE GAME RESERVE. A still developing game reserve
in the Lowveld in the northeastern quadrant of the
country. It is located along the Msulatane River. Its
35 square miles were proclaimed as a game reserve
by the King in 1968 and were placed under the care of
Mr. Terence Reilly (q. v.). It is bordered by another
15 square miles of Protected Area.

ELGIN, LORD. British Colonial Secretary, 1905 to 1908.
Several times during this period he rebuffed efforts to
have Swaziland handed back to the Transvaal before the
Union of South Africa became independent. Instead he
proposed that the Transvaal and Great Britain assist in
developing Swaziland. On the other hand, he also rebuffed a deputation of Swazis in London on November
21, 1907, when they requested revocation of the Concessions Partition Proclamation of 1907 (q. v.). He did
seem to promise, however, that Crown Land under this
proclamation would be turned over to the Swazis. The
British claim that there was no such intent and much
of the land was sold to others.

ELIZABETH II, QUEEN. Queen of England since 1953, when
the Ngwenyama, Sobhuza II, took one of his very rare
trips overseas in order to witness her coronation. As
a princess, Elizabeth visited Swaziland with her royal
parents and her sister on March 25, 1947.

ELYAN, SIR VICTOR. The first Chief Justice of independent

Swaziland, serving from 1968 to June, 1970.   After an
early legal career, he served in the Colonial Legal
Service in the Gold Coast from 1946 to 1955.   He then
came to southern Africa, serving the High Commission
Territories as Judge in the Court of Appeal, President
of the Court of Appeal, and Chief Justice of the three
Territories for various periods in the 1950's and 1960's.
In one such period, in 1964, he heard cases in Swaziland's High Court that arose out of the Havelock Mine
strikes.

EMA SWAZI.   A term used to denote all Swazi collectively,
recognizing them as a distinct entity.

EMABUTFO.   Plural of Libutfo.

EMADLOTI.   Plural of Lidloti.

EMAFIK AMUVA.   Variant: Labofik'emuva, means "late-
comers. "   Refers to clans who arrived in Swaziland
after the "true" Swazis had established themselves in
the land.   (See also TIKHONDZI.)   Some of these groups
were fleeing the effects of Zulu expansion.   Regardless,
these clans were incorporated into the nation, although,
their sibongo (clan names) still identify these people as
late-comers.   Among the clans considered to be in
this category are: Nkambule, Manyatsi, Nhlengetfwa,
Mtsetfwa, Hlatshwako, Tsela, Masuku, Dladla, Vilakati,
and Masilela.

EMAHIYA.   Plural of Mahiya.

EMAJOBO (plural).   Loin skins worn traditionally by Swazi
men over their mahiya (q. v.).   Made of the pelts of
small animals, one piece of skin hangs in front and one
behind; they are tied on the right hip.   At one time,
Swazi men did not wear emahiya, thus the emajobo
were larger and encircled more completely as a skirt
would.   A man is not properly dressed today without
his emajobo, and may abandon it only at his own village.   The comparable female clothing is a skin skirt,
sidwaba (q. v.).

EMAKHANDZAMBILI.   One of the three categories into which
Swazi clans are divided, the term means literally
"those found ahead. "   These clans were those of Nguni
or Sotho origin who were already occupying areas of

Swaziland when Sobhuza I came in with his followers.
Eventually they were incorporated into the Swazi nation,
but their clans are still not recognized as "true Swazis" (see BEMDZABUKO). The clans falling into the
category of Emakhandzambili are: Gama, Magagula,
Maziya, Kubonye, Mnisi, Maphosa, Gwebu, Shabangu,
Tabetse, Sifundza, Malindza, Bhembe, Shabalala,
Mncina, Makhubu, Mashinini, Msimango, Motsa, Mah-
langu, Zwane, Shongwe, Thabede, and Ngcomphalala.

EMALANGENI. The currency of Swaziland as of September
6, 1974. One Lilangeni (the singular form) is convert-
ible into one Rand (q. v.) at any time in Swaziland. Its
symbol is E (e. g. , E12 million). Each Lilangeni is
divisible into one hundred cents.

EMASOTSHA REGIMENT. Variant spelling of Masotja Regiment.

EMBO-NGUNI. Variant spelling of Bembo-Nguni.

EMLEMBE. A mountain on the border in northwestern
Swaziland at Havelock with a summit of 6, 109 feet.
Emlembe is also another name for the town of Have-
lock (q. v.).

ENRAGHT-MOONY, F. The British Special Commissioner
for Swaziland from 1902 to 1907. On February 22,
1907, after a proclamation by Lord Selborne amending
the Swaziland Administrative Proclamation of 1904, his
title changed to Resident Commissioner. He retired in
October of that year.

ESSELEN, D. J. The representative of the South African
Republic in the Triumvirate Government or Provisional
Government (q. v.), set up as a result of the First
Swaziland Convention (1890). This government set up
the first "civil service" in the territory, but was re-
placed in December, 1894 when the Third Swaziland
Convention was signed.

EURAFRICAN. A term used to indicate a person who is
descended from at least one European and at least one
African. There are about 4, 000 in Swaziland.

EURAFRICAN WELFARE ASSOCIATION. A small pressure
group representing members of the Eurafrican com-

munity in Swaziland. During the 1960's it was active
in constitutional matters as Professor Denis V.
Cowen served as an adviser both to the Association and to the
Swaziland Progressive Party. A member of the Association, Mr. A. Sellstroom, was chosen by the British
to represent the Eurafrican community in the 1963 constitutional talks in London. There he associated himself with the Alliance of Political Organizations (q. v.).

EUROPEAN ADVISORY COUNCIL (EAC). A body of Europeans set up as an administrative measure in 1921 in
order to deal with affairs affecting European residents.
Of its nine elected European members, five were from
southern Swaziland and four from the north. This was
the same year Europeans were made subject to a poll
tax. Prior to 1921, Europeans had been united on a
sporadic basis since the first "White Committee" (q. v.)
was established by King Mbandzeni in 1887. Meetings
of the EAC were held until 1949 when a new proclamation altered it. (See RECONSTITUTED EUROPEAN
ADVISORY COUNCIL). During the 1920's, the EAC
regularly informed the High Commissioner of their desire to remain free from ties with South Africa and their
preference for British aid, with the intention of encouraging more British settlers to immigrate.

EWING, CAPTAIN A. A sea captain, but a resident of Swaziland in the 1880's. He was a member of the "White
Committee" (q. v.) chosen in July, 1887, representing
the mineral concession holders. According to one account he was its Chairman (another source indicates
C. J. Swears was Chairman).

EXECUTIVE COUNCIL. A multi-racial administrative body
consisting of eight members, four from the British Colonial Government and four from Swaziland. Set up by
the 1963 Constitution, it was superseded by the 1967
Constitution's arrangements.

EZULWINI VALLEY (variant spelling: ZULWINI). Literally,
"the place of heaven. " A beautiful valley a couple of
miles south of Mbabane. It is the site of most of Swaziland's modern hotels and tourist areas.

-F-

FAIRLIE, MICHAEL JAMES. A civil servant in Swaziland
for many years, in November, 1972 he was declared
by the government a Prohibited Immigrant to Swaziland.
Prior to 1964 he had been Secretary for Political and
Social Welfare under the British Administration. In
1964 he became Minister of Labour, Information,
Broadcasting and Training as a member of the Executive Committee of the first Swaziland Legislative Council. Later he became Secretary for External Affairs
and Labour. He was very active in Mbabane cultural
activities, especially those involving music and theatre.

FAKUDZE, MBOVANE (variant spelling: MBOVANA). One
of Swaziland's most noted military leaders, he was
noted especially for his leadership in the Battle at Sekhukhune's Stronghold (q. v.) in 1879. In addition, he
was the indvuna at the Ndlovukazi's capital of Nkanini
when she (Sisile Khumalo, q. v.) came into conflict with
King Mbandzeni. Fakudze tried to persuade her not to
flee the country with her royal regiments as she indicated she would do. When he found her gone, however,
he reported it to the King, who sent regiments out which
captured and killed her.

FAKUDZE, MNGAYI. Leader of the Swazi forces against the
Zulus at the Battle of Lubuya (q. v.) in 1854.

FARMERS ASSOCIATIONS. Over a hundred organized groups
of Swaziland farmers with a total membership number-
ing over four thousand, they have done a lot to improve
the quality of farming in Swaziland. Each association
has a channel to the Agricultural Department for the
purpose of receiving information to be passed on to its
members. Some associations are now over thirty years
old. Although most of the associations provide for cooperation among members for such things as bulk pur-
chases, others have actually formed themselves into co-
operative societies (q. v.).

FEATHERSTONE, E. P. The British Resident Commissioner
for Swaziland from 1942 to 1946.

FERREIRA, J. J. One of the leaders in the "Little Free
State" area which eventually was taken from the Swazis
and declared to be part of the South African Republic.

Hunters originally, Ferreira and F. I. Maritz pleaded
with King Mbandzeni for land northeast of what is today
Piet Retief. After it was granted on October 3, 1877,
Boers moved in and the land was divided into small
farms. Later these farmers, led by Ferreira, protested to Mbandzeni that they would not recognize any
authority of the "White Committee" (q. v.). On February 6, 1880 the Alleyne Commission informed Ferreira
and his associates that they must move, as they had
been merely loaned the use of the land and Swazis
wanted it back. The squatters did not leave, and in
1893 the area was incorporated into the South African
Republic.

FILE. The successor to Lazidze (mother of King Mswati II)
as Ndlovukazi. File was Lazidze's subsidiary co-wife.
File's son, Prince Ndwandwa, later served as regent
for several years during the minority of Ludvonga, soon
to be Ngwenyama.

FIRST SWAZILAND CONVENTION. Also referred to as the
Convention of 1890, this agreement was based on the
recommendations of the Joint Commission (q. v.). The
Queen Regent of Swaziland, Gwamile Mdluli, had approved the establishment of a Provisional Government
(q. v.) to replace the "White Committee" (q. v.) in December, 1889. The South African Republic and Great
Britain formally signed the Convention on July 24, 1890.
In addition to providing for the formal offices of Government, it was again asserted (as in 1881 and 1884)
that Swaziland was independent and could not lose that
unless both Great Britain and the Republic agreed. It
also provided, however, for the transfer of the territory known as "the Little Free State" from Swaziland to
the South African Republic.

FITZPATRICK, HERBERT DANIEL G. A Swaziland Senator
from Independence until 1972. Born in 1909 and educated at St. Mark's School in Mbabane, he joined the
civil service in Swaziland in 1928. In 1944 he became
a district officer, and after a period in Palestine, returned to rural development work in Swaziland. He was
Secretary for African Affairs when he retired in 1956.
He was appointed to the committee for constitutional
talks in 1960. In 1964 he ran unopposed for a Legislative Council seat as an active member of the United
Swaziland Association. He was appointed Member for

Works, Power, and Telecommunications. In 1966 he
was appointed to the new constitutional committee, and
the next year was appointed to the Senate after the
elections.

FORBES, ALEX. Eldest son of David Forbes, Sr. (q. v.),
and discoverer of a gold-bearing reef with his partner,
C. J. Swears (q. v.), in November, 1884. It was in
northwestern Swaziland, not far from Mt. Ngwenya. In
mid-1886 the Forbes Reef Gold Mining Company (of
which Alex was a director) was founded to exploit the
deposit. This led to a great boom in prospecting, with
concessions granted that covered the country. He died
in Barberton in about 1885, less than 30 years old,
after having acquired enteric fever while claiming his
new discovery of gold near the De Kaap River.

FORBES, DAVID, SR. Born in the 1830's in Pitlochry, Scotland, he eventually became a successful hunter and
trader in the Zululand-Swaziland-Natal area. He later
turned to large-scale farming just west of Swaziland in
the Scottish settlement area of Alexander McCorkindale
(q. v.), his wife's uncle, near present day Amsterdam.
An attempt to mine diamonds at Kimberley in the 1870's
was unsuccessful; however, his son Alex (q. v.) discovered gold at Forbes Reef and the family's fortune
was made. He had nine children; several of them died
while young, but sons Alex, David, Jr. (q. v.), and
James had some significance in Swaziland's history.
David Sr. , besides being a Director of the Forbes Reef
Company, had a minerals concession with his brother
James (q. v.) for all Swaziland north of the Komati River.
It was granted them by King Mbandzeni on March 10,
1882.

FORBES, DAVID, JR. Born in South Africa in the late
1860's, he lived most of his life either in the eastern
Transvaal on the family property near Ermelo or in
Swaziland at Forbes Reef (his family's gold mine) or,
late in his life, on his two hundred thousand acres along
the Black Umbuluzi River (as described in his book, My
Life in South Africa, published in 1938). During his
life he was a farmer, miner (gold and coal), Scout and
later Captain during the Boer War--on the British side
--and cattle rancher. As a young man, he served as
an interpreter for the "White Committee" and the King
on occasion. Later he succeeded Captain Ewing as

Chairman of the Committee, which was eventually dis-
banded. His property, visited in this century by many
prominent Europeans, including royalty, consisted partly
of the huge Forbes Coal Concession along the Lubombo
Range in Eastern Swaziland. This concession had been
granted to his father, David Sr., and uncle James (q.
v.) who had found coal there.

FORBES, JAMES. Born in Pitlochry, Scotland, he was the
youngest of the three Forbes brothers to arrive in South
Africa. He joined his brother, David Forbes, Sr. (q.
v.) in the 1870's and tried diamond mining at Kimberley. Later, spending some time in Swaziland, he became very close to King Mbandzeni. While he was
trading for cattle with the Swazis, his nephew Alex (q.
v.) and their partner C. J. Swears (q.v.) discovered
gold near Mt. Ngwenya at a place to be called Forbes
Reef. The three formed the Forbes Reef Company in
1884 along with David Forbes, Sr. and London investors.
On March 10, 1882 King Mbandzeni had given David and
James the concession to mineral rights in Swaziland
north of the Komati River. This did not lead to much,
however, and James lived mostly at Forbes Reef. He
also discovered coal in eastern Swaziland. He was
selected temporary Chairman of the "White Committee"
on May 16, 1887, serving until July 31.
    James is also the name of the youngest of the
nephews of James Forbes (sons of David, Sr.). He remained in Swaziland also.

FORBES REEF. Now a "ghost town," this was once a thriv-
ing center of gold mining from the mid-1880's until
about the First World War. It is about 15 miles west
and north of Mbabane and about 5 miles east of the
South African border. The ruins of the old hotel and
the mine itself are still there. It was at Forbes Reef
that gold mining really began in Swaziland, the discovery being made by Alex Forbes (q.v.) and C. J.
Swears (q.v.) in the late 1870's.

FOREST PRODUCTS. The lumber and pulp produced in Swaziland has made this its third most valuable export.
Production in the northwest is handled by Peak Timbers
and Swaziland Plantations, in the Bunya area by the
Usutu Pulp Company, and in the South near Nhlangano
by Rand Mining Timbers. All practice harvesting and
replanting on a scientific basis.

FORRESTER, REV. ROBERT.   A member of the Swaziland
House of Assembly and a Deputy Speaker of it.   Formerly
a Headmaster, he owns Balegane Ranch near Balegane.
Appointed by the King to the House of Assembly upon the
death of Charles Mandy, he became Deputy Speaker.
He was reappointed after the 1972 elections.

FORSYTH-THOMPSON, PATRICK R.   Swaziland's Judicial
Commissioner, and a long time British civil servant,
serving in a variety of official capacities.   He was
Secretary for Local Administration in the mid-1960's.
Retired from British service after over forty years in
Swaziland, he has served as Chief Electoral Officer in
major Swaziland elections.

FOURIE, ETIENNE.   South African lawyer practicing law in
Mbabane in a partnership with Leo Lovell (q. v.).   He
was the magistrate in the trial of Dr. Zwane in 1963.
He was later suspended from the bench for associating
himself with a civil service protest.

G

GAIGER, SYDNEY.   Served several terms as Chairman of the
Mbabane Town Management Board in the 1960's and later
of the Town Council; he was also a member of the Reconstituted European Advisory Council.   A supporter of Carl
Todd (q. v.) during the 1962 struggle for a constitution, he
nevertheless ran as an independent on a law and order
platform in the 1964 Legislative Council elections. He was
not victorious.   He built the Swazi Inn into a major
hotel and inn while owning it between 1952 and 1966.

GAMA, JOHN.   Born in the early 1840's, he was an interpreter
for Allister Miller (q. v.) and was also in the employ of
King Mbandzeni.   A Swazi who was educated in Natal in
the nineteenth century, he also worked with Theophilus
Shepstone, Jr. to try to establish some of the earliest
geneological material on the Swaziland royal dynasty.

GAMA CLAN.   One of the Swazi clans classified as Emakhandzambili (q. v.), they came to settle near Mbabane at a place
called Dlangeni.   They have been given the charge to be
custodians of the royal graves there.   In the time of King
Sobhuza I, several of the Gama gained a reputation for
their ability to "doctor" armies in preparation for battle.

Sobhuza gave them a place to live near his headquarters.

GAMEDZE, REV. Dr. A. B.   Appointed Private Secretary
to His Majesty King Sobhuza II in June, 1974, he had
previously been a member of the Swaziland Government.
Born in 1921 in Swaziland's Shizelweni district, he
studied later in the United States at Wheaton College in
Illinois where he received a B. A. in Education and an
M. A. in Theology.   In 1968 he received an honorary
Doctor of Laws from Wheaton.   He has served as Chap-
lain and Lecturer at Fort Hare University in South
Africa.   In 1964 he became Vice President of the Swaziland Conference of Churches.   In 1973 he was elected
to be Vice-President of the Evangelical Church in Swaziland.   In May, 1967 he was nominated to the Senate
by King Sobhuza and became Minister of Education. He
was replaced in this position in July, 1971, and sent as
High Commissioner to the United Kingdom and Ambassador Extraordinary and Plenipotentiary to France,
West Germany and Belgium.   He was replaced in his
diplomatic positions in September, 1972.   That year he
had been involved in the Bank of Swaziland controversy,
having served as one of its directors.   Since leaving
the Diplomatic Corps he has been serving temporarily
as Secretary to the Swazi Nation.

GEGE.   A Swazi community three miles inside Swaziland on
a road fourteen miles from the South African town of
Piet Retief.   There are early rock paintings (q. v.) near
Gege.   Reserves of low-grade tocomite iron ore exist
near the town also.

GERMOND, ARNAULD.   First Speaker of the Swaziland Legislative Council.   Born in Basutoland of missionary
parents in December, 1905, he served for most of his
life in the Bechuanaland Government Service as Senior
District Officer and then Divisional Commissioner. He
retired to a home and land in Stegi (now Siteki) in the
early 1960's.   In 1963 he conducted an investigation into
the Big Bend labor disturbances, and later was appointed
Speaker of the Legislative Council in 1964. He died in
November, 1966.

GLADSTONE, VISCOUNT HERBERT.   First Governor-General
of the Union of South Africa, serving from May 31, 1910
until July, 1914.   In his dual role of Governor-General
and High Commissioner for the three High Commission
Territories, Gladstone was constantly at odds with the

British Colonial Office. He sympathized with Premier
Louis Botha, and advocated the transfer of Swaziland
and Bechuanaland to South Africa as soon as possible.
He felt that these areas could be used as homes for
surplus Natives in South Africa.

GLOUCESTER REGIMENT (Glosters). A British military unit
brought to Swaziland in July, 1965, one of a succession
of units brought in after labor disputes in 1963 threatened serious disorder. Only the First Battalion came
to Swaziland, replacing the North Lancashire Royal Regiment. It was replaced in April, 1966 by the Royal
Irish Fusiliers.

GOBA. A village in Mozambique, just across the
Swaziland border and forty-three miles from Lourenço
Marques. A railway was built from Lourenço Marques
to Goba in 1912, anticipating a railway across Swazi-
land which didn't come until 1964. It is located at
Umbeluzipoort, the most common crossing point into
Mozambique.

GOEDGEGUN. Now called Nhlangano (q. v.).

GOLD. A very important ore for Swaziland when it was
mined heavily between the 1880's and the First World
War. Production since then has been sporadic but
periodically profitable. Production at Forbes Reef was
important early in the period, but it was soon eclipsed
by that of the Pigg's Peak Mine (q. v.). As recently as
the 1960's there was good production from the She Mine
(q. v.). The value of gold purchased in Swaziland between 1907 and 1916 was £400, 000. From 1920 to 1949
the value was only £395, 000, but the She Mine produced £130, 600 between 1960 and 1966 when production
had to stop.

GOLELA. A small South African town on the border near
the southeastern corner of Swaziland. It is adjacent to
the Swazi town of Lavumisa, formerly called Gollel.
The twin towns constitute the end of the railroad line
from Durban. A South African border post strictly
regulates traffic into Swaziland, as political refugees
formerly used the area for escape from South Africa.

GOLLEL. A southeastern border town, since renamed
Lavumisa (q. v.).

GORDON HIGHLANDERS. A British military unit, the First
Battalion of which was airlifted from Kenya to Swaziland on June 13, 1963, in order to help restore order
after a series of strikes and labor disturbances in Swaziland. Their successful deployment, both in Mbabane
and at the Havelock Mine, prevented further violence.
About six weeks after their arrival they began to return to Kenya, being replaced by the North Lancashire
Loyal Regiment.

GRAAF, SIR DE VILLIERS. Leader of the South African
parliamentary opposition as head of the United Party
since 1956. The views of Sir De Villiers on a racial
federation either influenced or were parallel to a proposal for Swaziland by King Sobhuza II in 1960. The
King often mentioned an article by Sir De Villiers on
the subject.

THE GREAT TREK. A mass migration of settlers, especially Afrikaner Boers, from the Cape of Good Hope to
inland parts of southern Africa. This movement, primarily in the 1830's, resulted in many Whites settling
near or moving through areas claimed by the Swazis,
the first interaction between these peoples. More
Whites would follow.

GREAT USUTU RIVER (also: LUSUTFU RIVER). Sometimes referred to just as the Usutu River, this is the
Swazi river with the greatest water volume. Rising
near the headwaters of the Vaal River in the Transvaal, it enters Swaziland just north of Sandlane, about
half way down the country's north-south axis. Moving
due east, it travels in a straighter line than most
rivers, until it dips south a little, curves near Big
Bend, and then moves due east again. Leaving Swaziland at the town of Abercorn, it joins the Pongola River
at the South African border with Mozambique. The two,
once merged, are renamed the Maputo River and move
north-easterly to the Indian Ocean at Delagoa Bay. The
Usutu River is very important for the economy, servic-
ing several irrigation schemes, especially at Malkerns
and Ubombo. Among its tributaries in Swaziland are
the Umpiluzi, Little Usutu (Usushwane), Ngwempisi,
Mkondo, Mhlamanti, Mzimpofo, Mhlatuzane, Mtindekwa,
Mhlatuze and Nyetane Rivers. Thus it drains most of
the center of the country as it crosses from west to
east. Additionally, the river plays a part in Swazi

ritual. To begin the great annual ceremony, the Ncwala (q. v.) men are sent with sacred vessels to get water from three rivers important to the Swazi and from the Indian Ocean. Traditionally, they travel to the point where the Usutu (now the Maputo) River reaches Delagoa Bay.

GREEN, NELL. A co-founder and director of the Sebenta National Institute (q. v.), the important adult education for literacy group. She was a former member of the South African Black Sash women's protest movement. She and her husband Hal moved to Swaziland in 1961 in conjunction with his job building the Swaziland Railway, and they left in 1965.

GRENDON, ROBERT. A Eurafrican man from Natal who was brought to Swaziland by Queen Regent Gwamile. He was to serve as tutor for her grandson, the future Ngwenyama, Sobhuza II.

GREY, GEORGE. A special commissioner appointed by the High Commissioner, Lord Selborne, to actuate the provisions of the Concessions Partition Proclamation of 1907 (q. v.). He had the difficult and unenviable task of dividing the land held by concessionaires and returning one-third of it to Swazi use. He arrived in Mbabane in November, 1907, began his work two months later, and finished early in 1909. He was successful in limiting Swazi migration to a minimum and in giving the Swazis a fair share of the better land. There were few objections to his division itself.

GRIFFIN, SIR ARTHUR. An appointee of the British Government who has vitally affected transportation in Swaziland. He and L. C. Reynolds were appointed in 1956 to investigate communications in the country. Their report resulted in a plan for a primary road system for Swaziland, much of it soon implemented with Colonial Development and Welfare Funds. In September, 1960 Griffin, then advisor on economic development to the High Commissioner for Basutoland, Bechuanaland and Swaziland, along with Mr. L. A. W. Hawkins (q. v.), began discussions on behalf of the Swaziland Government with the Portuguese Government concerning a rail link with Mozambique. The Swaziland Railway also eventually became a reality.

GROENING, FRANK. A Eurafrican member of the Ngwane
National Liberatory Congress during much of the 1960's,
he was an NNLC candidate for the Legislative Council
in 1964. He received 1, 800 votes in a losing effort.
He was active in organizing some of the strikes in
Swaziland in 1962 and 1963, and was arrested, tried,
and acquitted for this activity. In February, 1967 he
resigned from the NNLC, bitterly critical of its leader
Dr. Ambrose Zwane.

GUNDWINI. An area about eight miles south of Manzini, and
the site of an important kraal once governed by Logcogco (q. v.). It is especially important as the location
of numerous lusekwane trees, branches and leaves of
which are picked by youths during the first day of the
Incwala ceremony (q. v.).

GWAMILE, QUEEN MOTHER see MDLULI, QUEEN
GWAMILE

-H-

HAILEY, LORD WILLIAM MALCOLM. A long-time official
in the British colonial service, his interests switched
to Africa after he promoted constitutional changes leading to Indian independence. In addition to his famous
An African Survey, he has written two other books
dealing with Swaziland: Native Administration in the
British African Territories, Part V, The High Commission Territories, and The Republic of South Africa and
the High Commission Territories. His advice to British
colonial officials, mirrored in his book on Native Administration, is considered to have been an important
guide in the shaping of British policy toward Swaziland
between the 1940's and Independence.

HARCOURT, LEWIS. British Colonial Secretary from 1910
to 1915. In this position he firmly and successfully resisted the pressures from both South African Prime
Minister Louis Botha and High Commissioner Herbert
Gladstone to begin immediate negotiations for the transfer of both Swaziland and the Bechuanaland Protectorate
to the Union of South Africa. He used the unsettled
land apportionment question in Swaziland as an immediate excuse for delay.

HARDING, SIR EDWARD. High Commissioner of the United
Kingdom for South Africa and for Basutoland, the
Bechuanaland Protectorate and Swaziland from January,
1940 until May, 1941. In his capacity as permanent
under-secretary of the Dominions Office from 1930 until
1939, he helped shape policy designed to resist attempts
by the Union of South Africa to secure the transfer to
it of Swaziland and Basutoland. African opposition to
transfer was one of his major arguments in opposing
South Africa.

HARLECH, LORD (SIR WILLIAM ORMSBY GORE). High
Commissioner of the United Kingdom for South Africa
and for Basutoland, the Bechuanaland Protectorate and
Swaziland from May 24, 1941 to May 13, 1944. In
disagreement with the Dominions Office, Lord Harlech
believed that a deal should be arranged with General
Smuts to grant transfer of Swaziland to South Africa but
involving minimal change for Bechuanaland and Basutoland. He felt Swaziland was too small for efficient administration and British rule was unpopular there. It
would be better to transfer it to Smuts, he felt, than
to wait until after the Nationalists came to power in
South Africa.

HAVELOCK (also: EMLEMBE). A city of over four thousand inhabitants, including about five hundred of European descent, it is located in the northwestern part of
Swaziland on the border with South Africa. Named
after Sir Arthur Havelock, it is the site of one of the
largest asbestos mines in the world. It was also the
site of a major strike in May and June of 1963 which
resulted in the bringing in of British troops.

HAVELOCK, SIR ARTHUR E., 1844-1908. Governor of Natal
from 1885 to 1889. The city of Havelock was named
after him in 1886 by two prospectors who had a concession to mine gold in the vicinity. During his service
in Natal, he defended the right of Swazi independence so
long as existing ruling institutions were successful.

HAVELOCK ASBESTOS MINE. Opened in 1939, and owned by
New Amianthus Mines, Ltd., a subsidiary of the British
asbestos firm, Turner, Newall and Company. It is one
of the five largest producers of chrysotile asbestos in
the world. Production rose from R84, 328 in 1938 to
R965, 668 in 1940. By 1952 it reached R5, 000, 000 and

remained there for a number of years. In 1968 production was worth R6 million. The asbestos is carried
from high in the mountains to Barberton, a distance of
twelve and a half miles, by cableway. There are indications that it will continue to be a major source of
revenue and jobs for the country until about the year
2000. In 1973, 40 per cent ownership was transferred
to the Swazi nation. Low wages for Swazi at the mines
precipitated a strike beginning May 20, 1963, by between
two and three thousand workers led by Dr. Zwane and
Dumisa Dlamini of the Ngwane National Liberatory Congress. Arrests were made but the strike spread. After
several weeks of disorder, British troops stationed in
Kenya, the Gordon Highlanders (q. v.), were brought in
to quell the strikes.

HAWKINS, LEONARD ARTHUR WYON. Chief Executive
    Officer and Chairman of the Board of the Swaziland
    Railway until his death, February 13, 1972. In Septem-
    ber, 1960 he and Sir Arthur Griffin (q. v.) began nego-
    tiations with the Portuguese Government for the Swazi-
    land Government regarding a rail link with Lourenço
    Marques, Mozambique. After taking part in feasibility
    studies, he came to Swaziland in 1961 to supervise con-
    struction of the railway, and was subsequently respons-
    ible for a major part of its later success. In addition,
    he was responsible for resolving major problems in
    the Malkerns Valley pineapple industry, finally becoming
    Chairman of the Board of Libby's (Swaziland), as well
    as serving on the Board of the Standard Bank, the Swa-
    ziland Building Society and other companies.

HELEHELE. A central Swaziland town located about five
    miles east of Manzini on the major cross-country road,
    at the spot where this road meets one of the main roads
    heading south toward Hlatikulu, Gollel and other south-
    ern Swaziland towns.

HER MAJESTY'S COMMISSIONER FOR SWAZILAND. A post
    established by the Sandy's Constitution of 1963, replac-
    ing the previous position of Resident Commissioner when
    it went into effect in January, 1964. Power in the po-
    sition would be roughly equal to the right of veto over
    any legislative council enactments. Mineral rights were
    left in his hands to grant or refuse after "consultation"
    with the Ngwenyama. The post lapsed at Independence.

HERTZOG, GENERAL JAMES BARRY MUNNIK. Prime Minister of the Union of South Africa from 1924 until 1939. Several early breaks with Great Britain over policy matters made British concessions to Prime Minister Hertzog on the question of the transfer of the High Commission Territories to South Africa very unlikely. Nevertheless, from less than four months after his installation as Prime Minister in 1924 until the Thomas-Hertzog concordat of 1935, Hertzog applied constant pressure to Great Britain on the subject of the transfer of Swaziland and Bechuanaland to South Africa. British Colonial and Dominion Offices successfully resisted and delayed him during this period. Finally, in mid-1935, the Secretary of State for Dominion Affairs, J. H. Thomas, and Hertzog agreed on an indefinite delay. During this delay, South Africa and Great Britain would cooperate on projects which would so greatly improve conditions in the High Commission Territories that their citizens would feel great good will toward South Africa, and eventually, willingly agree to a transfer to South African control, it was assumed.

HHOHHO (variants: HOHO and HORO). The northernmost of the four Administrative Districts of Swaziland, at 1,378 square miles it is the smallest of the four in area. It has a population of about 100,000; its largest city and headquarters of the District is Mbabane. The District's assets include the country's major mining regions: Havelock, Ngwenya, and Pigg's Peak. Under the 1963 administrative revision, the Pigg's Peak and Mbabane Districts were merged to form Hhohho.
    The town of Hhohho is the northernmost town in Swaziland, three miles from the South African border. Under both Ngwane III and Mswati II it became the King's administrative capital.

HIGH COMMISSIONER OF THE UNITED KINGDOM FOR BASUTOLAND, THE BECHUANALAND PROTECTORATE, AND SWAZILAND. The title of the chief administrative officer of the United Kingdom directly responsible for the affairs of Basutoland, the Bechuanaland Protectorate, and Swaziland. The position was instituted in May, 1910, when it was a joint appointment of the Governor-General of the Union of South Africa. The latter assignment was separated from the post of High Commissioner in January, 1931. The position lapsed in 1964.

HIGH COMMISSION TERRITORIES. The common term used
to designate the three territories: Basutoland, the
Bechuanaland Protectorate, and Swaziland. Based on
the title of their chief colonial administrator, the High
Commissioner, the term was generally applied to the
three areas until their independence in the 1960's.

HIGH COURT OF SWAZILAND. Presided over normally by
the Chief Justice, the head of the judiciary, it is a
superior court of record. It has unlimited original
jurisdiction in civil and criminal matters in Swaziland,
and appellate jurisdiction as prescribed by any law currently in force in the country. Under it are Subordinate Courts, Swazi (traditional) Courts, and superior to
it is the Court of Appeal. Except where altered by
statute, Roman-Dutch common law is the common law
of the country.

HIGHVELD. A mountainous area along the western side of
Swaziland, the altitude averages 3, 500 to 4, 500 feet
above sea level. The highest altitudes are the summits
of Mt. Emlembe (6, 109 ft.) and Mt. Ngwenya (6, 002
ft.). The area is cut through by numerous river valleys
and gorges, with waterfalls not uncommon. The Highveld is really an extension of the Drakensberg chain of
mountains that rises through Lesotho and the Republic
of South Africa. The hillsides are mostly grassland,
except for areas planted and tended by the Usutu Pulp
Company. The siSwati term for the Highveld is Inkangala. Much of Swaziland's mining is in this area.
The Highveld receives between 40 and 90 inches of rain
a year, and has a temperate but humid climate.

HILL, ROLAND. A South African he was Chief Justice of
Swaziland from December, 1972 to December, 1973.

HLATHIKULU (variant: HLATIKULU). A town in the southwestern part of the country, with a population of about
1, 000, mostly Swazi. The name means "Big Bushes. "
Located near the scenic "Grand Valley" of the Mkondo
River, it is a hub for bus traffic, partly because it is
a link for bus travel between Manzini and Piet Retief,
South Africa. It also has a large hospital. Before the
administrative changes of December, 1963, Hlathikulu
was also the name of one of the six districts of the
country, since renamed the Shiselweni District.

HLOPHE, ABEDNEGO RUSENI. An important member of the
Swazi National Council, and Minister of Agriculture
since Independence. Born at Lozita, January 13, 1922,
he was educated at the national schools and at St.
Chad's College in Natal and the University of Sussex in
England. He became clerk to the Standing Committee
of the Swazi National Council, and from 1951 to 1962
was private secretary to King Sobhuza II. He served
on the Constitutional Committee from 1961 to 1963, and
was a delegate to London Constitutional Conferences in
1963 and 1968. He has stood successfully in elections
in 1964, 1967, and 1972, each time being elected as an
Imbokodvo member to Parliament from the Mbuluzi
constituency. From 1964 until he became Minister of
Agriculture, he served on the Executive Committee of
the Legislative Council as Minister of Local Government and Social Services, with responsibility for cooperatives, social welfare, and community development.

HLOPHE, LOSHINI. One of the advisers to King Sobhuza II
who accompanied him to London in December, 1922, to
present a petition to the British Government protesting
the Partitions Proclamation.

HLOPHE, MAHAGANE. Indvuna of King Ndvungunye's administrative capital at Shiselweni around the beginning
of the nineteenth century.

HLUBI. The rightful heir to succeed his father Ludvonga I
as Swazi Ngwenyama. However, his mother had two
other sons, a pattern not acceptable for Swazi Kings
according to Swazi custom. Thus Dlamini III, his half-
brother, became King. This took place probably in the
late seventeenth or early eighteenth century.

HLUTI. A town located in Swaziland about eight miles north
of the South African border. One report indicates that
the Zulu King, Dingane, brother of Chaka, died somewhere east of this area. He is reportedly buried near
there.

HOHO. Variant of HHOHHO.

HOLTHAUSEN, I. The man responsible for stimulating the
growth of the asbestos industry in Swaziland. A resident of Barberton, he rediscovered a deposit of chrysotile asbestos along the banks of Dudusi Creek in north-

west Swaziland in 1918.   This deposit had been noticed
over a decade earlier but was ignored by the gold prospectors.

HONEY, SIR DE SYMON.   Appointed Government Secretary
(assistant to the Resident Commissioner) of Swaziland
in 1907.   He later served as Resident Commissioner
from 1917 to 1928.   In this capacity, he accompanied
King Sobhuza II and the Swazi delegation to London in
1923.   Interested in history, he collected historical material on the Swazi people which is found in some of
the Official Year Books of the Union of South Africa.

HOULTON, SIR JOHN WARDLE.   Speaker (later, President)
of the Senate until he retired in May, 1973.   He came
to South Africa in 1950, and while living in Swaziland
he was made Legal Secretary.   In 1965, he became
Speaker of the Legislative Council, and two years later
he became Speaker of the Senate.   For many years he
wrote lead editorials in the Times of Swaziland.   He
died November 9, 1973.

THE HOUSE OF ASSEMBLY.   The larger of the two houses
of Parliament (q. v.) under the 1967 and Independence
Constitutions.   It consisted of thirty members--twenty-
four elected from eight three-member constituencies and
six appointed by the King.   In addition, the Attorney-
General (q. v.) was an ex-officio member without a vote.
Exclusive power to initiate legislation on taxation and
financial matters belonged to the House of Assembly.
The Speaker was its presiding officer.   (See also
PRIME MINISTER.)

HOWICK, LORD see SIR EVELYN BARING

HUGGARD, SIR WALTER (1883-1957).   A judge of the High
Courts of the High Commission Territories for some
years after his retirement from the British Colonial
Service.   He was first appointed judge in 1937.   He
also served as Legal Adviser to the High Commissioner
and was Acting High Commissioner from January, 1940
to May, 1941.   He briefly served as High Commissioner
from June 23, 1944 to October 27, 1944.

HULETT, GEORGE.   A solicitor from Natal, he was appointed as Chief Secretary to the Swazi nation on August 28, 1894, and was confirmed in this post by Queen

Mother Labotsibeni.   He sailed to England with the Deputation of 1894 (q. v.) as legal advisor to the group
and was a witness to the negotiations.

HYND, DR. DAVID.   A medical missionary of the Church of
the Nazarene, he and his wife arrived in Swaziland in
1925.   In 1927 he helped found a hospital at Manzini.
He became director of the Swaziland branch of the Red
Cross in 1932 and continued until 1957.   In 1963 he
was sent as an Independent to serve on the Swaziland
delegation at the London constitutional conference.   He
has also been President of the Swaziland Council of
Churches in recent years.

-I-

IMBOKODVO NATIONAL MOVEMENT   (variants: MBO-
KODVO, IMBOKODO).   The victorious party in the
three parliamentary elections held in Swaziland in 1964,
1967, and 1972, and thus the ruling political party of
Swaziland since 1964.   Described by many as "The
King's Party," its early strength did indeed derive
from its support by the King and the Swazi National
Council.   Since then it has gained the active support
and membership of numerous leaders from the other
political parties, who were unable to match the traditional charisma of the King.   It was formed by the
Swazi National Council (q. v.) in 1964 on advice from
South African advisers after the British made it clear
that elections would be held.   After his success in unit-
ing the Swazi people in a January election, the "reindeer referendum" (q. v.), King Sobhuza II and the SNC
decided to beat the British at their own game.   At a
national meeting in the Royal Kraal on April 17, 1964,
Sobhuza announced that, since the people had stuck together like an Imbokodvo ("Grinding Stone," a very
hard and unbreakable rock) in the earlier election, they
"should remain as such."   Some say that he added,
"And Makhosini should take the lead."   Prince Makhosini Dlamini (q. v.) then did lead the Imbokodvo to electoral and political successes, for a while with the aid
of Dr. George Msibi (q. v.) as Secretary General.   The
party supported Swazi traditions and the power of the
King, and received thereby massive support from traditionalists.   Likewise, cooperation during the 1964 elections with the United Swaziland Association (USA), made

up of Europeans, brought it much White support. After
winning the 1964 elections decisively, however, the
party abandoned a couple of its early positions, such
as close ties with South Africa and restricted voting
rolls, thus attracting members of the defeated political
parties by adopting large parts of their platforms. Its
leadership, under Prince Makhosini, has continued to
attract widespread support, which is by no means un-
animous. While the party does have an organizational
structure with officials and local branches, its support
still is heavily based on its indirect ties to the Swazi
National Council.

IMMIGRATION AMENDMENT ACT of 1972. A law passed
by the House of Assembly on November 13, 1972, as
an amendment to the Immigration Act of 1964. It provides for appointment of a Special Tribunal to decide
whether or not an individual is actually a citizen of
Swaziland. The person must prove his claim before
the Tribunal, subject only to appeal to the Prime Minister. The regular court system is not to be involved
at all. The law was passed after Thomas Ngwenya
(q. v.), an elected member of the Opposition in the
House of Assembly, was declared to be not a Swazi citizen, and later was made a prohibited immigrant by the
Government. The High Court and Court of Appeal then
reversed this action. This law then set up a Tribunal
to avoid the other courts, but the Court of Appeal
found, in March, 1973, that the law was unconstitutional. Two weeks later the King declared the Constitution to be unsuitable to the nation's needs and thus
cancelled it. A month later (May, 1973), the King's
Order-in-Council reinstated the Special Tribunal for
Immigration cases.

IMPALA RANCH. A large cattle holding ground in northeastern Swaziland between the White Umbeluzi River
and the Black Umbeluzi River.

IMPALAMPALA. A traditional hunting horn of the Swazi,
preferably made from a very narrow and twisted horn
of a kudu bull. It produced a greater volume of sound
than the luveve (q. v.). It has been used by herdsmen
to lead their cattle and was sometimes used by Swazi
warriors. Today it has been replaced for the most
part by brass instruments.

IMPI.   An army.   It is an Nguni word sometimes used to
describe Swazi fighting units, although emabutfo (q. v.)
is more commonly used.   Emabutfo could be combined
to serve as an impi.   The term is used most frequently
to describe the highly trained and organized fighting
units developed by the Zulu, especially under the influence of their great leader Chaka.

IN-.   Words beginning with these two letters are in some
books also printed properly beginning with the letter
"N, " since the "I" is more of a phonetic contribution.
This also holds true for a couple of other combinations,
especially "Im-. "

INCORPORATION INTO SOUTH AFRICA.   The process by
which Swaziland and the other two High Commission
Territories might be absorbed into the Union (later, Republic) of South Africa.   Although the South African Act
(q. v.) allowed for this possibility, it made absorption
contingent upon the approval of each of the three Territories.   Great Britain insisted on this and most of its
colonial officials safeguarded it.   South African attempts
to incorporate Swaziland were most notable in 1913,
1927, 1933, 1935 and 1937.   After the Nationalist Party
came to power in South Africa in 1948, British reluctance to allow transfer grew quickly, especially as
Apartheid was being implemented.   Dr. Verwoerd made
a kind of appeal to the Territories in 1963, but by this
time Great Britain was adamant in its refusal.

INCWALA   see   NCWALA

INDEPENDENCE CONFERENCE.   Held at Marlborough House
in London from February 19 to February 24, 1968. The
Swazi delegation was led by the Prime Minister, Prince
Makhosini Dlamini, and did not contain representatives
from opposition parties.   Nevertheless, Dr. Ambrose
Zwane and Mr. Kingsway T. Samketi of the NNLC gained
attention by prostrating themselves on the steps of the
conference building until taken away by police.   The
Conference itself resulted in agreement on the Independence Constitution (almost exactly the same as the 1967
Constitution) and the date for independence, September
6, 1968.   The British also relinquished the determina-
tion of mineral rights to the Swazi King, but did not
promise Swaziland extra financial aid to gain back land
alienated in the past century.   The latter was a dis-

appointment to the Swazi delegation.

INDIAN OCEAN. Touching the southeastern coast of Africa
in places as close as forty-five miles from Swaziland,
this great ocean plays several roles in Swazi history.
Traditionally, the founder of the Swazis, Dlamini, led
his followers along the Komati River to Delagoa Bay on
the Ocean and dwelt in that area for perhaps two centuries before moving inland. Even today that is re-
called in the Ncwala ceremony by sending runners to
the ocean for ceremonial waters to renew the King.
There are similar references in other rituals about how
one must "go to the sea. " In the last century the subject of going to the ocean has been discussed concerning a Swaziland Railway (q. v.) either to Delagoa Bay or
Kosi Bay. This was finally completed in 1964. Today
the Indian Ocean bears the ships carrying Swazi iron
ore to Japan.

INDIRECT RULE. A pattern of colonial government developed especially by the British and credited primarily to
Lord Lugard who utilized this concept both in India and
Northern Nigeria. This system, in contrast to Direct
Rule, leaves traditional leaders in their positions, while
at the same time imposing foreign rule by requiring the
traditional leaders to implement the orders of the colonial power. For the most part this system, used
commonly in British colonial Africa, was not followed
in Swaziland (see PARALLEL RULE), with the exception
of a series of Administration Proclamations in 1950.
Even these left loopholes for the traditionalists, however.

INDLOVUKATI. A commonly used variant of Ndlovukazi.

INDLUNKULU. The great hut, one of the three key structures in a Swazi homestead. (see SIBOYA and
LILAWU.) It is the sine qua non of the homestead and
normal relations within the homestead are restricted
until it is ready. It is the embodiment of the lineage
of the headman. Decorated with the skulls of cattle
sacrificed to the ancestors, it is used for rituals and
as a family shrine. It is cared for by the headman's
mother or, on her death, her designated successor as
"mother. " Wives are normally forbidden access but the
headman's children are not, emphasizing its significance
to the patrilineal lineage. Wives are given their sepa-

rate huts for sleeping, cooking, and storage. The
above description applies to all homesteads, but is of
special significance when the indlunkulu in question is
that of the King himself. His is a magnificent structure (of traditional design and materials) which is regularly refurbished by the men of the nation.

INDUNA (variant: INDVUNA [q. v.]). INDUNA is more
commonly used among the Zulus and Xhosas, whereas
indvuna is used among the Swazis.

INDVUNA (plural: TINDVUNA). Variously translated as
"counsellor, " "second in charge, " "governor, " and
"representative. " In any case he is a commoner chosen
by the King, usually from one of four clans (Fakudze,
Nkambule, Zwane, and Hlophe), to serve in an official
capacity in one of the royal villages. The King relies
on his tindvuna to counsel him and to serve as an in-
termediary between the King and the people of each of
the royal villages. The position is not necessarily
hereditary but may stay in the same family. An indvuna may be dismissed only by the King sitting in
council, not by the King alone. Duties of an indvuna
may be to hear cases and give judgments, organize
labor in the fields, watch over the distribution of royal
cattle, interview strangers, arrange for national rituals,
advise the King on popular opinion, and even to join
with senior princes in rebuking an erring King or Queen
Mother. In addition to its application at the national
level, the title indvuna is given to individuals serving
in similar positions under chiefs at lower levels of the
Swazi nation.

INDVUNA LENKULU. The man chosen to be indvuna (q. v.)
over a new royal capital (rather than just one of the
royal villages), thus called the "great councilor. " Es-
sentially his role is that of an indvuna, but more significant because his locus of power is the capital itself.
Although commoners, tindvuna (plural) lenkulu have been
known to conspire with princes and queen mothers
against Kings, and at least two were executed for trea-
son. The indvuna lenkulu will always appoint a younger
assistant who, if he serves well, may succeed to the
position upon the death or disability of the indvuna lenkulu.

INGWAVUMA RIVER. Draining much of the southern Swazi-

land watershed, this river begins north of Nhlangano in
the southwestern part of the country and flows due east.
It breaches the Lubombo Mountains at Ingwavumapoort
and flows north as it enters Natal where it merges with
the Pongola River before the latter merges with the
Usutu River.

INGWENYAMA.   A commonly used variant of Ngwenyama.

INHERITANCE FUND   see   LIFA FUND

INKANGALA.   The siSwati word for the Highveld.

INKHOSATANA YELIVE.   Princess of the country, a term
    applied to any full sister of the King.   Among the
    women of the country she is considered next in rank
    after the Ndlovukazi and the King's leading wives. She
    will usually take little part in the central government
    since, after marriage, she will not reside in the capi-
    tal; however, she does have an important voice on the
    council choosing an heir to the kingship.

INKONYAMBA.   The Swazi God of the underworld, who takes
    the form of a great horned snake.   Believed to dwell
    in the heart of the Ngwenya Mountains, he deterred
    Swazis from mining anything except the summit (for
    iron).

INKOSI.   A variant of Nkosi.

INSANGU.   Marijuana, also called Indian hemp.   This is one
    of several terms used in Swaziland and other parts of
    southern Africa to denote this drug.   (See DAGGA.) Al-
    though it has been legislated against and many convic-
    tions have taken place, its use is still not rare.   At
    one time historically it was given to the Swazi army to
    smoke before going into battle in order to make the
    warriors "fearless. " It was also used by the praisers
    who sang praise poems to the King and other notables.
    It supposedly stimulated their brains.   Modern pharm-
    acognosists would seriously dispute the beneficial effect
    of the drug on the quality of both the battles and the
    praise poems.

INSILA (plural: TINSILA).   A person who has been linked
    with the King in a very special "blood" ceremony. (A
    second definition, of less broad significance, is "body

dirt. ")   When the young King nears the age of puberty,
the councillors send to certain lineages of the Midluli
and Motsa clans to bring a youth of approximately the
same age.   A ritual then takes place at the royal village where incisions are made in each insila and the
King in order to allow the blood to mix in their wounds.
Medicines are also rubbed into the cuts.   The cuts on
the right side of the King are mixed with the blood of
the Mdluli insila and on the left side with the blood of
the Motsa insila.   The theory behind the ritual is that
danger originally intended for the King will first enter
the insila, thus reducing the chance of harm to the
King.   The link between the tinsila and the King is
strong for the rest of their lives, and they are often
linked in rituals.   Shortly after the King selects his
first two wives (also from specific clans), the tinsila
must marry.   Usually the first wife of each is selected
by the queen regent and the council.   When the tinsila
are married, two youngsters are chosen from other
clans to serve as junior tinsila.   One from the Matsebula clan becomes junior insila of the right side and
one from the Nkambule clan becomes junior insila of
the left side.   No blood ceremonies take place, however,
and a junior insila serves only as an attendant and does
not get promoted to senior insila.   When the first two
junior insila get married, a Mdluli becomes another
right hand insila, and a Thwale becomes another left
hand insila.   The death of the King removes all tinsila
from office.

INYANGA   (plural: TINYANGA).   A specialist in any of
several professions or handicrafts, including such as
blacksmiths, carpenters, potters, medicine men, and
diviners.   Practitioners of pharmacognosy, the tinyanga
work with products of nature in attempting to cure ill-
nesses, but it is preferable for them to link these with
a knowledge of ritual handed down through their family.
Usually working alone, the inyanga emphasizes the material "medicine" rather than the ritual or an incanta-
tion.   Tinyanga are rated by the Swazi at several levels
of competence, and thus are not equally sought after.
(See also TANGOMA.)

IRON ORE.   Now one of the main sources of revenue and exports for the country, it meant little as late as 1955.
Despite evidence that Stone Age men had worked as
early as 25, 000 B. C. among the deposits in the Ngwenya

Mountains, no serious efforts were made until after a 1955 report of the Geological Survey Department. The Swaziland Iron Ore Development Co. Ltd. was formed in 1957 and was granted prospecting and mining rights. Almost as important as the ore itself, the need for transporting it and the guarantee of a customer for a railroad spurred the development of a Swaziland railway which then made possible many other export industries along its right of way.

IRRIGATION SCHEMES. Financed for the most part by the Commonwealth Development Corporation (q. v.), irrigation projects have diverted the plentiful waters of Swaziland to enable large scale production of sugar, rice, and citrus fruits especially. The Lomati, Umbeluzi, Great Usutu, and Mhlatuzane Rivers in the Middleveld, and the Komati and Great Usutu Rivers in the Lowveld are principal sources of the irrigation waters.

IZWI LAMA SWAZI. Literally, "The Voice of the Swazi. " A vernacular newspaper founded in 1934 by John J. Nquku (q. v.). He served as its editor until the Bantu Press took over its publication. It was a weekly newspaper until its demise in 1964.

- J -

JACKSON, REV. JOEL. Anglican missionary who began the Holy Rood Mission near Piet Retief along the Ndlotane River on December 25, 1871. His Bishop, Thomas Wilkinson, had received permission after visiting Queen Mother Thandile and the Swazi council. In 1881, King Mbandzeni invited Rev. Jackson to start a mission school at Luyengo for the education of his son, Bhunu. However, Bhunu did not attend the school. About six years later, Rev. Jackson was chosen by King Mbandzeni as one of his representatives on the "White Committee" (q. v.). (Two amusing incidents concerning his missionary efforts are portrayed in David Forbes' book, My Life in South Africa.)

JAPAN, ECONOMIC RELATIONS WITH. Aside from trade with South Africa and Great Britain, nothing has been more pivotal for the economy of Swaziland than the agreement with two major Japanese steel companies to export large quantities of Swaziland's iron ore to Japan.

In addition to its expected effect on Swaziland's economy, it guaranteed the viability of a railway through
Swaziland. In addition to financing other mineral exploration, Japan has built in 1973 a radio and TV assembly plant, its products to be exported to Europe,
Australia, and Africa.

JOINT COMMISSION. A commission chaired by Sir Francis
de Winton (q. v.) and consisting of several representatives each from the British government and the government of the Transvaal. It was appointed in 1889 to
visit Swaziland and investigate its internal affairs, and
to make recommendations that would satisfy both Great
Britain and the Transvaal. It arrived November 30,
1889, several weeks after King Mbandzeni died. Its
recommendations, agreed to by the Queen Regent on
December 18, 1889, and formalized the following March
in the First Swaziland Convention, 1890 (q. v.), included
the following: a Provisional Government (q. v.) representing the Swazis, the British, and the Transvaal would
replace the "White Committee, " but with no jurisdiction
over purely Swazi matters. Also, the South African
Republic would receive the right to build a railway
through Swaziland to Kosi Bay. A high court should be
formed and it would decide on the validity of all concessions. Likewise no new concessions would be allowed without the approval of the British High Commissioner and the President of the South African Republic.

JOINT COUNCIL OF SWAZILAND POLITICAL PARTIES. An
ad hoc alliance formed by four of Swaziland's political
parties on June 1, 1964. The several segments of the
Swaziland Progressive Party, and the Ngwane National
Liberatory Congress tried to get Sir Brian Marwick to
persuade the King to stay out of politics. This was
just several weeks before the election. The parties did
not, however, agree to present a common slate of candidates in the election. Just after the election (in which
only the King's party was successful) they got together
again, led by Obed Mabuza (q. v.). Other members of
the Joint Council included Macdonald Maseko, Austin
Nxumalo, and Sifunti Matsebula (all q. v.). The Joint
Council was relatively disorganized, however, as members resigned (Dr. A. Zwane) or were expelled (J. J.
Nquku) or failed to be active. In August, 1965, its
leaders were Mabuza (President), Maseko (Vice-President), and Austin W. Nxumalo (Secretary-General). In

July, 1966, Mabuza and Dr. Zwane held talks and
agreed to reunite as the Swaziland United Front (q. v.),
with Nxumalo continuing as Secretary-General.   Dr.
Zwane's NNLC never fully integrated with the United
Front, however, and the groups had candidates running
against one another in the 1967 elections.

JOKOVA, PRINCE (variant: JOKOVU).   A senior member
of the Swazi Council and a chief during the latter part
of the nineteenth century.   Believing that Swazis and
Europeans should each have their controls over their
own systems of justice, he argued against the Europeans
concerning the Swazi right to kill their evil-doers, but
argued for the Europeans in trying to persuade King
Mbandzeni to allow them their own courts (through the
"White Committee, " q. v.).

THE JUDICIAL SERVICE COMMISSION.   A three-member
commission which advised the King on certain high judicial appointments and which on its own authority appointed the Registrar and Assistant Registrar for both
the Court of Appeal and the High Court as well as all
magistrates and other court officers for any court designated by Parliament.   This Commission consisted of
the Chief Justice as chairman, plus the chairman of the
Public Service Commission, and a person of judicial
experience appointed by the King on the advice of the
Chief Justice.   The Commission was abolished by the
King in April, 1973, after the Ngwenya dispute.

-K-

KADAKE.   Two miles east of the South African border, this
town is the western terminus of the Swaziland Railway
which was opened at Kadake by the King on November
5, 1964.   Ka-Dake is named after Johan Darke, a
trader from Zululand who set up a store and inn below
Ngwenya Mountain in the 1880's.

KANGWANE.   A Swazi word used as a synonym for Swaziland.   It means "the place (or country) of Ngwane. "

KARANGA.   Ancestors of today's Swazis, they are a group
of people who, five hundred years ago, lived north of
the Zambezi River but moved south to the area between
the Limpopo and Sabi Rivers.   Some of them were

called Emalangeni, but called themselves Vhambo. The
Portuguese saw them near the Limpopo River about
1589. The term Vhambo evolved into Bambo--Bembo--
Embo. Thus we have the Bembo Nguni (q. v.), of which
group Dlamini (q. v.) was.

KHONTA see KUKHONTA

KHOZA, ARTHUR RAY. Permanent Secretary in the Swaziland Ministry of Justice. A university graduate, he had
been active with the Ngwane National Liberatory Congress in the mid-1960's. In 1965 he was named Acting
Secretary General and Secretary for Publicity and Education. Frustrated with personality disputes and leadership splits within Dr. Zwane's party, he resigned in
September, 1966, despite having spent several months
at an ideological institute in Ghana. Later he joined
the Imbokodvo National Movement, eventually becoming
private secretary to the Prime Minister. Before joining the Ministry of Justice on December 1, 1971, he
had been Permanent Secretary for Works, Power, and
Communications. In 1973, he was appointed Secretary
to the Royal Constitutional Commission.

KHUMALO, SISILE. Also known as la Mgangeni. A wife of
Mswati, her son Ludvongo became King Ludvongo II in
a controversial decision by the Royal Council (see
MBILINI). Sisile became Ndlovukazi and her capital
was set up at Nkanini (q. v.). When Ludvonga died after
only four years as King at the age of twenty-one, he
had no heir. The Royal Council asked Sisile to choose
a "replacement" son from Mswati's other sons. She
chose an orphan, Mbandzeni (q. v.). A conflict later
developed between King Mbandzeni and the Ndlovukazi
Sisile over a girl he married and by whom he had a
son. When the son died, Sisile tried to flee the country
accompanied by some royal soldiers. With great re-
gret, Mbandzeni sent two emabutfo after her with orders
to kill her, but only after removing the symbol of her
royal office from her head. This was done as they
caught her a little west of where Mbabane now is.

KHUMALO, ZONKE AMOS. Deputy Prime Minister of Swaziland since 1971 and member of the House of Assembly
from the Usutu constituency. Born in 1927 at Zombode
and educated in Swazi schools, he was elected to the
Legislative Council in 1964 as a member of Imbokodvo.

He has been reelected in both 1967 and 1972, and
served as Minister of State for Foreign Affairs before
being appointed Deputy Prime Minister.

KING OF SWAZILAND. The word "King" is not indigenous
to the Swazis, but the word Nkosi is a rough equivalent
despite the fact that it can be applied to lesser chiefs
as well. The most appropriate title given to the main
ruler of Swaziland is Ngwenyama (q. v. for a summary
of his role in traditional Swazi affairs). The use of the
word "King" became common only after the British became active in Swaziland (and even they preferred the
term "Paramount Chief"). To a great extent the role
of the King of Swaziland in modern life is the story of
King Sobhuza II (q. v.), who has ruled for over fifty
years. Educated and dynamic, he has made his position
an extremely powerful one. Starting with his challenges
to Great Britain in the 1920's, he has shown determi-
nation to return his country to his people's control,
both politically and economically. Asserting the Swazi
ruler's traditional right over all his people's land as
its trustee, he constantly tried to reaquire control over
land and mineral rights. He finally succeeded in this
with the Independence Constitution and subsequent legislation. Resisting British attempts to make the King
merely a figurehead, King Sobhuza II organized a coalition with Europeans in Swaziland, and later formed
the Imbokodvo National Movement (q. v.), a political
party successfully designed to beat British plans while
using Great Britain's own ground-rules. Finally in 1973
he succeeded in overthrowing the Independence Constitution, calling the Westminster model "unsuitable" for
Swaziland. He plans to institute a new Constitution which
is expected to return considerable power to the King and
his followers. See Appendix B for a list of recent kings.

THE KINGDOM OF SWAZILAND. The full and complete name
of the country of the Swazis as internationally recognized.

KOMATI RIVER. Starting near the Transvaal town of Carolina, some sixty or so miles west of Swaziland, the
river follows an erratic path before it enters Swaziland
about six miles south of Havelock. It flows due east to
Balegane, where it starts north and east, exiting the
country near Bordergate. It then flows through the
Transvaal where it is joined by the Lomati River. Later,

as the Incomati River, it loops through Mozambique to
join the Indian Ocean at the north end of Delagoa Bay.
The waters of the Komati are used for an important
irrigation scheme in the Tshaneni-Mhlume area.   Its
waters are also gathered in sacred vessels for the beginning of the annual Ncwala rites.

KOPJE.   A "hill" in the Afrikaans language, frequently used
by South Africans in Swaziland.   It is a term used by
many non-Afrikaners.

KOSI BAY.   An Indian Ocean inlet roughly fifty miles due
east of southern Swaziland and ten miles south of the
Mozambique border with South Africa.   It became im-
portant in the 1880's and 1890's when the South African
Republic wanted access to the ocean.   If they could get
Swaziland from the British (effectively accomplished by
the Third Swaziland Convention, 1904, q. v.), they needed only a little more land plus British rights to Kosi
Bay.   A railroad across that area was also envisioned.
The British prevented this by concluding an agreement
with the ruler of Tongaland (see TONGA) which included
Kosi Bay.   Thus the South African Republic lost much of
its interest in Swaziland.

KRAAL.   An enclosure for cattle and other livestock, also
used sometimes for other purposes (see SIBOYA).   It is
an Afrikaans (q. v.) word, not unlike the American term
"corral" in meaning.   It is in common use throughout
southern Africa.   It is sometimes used to indicate the
whole enclosed dwelling area belonging to a family.

KROGH, JOHANNES C.   Formerly a landdrost at Wakker-
stroom, he was appointed in February, 1895, by the
South African Republic as Special Commissioner for
Swaziland when the Boer Government assumed the
country's administration.   The Swazis called him Nko-
seluhlaza.   As Special Commissioner (equivalent to
Resident Commissioner), he became part of the controversy over the setting of the boundary between Swaziland
and Portuguese Territory on the east in 1897.   He was
a member of the boundary commission.   He also was
Commissioner during the affair when King Bhunu
(Ngwane V) was charged with the murder of indvuna
Mbhabha Sibandze (q. v.) in April, 1898.   Hundreds of
warriors protested their King being brought to trial.
This resulted in a counterforce of burghers and troops,

but no battle ensued. With the coming of the Boer War
in October, 1899, Krogh issued an official notice advis-
ing all Europeans except those called for military service to leave Swaziland immediately. After the British
Order in Council of June, 1903, Krogh helped rule Swaziland from Pretoria.

KRUGER, STEPHANUS JOHANNES PAULUS. President of
    the South African Republic during the Anglo-Boer War.
    President Kruger made little attempt to discourage his
    people from settling in Swaziland for purposes of farm-
    ing or mining, as he saw Swaziland to be a logical
    addition to the Transvaal, especially in view of his de-
    sire to use it as an outlet to the sea. As a result, he
    was involved in a series of agreements with Great
    Britain that ultimately placed Swaziland under his rule.
    (See FIRST, SECOND and THIRD SWAZILAND CON-
    VENTIONS.) When Britain cut off his access to the sea
    at Kosi Bay by annexing Tongaland (see TONGA) in
    1897, Kruger's interest in Swaziland folded.

KUBUTA. A town located along the road from Hlatikulu to
    Sitobela, in south-central Swaziland. It is in the middle
    of a major irrigation scheme stemming from the Mhla-
    tuzane River which flows through this banana-producing
    area. There is also a small airstrip nearby.

KUKHONTA. A voluntary bond of homage and allegiance
    offered to a superior. Commoners khonta (verb form)
    to a chief, chiefs khonta to the King. It involves legal
    and economic obligations on both parties. The nature
    of the bond will vary under differing circumstances. A
    commoner may khonta to a wealthy commoner in order
    to gain benefits his kinships ties can not offer. The
    relationship is mutually beneficial but may be terminated
    by either party.

KUPER, DR. HILDA. The most knowledgeable foreign scholar
    on the subject of the Swazis, her numerous works may
    be found in the bibliography under both Kuper and
    Beemer, her maiden name. She is presently writing
    the approved biography of King Sobhuza II. Born in
    Rhodesia, she received her doctorate in Anthropology
    at the London School of Economics. She has taught at
    Witwatersrand University and the University of Natal,
    among others, and has been head of the Anthropology
    Department at the University of California at Los Ange-

les. Her original research in Swaziland began in 1934,
and resulted in numerous articles and several books.

KWALUSENI. A Royal Village located about a mile north of
the main highway between Matsapa and Manzini. In
1973 it became the site of a Swaziland campus of the
University of Botswana, Lesotho and Swaziland (q. v.).

-L-

LABOTSIBENI, QUEEN. Another name of Queen Gwamile
Mdluli.

THE LADY ELEPHANT. The main expression of praise used
to describe the Queen Mother, it is actually the translation of the Swazi word Ndlovukazi (q. v.). The elephant and the lion are considered to be the two most
important and regal of the African animals. Other
praise names used to describe the Queen Mother are:
"The Earth, " "The Beautiful, " "Mother of the Country,"
and so on.

LAGDEN, SIR GODFREY YEATMAN. British administrator
of native territories. Most of his career was spent in
Africa, with his longest service in Basutoland. He
served in Swaziland during 1892 as British representative in the Triumvirate or Provisional Government. In
June, 1903, as a result of a British Order in Council,
he was put in charge of Swazi affairs in Pretoria, as
Swaziland was ruled until 1907 as if it were to be an-
nexed to the Transvaal.

LAMAKHASISO. One of the favorite wives of King Mswati II,
and the chief wife of his royal household at Hhohho.
Her son, Mbilini (q. v.), expected to succeed his father,
and when a half-brother, Ludvonga, was chosen over
him, Mbilini went on a rampage.

LAMGANGENI. An alternate name for Queen Mother Sisile
Khumalo.

LAMNDZEBELE (also: LAKUBHEKA). A wife of King
Ngwane III, she became Queen Mother with her residence at "old" Lobamba when her son, Mdvungunye became Swazi Ngwenyama. She was a daughter of Kub-
heka Mndzebele. She lived in the late eighteenth and

early nineteenth centuries.

LAND SETTLEMENT SCHEMES. A series of three land
    purchase programs financed by the British during the
    1940's which added thousands of acres to that previously
    owned by the Swazis. They were in response to con-
    tinued appeals by King Sobhuza II to the Colonial Gov-
    ernment. The first of these programs was implemented
    in 1944.

LAND SPECULATION CONTROL ACT. An act of the Swazi-
    land Parliament passed in December, 1971. It provides
    that land transactions between other than two Swaziland
    citizens must receive prior approval from a Land Con-
    trol Board. The Board should consider the intended use
    and development plans of the purchaser, so as to dis-
    courage speculators. A Land Control Appeals Board
    was also established solely to hear appeals from Con-
    trol Board decisions. The law was very controversial
    when passed and implemented.

LANGENI. Literally: "In the sun." Variant: ELANGENI.
    The administrative capital of King Sobhuza I, a home-
    stead established in central Swaziland near the present
    capitals. The senior prince there was Phangodze.

LANGOLOTJENI (variant LANGOLOTSHENI). An alternate
    name for Queen Mother Lomawa.

LANQABANE (actually: LANQABANE MNISI). A man living
    near the foot of the Mdimba Mountains (near the site of
    Lozithehlezi today) in the early nineteenth century. It
    was he who, when introduced to King Sobhuza I by
    members of the Maseko clan, showed Sobhuza and his
    followers the famous caves in the Mdimba Mountains.
    These caves later saved the lives of Sobhuza's people
    many times as they evaded the Zulus.

LANSDOWNE, LORD. British Minister of State for Colonial
    Affairs for a time in the 1960's. He presided at the
    January, 1963, London Constitutional Conference involv-
    ing Swazi representatives and the colonial officials. He
    also visited Swaziland in April, 1963, concerning the
    constitution. His stay in Mbabane prompted a gathering
    of several political party leaders and about four hundred
    supporters. When they tried to present him with alter-
    native constitutional proposals, they were dispersed by

police using tear gas.

LAVUMISA. Formerly Gollel, it is a town of about eight
hundred people located on the southern border and near
the eastern border of Swaziland. It is immediately
across the border from the South African town of Golela.
As a railhead of South African Railways, Lavumisa is
the country's second busiest entry point. Trains arrive and depart frequently to Durban and other major
South African cities. The name change was made in
1969, using the name Lavumisa which had been used
for an area near Golela. Lavumisa had been a daughter
of Zwide (q. v.) and the mother of Tsekwane, one of the
refugees in the Malambule affair (q. v.) who had returned to Swaziland.

LAZIDZE. Daughter of Zidze (also, Zwide), chief of the
Ndwandwe peoples, and the main wife of King Sobhuza
I. Also known as Thandile, she was chosen at about
the age of ten to be Sobhuza's wife. As the mother of
Mswati II, she became a very important Ndlovukazi,
and resided at Ludzidzini. Before bearing Mswati she
had a girl, Mzamose. Her influence on Swazi history
continued during the reigns of her grandsons, Ludvonga
II and Mbandzeni, as her advice was frequently sought.

LEGISLATIVE COUNCIL. A multi-racial law-making body
established by the 1963 Constitution. It consisted of
thirty-one members chosen by five different methods including three categories: election, appointment, and ex-
officio membership. The elections for this Legislative
Council took place in June, 1964. It remained until it
was replaced by Parliament (q. v.) under the 1967 Constitution.

LEIBRANDT, DR. V. S. Appointed to the Swaziland Senate
in May, 1972, Dr. Leibrandt had been an active member of the multi-racial Swaziland Democratic Party in
the early 1960's until he was expelled from it at the
party congress in October, 1964.

LE ROUGETEL, SIR JOHN. The British High Commissioner
for southern Africa from October 2, 1951 until February
2, 1955, a relatively uneventful period for Swaziland.

LESOTHO. Formerly the British colonial territory called
Basutoland until Independence Day, October 4, 1966. It

is a relatively homogeneous nation of Sotho (q. v.)
peoples, usually referred to as Southern Sotho.   Sharing a common past with Swaziland as one of the three
former High Commission Territories, it has a certain
amount of interaction with Swaziland, especially through
membership in the South African Customs Union (q. v.),
and as partners in the University of Botswana, Lesotho,
and Swaziland (q. v.), as well as membership in the
Commonwealth (q. v.).   It is about two hundred miles
southwest of Swaziland.

LIBANDHLA (variant: LIBANDLA, also, LIBANDLA LAKA
    NGWANE).   Council of the Ngwane nation.   A general
    council representing the nation in advising the King. It
    consists of all chiefs, bantfanenkosi, and other people
    who have been chosen to it because of their importance,
    intelligence, expertise or other contributions.   It rep-
    resents the people and their opinion.   The liqoqo (q. v.)
    sits together and introduces the subjects for discussion,
    which is very open and often heated.   The King may or
    may not choose to sit in on the debates, but he is in
    attendance when a consensus has been reached.   The
    King announces what he feels is the decision of the li-
    bandla and gives his approval to it.   The decision then
    becomes law.   The King's principal indvuna takes the
    lead both in summoning councillors to the meetings
    (which were not regularly scheduled) and in the running
    of the meetings themselves.   In recent years partisan
    political controversies have brought modern issues into
    this traditional council.   It now meets regularly once a
    year, during the winter, sitting for about a month.   A
    Standing Committee appointed by the Ngwenyama in Li-
    bandhla keeps in close contact with the Government.

LIBUTFO.   Class or regiment.   While age regiments (plural,
    emabutfo) exist both for men and for women, women's
    groups are much less formal and much less significant.
    The men's emabutfo, however, play important roles in
    the social and political organization of the Swazi.   A
    new libutfo is organized periodically (usually five to
    seven years) by the King and it is given its own special
    name.   The young men included in this libutfo are thus
    identified with this regiment and each other for life.
    They have certain societal roles depending on the age
    of the regiment, with men of fighting age, for example,
    representing the defense of the community.   During the
    nineteenth century these regiments served as royal war-

riors, especially in conflicts with the Sotho and with other Nguni groups. Today they are called upon periodically to perform labor for the King or for the Swazi nation and to participate in certain rituals. The labor may involve the royal herds, the Queen Mother's fields, or even something like road-building. A member of a libutfo can not get married until the King has given permission for that regiment to marry. A libutfo cuts across family, clan, and geographic lines, thus creating a different kind of national unity. "Age mates" (members of the same libutfo) become very close and develop bonds stronger than those between many kinsmen. Group responsibility for one another develops. Nevertheless, the whole libutfo system has become less significant with the advent of organized education and Westernizing influences. In spring, 1973, however, King Sobhuza called the emabutfo to serve again as a defense force for the country.

LIDLOTI. An ancestral spirit--also, a snake, since ancestral spirits do not manifest themselves except in the form of snakes. Ancestral spirits (plural emadloti) play an important role in Swazi life. Illness and other mishaps are frequently blamed on ancestors. Ancestors are also believed to have more wisdom and power than the living. Appeals are made to the dead ancestors through the head of the family who will make offerings and address the dead. Special songs and rituals also exist for the purpose. Of course, the most important of the nation's emadloti are the ancestors of the King, since the spirit exists in all persons and the more powerful a person was in life, the more powerful his spirit will be after death. Approval and even advice from the emadloti is often sought before an important decision is made or act is performed.

LIESCHING, SIR PERCIVALE. British High Commissioner for southern Africa from March 4, 1955, until the beginning of 1959. When retiring, he said that while the High Commission Territories were moving toward a greater degree of self-government, this did not imply that they would ever advance as far as Ghana, that is, to full independence within the Commonwealth.

LIFA FUND. A Swazi financial arrangement begun in 1946 for the purpose of raising money to buy back land from the Europeans in Swaziland. Under an order made by

the King-in-Council (Ngwenyama-in-Libandhla), cattle
are periodically taken from the herds of Swazis with
more than ten head, and they are then auctioned with
the proceeds going into the Lifa Fund. This also had
the effect of helping to control overgrazing in some
areas. Resentment by both cattle-owners and local
chiefs combined with some local scandals over use of
the money to bring a halt to the program. A 1963 report indicates, however, that 268, 093 acres had already
been purchased from the Lifa Fund.

LIGUBU. A native Swazi musical instrument, a strung wood-
    en bow with inverted calabashes as resonators. It is
    played somewhat like a guitar, and a piece of strong
    grass is used as a pick.

LIHLANZE. SiSwati term for Lowveld (q. v.).

LILANGENI. Singular of Emalangeni (q. v.).

LILAWU. The bachelors' quarters, or barracks; one of the
    three basic structures in the traditional Swazi home-
    steads. (See also SIBOYA and INDLUNKULU.) The
    lilawu housed unmarried men and male visitors, and
    was placed near the entrance to the homestead in order
    to guard it. When used in context with a young king,
    however, lilawu refers to the site of his new quarters
    as he lays the basis for a new capital away from that
    of his parents. As such, it then eventually becomes
    his administrative headquarters while he is King.

LILOBOLO see LOBOLA

THE LION. The main expression of praise used to describe
    the King of Swaziland, it is actually the translation of
    the Swazi word, Ngwenyama (q. v.). The lion and the
    elephant are considered to be the two most important
    and regal of the African animals. The lion is thus used
    as a symbol representing the King. Other praise
    names for the King include: "The Sun, " "The Milky
    Way, " "The Bull, " "Obstacle to the Enemy, " and "The
    Great Mountain. "

LIQOQO. A council at the national level that consists of the
    closest advisors to the King. Membership consists of
    the King's chief uncle plus the indvuna of the chief vil-
    lage, the tindvuna of royal villages and others, presum-

ably the wisest men in the nation, who are appointed
for life. Many of the members will be of the royal
clan, the Nkosi Dlamini, but this is not necessary.
There is no fixed limit, so new members may be appointed as the King, his uncle, and the chief indvuna
(the appointment committee) see fit. This council plays
a very important role in Swazi government, as the King
is expected to heed his advisers. The liqoqo is expected to relay to the King the ideas of the nation and
to keep him informed on matters needing his attention.
It should also advise him of matters that should be discussed at a meeting of the libandhla (q. v.).

LISOKANCANTI. Meaning "the first circumcised, " it refers
specifically to the first son of the first wife in a polygamous homestead, even if sons of other wives were
born first. The lisokancanti becomes a close advisor
of his father, and is usually told by his father who is
to be considered the heir after the father's death. This
is especially important when the father is an important
man. The lisokancanti never becomes chief or headman, but he will often serve as Regent or in another
capacity for the young heir. He continues to serve in
a number of capacities for his younger half-brother, and
is expected to take the lead in council when hearing
complaints brought by someone against the chief.

LITTLE FREE STATE (also KLEIN VRYSTAAT, in Afrikaans). A little Boer Republic located on land originally belonging to the Swazis. The land was granted
on October 3, 1877, by King Mbandzeni to two hunters,
J. J. Ferreira and F. I. Maritz. It consisted of fifty
square miles northeast of the present town of Piet Retief (q. v.). As other Boers settled there and the land
was divided into small farms, the King allowed them to
choose their own indvuna (q. v.) from among themselves.
They called this their own government of "The Little
Free State, " which they formally declared on March 10,
1886. Attempts by Mbandzeni to evict them because of
this failed, despite intervention for the Swazis by a
Royal Boundary Commission. On May 2, 1891, the area
was incorporated as a part of the Piet Retief district of
the South African Republic. This had been sanctioned
by Article 24 of the First Swaziland Convention of 1890
between the British and the Republic. Such action had
been recommended by the Joint Commission (q. v.) the
previous year.

LITTLE USUTU RIVER.   Also called Usushwane River (q. v.).

LIVE LAKANGWANE.   The country (or nation) of the place
   of Ngwane.   Ngwane is the name of the recognized first
   founder of the nation as it is now known.   (See
   NGWANE.) Sometimes the word <u>umhlaba</u> (arable lands)
   replaces live in this phrase.   In the period preceding
   independence there was considerable conjecture that the
   name Swaziland might be changed to Ngwane at independence, just as Basutoland and Bechuanaland changed
   their names.

LOBAMBA.   As the <u>Ndlovukazi's</u> village, it is the capital of
   the Swazi nation.   It also houses the modern parliamentary buildings as well as an official residence of the
   King, the Swazi National Council offices and the National Stadium.   Further development is still going on.
   It stands on the site of a previous royal village called
   Nkanini, and is located on the main road halfway between Mbabane and Manzini, and is perhaps twenty
   miles west of the geographical center of the country.
      The name Lobamba was originally used by Ngwane
   II as the name of his first village in what is now southeastern Swaziland.   He died there, and pilgrimages are
   still made to a cave there where he and other Swazi
   kings have been buried.   Likewise, Sobhuza I called his
   headquarters Lobamba, when he built it about 1820 near
   the Mdimba Mountains.   It is now sometimes referred
   to as Old Lobamba.
      It should be recalled that the nation's capital is the
   village of the Ndlovukazi, and thus changes when monarchs change.   King Sobhuza II has set up his village
   at Lozita, about five miles southeast of Lobamba. When
   it eventually becomes necessary to choose a successor,
   the new Ndlovukazi will take residence at Lozita, which
   will become the new capital.

LOBOLA (variant: LOBOLO, also LILOBOLO).   A payment,
   almost always in cattle by a man to the father of his
   bride for the purpose of legitimizing the marital union
   and guaranteeing his family's claim to all of the woman's children.   The practice is very wide-spread
   throughout Africa as well as in Swaziland.   Among the
   Swazis the custom has been to "pay" ten cattle plus two
   (used for special ceremonial purposes), although the
   "price" may be higher if demanded by the father. Princesses especially will bring more cattle, and any chief

or the King himself will certainly be expected to "pay" considerably more for a bride. The cattle from the man may well have been donated from the herds of his father or other family members (especially for his first wife), and the father of the bride may well distribute many of the cattle to other members of his family. Payment of some of the lobola cattle may be delayed if the father of the bride consents. The tradition of lobola is still practiced in Swaziland today but not as universally as it once was.

LOCH, SIR HENRY BROUGHAM. Governor of the Cape Colony and British High Commissioner in South Africa from 1889 to 1895, a period of bitter relations between the British and Transvaal governments. Meeting the Transvaal's President, Paul Kruger, at Blignant's Pont on the Vaal River, March 12 and 13, 1890, he signed for the British the First Swaziland Convention, 1890 (q.v.), approving the recommendations of the Joint Commission (q.v.). On November 13, 1893, they signed the Second Swaziland Convention, 1893 (q.v.); and subsequently the Third (and last) Swaziland Convention, 1894, (q.v.), on December 6, 1894. The latter agreement made Swaziland a protectorate of the South African Republic in order, as Loch said, "to avert war between the two white peoples of South Africa."

LOGCOGCO, PRINCE (variant: LOGQOGQO). A son of Ngwenyama Mswati II, and half-brother of Ludvonga II and Mbandzeni, he was an important Swazi councillor for many years. He met with the Joint Commission (q.v.) in 1889 to discuss its purpose. He was a member of the Deputation of 1907 (q.v.) that traveled to London to protest British land concession arrangements. Also, as grand-uncle of young Mona (later King Sobhuza II), he assisted as an adviser to Queen Regent Labotsibeni before Mona became Ngwenyama.

LOJIBA. Principal wife of King Ndvungunye. Since she had no child of her own, she adopted Somhlolo (to become King Sobhuza I) after the death of Ndvungunye. This occurred about the year 1815.

LOMAHASHA. A Swazi border town high in the Lubombo mountains in northeastern Swaziland. Across the border is Nomahasha, Mozambique. The town is named after Chief Lomahasha Mahlalela, an important chief in the

area during the 1890's. There were bitter disputes at
this time between Great Britain, Transvaal and Mozambique over their borders in this area. The dispute was
resolved after two decades, but included a curve around
a Portuguese military post, now Nomahasha. Lomahasha was used as a base by Ludwig Steinacher (q. v.)
during the Boer War.

LOMATI RIVER (also: MLUMATI or UMLUMATI RIVER).
Starting in the Transvaal region of South Africa south
of Barberton, it cuts through the northernmost area of
Swaziland before exiting east of Hhohho. It then wends
along an extremely crooked path until it joins the Komati River, under which name it heads north to Komati
Poort. It joins other rivers at that mountain gorge and
winds through Mozambique, flowing into Delagoa Bay.

LOMAWA, QUEEN MOTHER. Wife of King Bhunu and mother
of the present Ngwenyama, Sobhuza II. She spent her
first two decades as Queen Mother under the strong
personal influence of Queen Mother Regent Labotsibeni,
who died in 1925. Lomawa herself died in 1938 and
was succeeded by her sister and co-wife, Nukwase
(q. v.) as Ndlovukazi. Lomawa Ndwandwe (Nxumalo),
also called Langolotsheni, was the daughter of a chief
in southern Swaziland.

LONDON CONSTITUTIONAL CONFERENCE OF 1963. Lasting
from January 28, 1963, to February 12, 1963, this
conference attempted to get final agreement on the first
modern constitution for Swaziland. Constitutional discussions had been taking place in Swaziland for several
years. The British invited six representatives from the
Swazi National Council, four from the Reconstituted
European Advisory Council, one each from the Swaziland Democratic Party, the Mbandzeni Convention Party,
the Eurafrican Welfare Association, and the Nquku
branch of the Swaziland Progressive Party (thus pro-
hibiting Dr. Zwane of the SPP from being a legal delegate), and an independent missionary doctor, Dr. Hynd.
It quickly became obvious that the conference was torn
by disagreement, although a temporary "Alliance of
Political Organizations" (q. v.) was formed, and virtually no real progress was made. Issues of importance
were: the extent of white representation in the Legislative Council, the one-man, one-vote election system,
and the control of mineral and land rights. The ulti-

mate lack of agreement led to the closing of the conference and, several months later, the imposition of a
constitution by Great Britain.

LONDON CONSTITUTIONAL CONFERENCE OF 1968   see
    INDEPENDENCE CONFERENCE

LONDON CONVENTION OF 1884   see   CONVENTION OF
    1884

LONG, ATHEL C. E.   Deputy Queen's Commissioner at the
    time of Independence.   He came to Swaziland in 1961
    as Government Secretary, later called Chief Secretary.
    In this capacity he was one of the officials who ordered
    police to use tear gas to control the "porridge riot" of
    April, 1963.   He became an ex-officio member of the
    Executive Committee of the Legislative Council in 1964,
    serving until internal self-government in April, 1967,
    when he was made Deputy Queen's Commissioner. He
    also served on the committee to draw up a Constitution
    in 1966.

LONGCANGA, PRINCE.   A half-brother of Ngwenyama
    Mbandzeni, he was appointed leader of the Deputation
    of 1894 (q. v.).   This was a delegation of Swazis who
    went to London to ask Queen Victoria to declare a pro-
    tectorate over Swaziland rather than allow it to be
    handed over to the South African Republic.   His re-
    quests were nevertheless rejected by Lord Ripon and
    the Deputation returned home.

LOURENÇO MARQUES.   The terminus of the Swaziland Rail-
    way and the principal port for Swaziland, located at
    Delagoa Bay on the Indian Ocean in Mozambique.
    Only about forty-five miles from the Swazi border,
    this cosmopolitan city of about 200, 000 is a pop-
    ular place for Swaziland residents to go for a week-
    end or a brief vacation.

LOVEDALE MISSIONARY INSTITUTION.   A large educational
    institution established by missionaries in Alice, South
    Africa, in 1826.   It has been an important source of
    learning, especially at the secondary level, for south-
    eastern Africans.   In 1916 young Sobhuza was sent there
    along with eight other young Swazis. He returned to
    Swaziland after almost three years at Lovedale in order
    to prepare for kingship.

LOVELL, LEOPOLD.   Swaziland Minister of Finance from
1967 to 1972.   Born in the Cape Province of South
Africa, he served in South Africa's Parliament from
1949 to 1958 as a member of the South African Labour
Party.   He settled in Swaziland in 1961 and shared a
law office with Etienne Fourie.   Appointed to the House
of Assembly by King Sobhuza in May, 1967, he quickly
became Minister of Finance, Commerce, and Industry,
later just Minister of Finance.   He got into a dispute
with Prime Minister Makhosini Dlamini in late 1971 over
the Land Speculation Control Act and was not reappointed to Parliament in 1972.

LOWVELD.   Also Bushveld, it is the region of Swaziland between
the Middleveld on the west and the Lubombo Mountains
on the east.   Covering more than 2, 200 square miles
in a belt from north to south, it is a rolling lowland
with occasional ridges.   The elevation ranges from 500
to about 2, 300 feet above sea level, but is mostly under
1, 000 feet.   Vegetation ranges from thorny bush to
sweet grass, the latter fostering a degree of cattle
raising, especially since the Government Malaria Control team virtually eliminated that disease in 1958.   The
Lowveld is called Lihlanze by the Swazi (although a variant Ihlanze is used in one publication).   The area receives between 20 and 35 inches of rain a year and has
an almost tropical climate.

LOYD, SIR FRANCIS A.   (variant: LLOYD).   Held the post
of Her Majesty's Commissioner representing the British
Government in Swaziland from May, 1964 until Swaziland's independence, September 6, 1968.   Loyd's appointment, replacing Sir Brian Marwick (q. v.), indicated
a British swing away from support of the emerging nationalist parties and towards support of the traditional
elements led by King Sobhuza II.   Loyd presided over
the dissolution of British colonial control of Swaziland.

LOZITHEHLEZI.   Abbreviated form: Lozita or Lozitha. The
principal residence of the Ngwenyama, Sobhuza II, and
thus the Swazi national administrative and military
headquarters.   It is about five miles southeast of Lobamba and three miles northwest of Matsapa, but off
the main roads.

LUBELO.   Son of Udlakadla and leader of the Mngometfule
clan at the time of King Mswati II.   His people lived

near the Lubombo Mountains in southern Swaziland when
they lost a major battle to Mswati and his men.   Lubelo was killed, but his infant son, Mbikiza, survived
and was raised to maturity by the maternal grandfather
of King Sobhuza II.

LUBOMBO MOUNTAINS (variants: LEBOMBO, LOBOMBO).
A range of mountains running along the eastern edge of
the Lowveld.   Broken only by the gorges of three major
rivers, it is an impressive escarpment of about 2,000
feet.   One important town, Siteki (q.v.) is in the mountains, along with a couple of border towns, notably
Lomahasha (Swaziland) and Nomahasha (Mozambique).
The area contains about 600 square miles in Swaziland,
and includes both cattle ranching and some farming.
The area receives between 30 and 45 inches of rain a
year and has a sub-tropical climate.

LUBOMBO DISTRICT.   One of the four administrative districts of Swaziland, it consists of 2,036 square miles
along the eastern side of the country.   It starts slightly
north of Tshaneni in the north, and extends south to
within ten miles of the southern border at Gollel.   At
some points it reaches close to the center of the country.   Among its major towns are Tshaneni, Mhlume,
Siteki, and Big Bend.   This district was called Stegi
before the 1963 administrative reforms.   Siteki is the
administrative headquarters of the district, the total
population of which is about 85,000.

LUDVONGA I.   A son of the Ngwenyama, Mavuso I, Ludvonga served as Ngwenyama of the Swazis in the early
eighteenth century.   He became ruler only because of
the actions of the mother of his half-brother, Magudulela (q.v.).

LUDVONGA II (variant: LUDONGA).   The son of Mswati II,
he was chosen to succeed his father as Swazi King.   He
was seventeen years old at the time in 1868.   His
mother, Sisile Khumalo (q.v.) became Ndlovukazi, and
his uncle, Prince Ndwandwa served with her as regents.
Ludvonga died four years later without an heir.   Prince
Ndwandwa was accused of having him murdered and was
clubbed to death on orders from the lusendvo (council).
Ludvonga was buried at Dlangeni on the Mdimba Mountains.

LUDZIDZINI.   The site of an important royal residence during the nineteenth century.   Queen Mother Thandile
(Lazidze) lived there during the reign of her son,
Mswati II.   The senior indvuna there was Sandlane
Zwane (q. v.).   Its location in the center of the country
persuaded Mswati to station three of his military regiments there.   On July 1, 1875, it was the site of the
signing of an agreement between King Mbandzeni and a
Boer delegation.   It was a mutual recognition and aid
agreement.

LUKHELE, DOUGLAS.   Appointed Deputy Attorney-General of
Swaziland in May, 1973.   Born in 1932, he was educated in both Swaziland and Pretoria, South Africa.   He
received a B. A. from Fort Hare University College,
and then joined a Johannesburg law firm, practicing
there from 1955 to 1964.   In 1960 he participated in
some of the early constitutional talks with British officials.   He was chosen to be a Swazi Senator after the
1967 elections, a position he held for five years.   He
was reappointed by the King in May, 1972.

LUSABA RIVER.   A boundary between the Sotho and Swazi
peoples over a century ago, it retains significance annually during the Ncwala (q. v.).   In order for the
Ncwala to begin, specially chosen men must carry
sacred containers to collect water from four sources,
one of which is the Lusaba River.

LUSEKWANE.   A species of acacia, this tree (or shrub)
grows sparsely in Swaziland and also near the Indian
Ocean coast.   It is considered sacred by the Swazis.
As part of the Ncwala ceremony, youths who have
reached puberty are expected to go out on the night of
the full moon to travel to Gundwini to cut the largest
branch they can carry and bring it back to Lobamba at
dawn.

LUSENDVO.   A family council or kinship council, consisting
of all male relatives belonging to a clan.   In practice,
however, usually only the closer relatives are involved.
The lusendvo can be called to advise a man on important matters, or to come to his aid in times of need.
If there is a question as to who the proper heir is, the
lusendvo will decide (in this case with the addition of
several closely related females).   The lusendvo also
helps adjudicate family disputes when necessary.   In

the case of a local chief, the lusendvo fills the position
occupied at the national level by the liqoqo (q. v.).

LUSUTFU RIVER.   Another name for the Great Usutu River,
(q. v.).

LUVEVE.   A traditional horn used by the Swazis to call
people when a hunt has been arranged.   The basis of
it is usually a buck's horn covered by the skin of a
beast's tail.   It is also used to encourage the dogs during the hunt, and has been used by the herdsmen of the
royal herds.   It is said that the Swazis were routed in
one battle against the Sotho when the latter bewitched
them by sounding a luveve made of the bone of a man's
leg.

LUYENGO.   Along the edge of a major irrigation scheme, it
is a small community about three and a half miles south
of Malkerns in west-central Swaziland.   Near the Great
Usutu River, Luyengo has attained importance recently
with the locating there of the Swaziland Agriculture College (q. v.) and Agricultural Research Station, and also
as the temporary site of a Swaziland campus of the
University of Botswana, Lesotho and Swaziland.

LYDENBURG REPUBLIC.   A short-lived Boer Republic which
was founded first in a town called Andries Ohrigstad in
1845, but two years later was moved to another area
which was called Lydenburg (Lyden means "suffering")
because of deaths due to fever.   The leader of the
Boers here was Willem Joubert.   The Boers claimed
to have a treaty with King Mswati giving them ownership
of a very large portion of land north and west of Swaziland in exchange for a hundred head of cattle.   Its
legality is questionable in that it was signed "for
Mswati" in July, 1846, by Somcuba, a Swazi who had
fled the country years earlier as a fugitive.   The Swazis continued to raid other Africans in the "ceded" region for many years.   When gold was found in the area
(which included the modern districts of Lydenburg, Mid-
delburg, Barberton, and Carolina) in the 1870's, return
to the Swazis became impossible.   Meanwhile the Lydenburg Republic joined the South African Republic (q. v.) in
1860.

-M-

MABUZA, OBED MPANGELE. A significant political activist
and party leader for about a decade in Swaziland, especially during the 1960's. Having been a member of
the Swazi National Council for fifteen years as well as
a high-ranking member of the Swaziland Progressive
Party, Mabuza was appointed to the first Constitutional
Committee in 1960, along with fellow SPP members
J. J. Nquku and Dr. Zwane. There was a clash in
these meetings between the SPP members and Swazi
traditionalists over the extent of modernization of politics in the new Constitution. Thus Nquku was dismissed from the committee and, after consulting with
Dr. Denis Cowen (q. v.), Mabuza and Zwane also resigned on June 11, 1961. Mabuza and Zwane had various conflicts with Nquku's strong-handed methods within
the SPP and were suspended from office once, but
stayed in the party. Zwane finally created his own
party in January, 1962, while Mabuza waited until
August, 1962. At that time, during a party constitutional conference with Nquku presiding, Nquku was suspended from office and K. T. Samketi was elected President, with Mabuza chosen as Secretary General. Later
Samketi joined Zwane, and Mabuza became the leader
of his version of the SPP. Mabuza was a moving force
in organizing the Joint Council of Swaziland Political
Parties (q. v.) when it got together on June 1, 1964. It
failed in its unity function, however, and the splintered
parties lost the elections badly, Mabuza's party getting
only one vote for every four hundred cast. Mabuza received thirty-four votes himself. When Nquku was expelled from the Joint Council in March, 1965, Mabuza
was unanimously elected to replace him as Chairman of
its Executive Council. Its name was changed in 1966
to the Swaziland United Front and also absorbed the
Umvikeli Wabantu National Movement, with Mabuza as
President. United Front candidates in the 1967 elections received only one out of every three hundred votes.
Nevertheless, Mabuza protested the new constitutional
arrangements and even flew to London in 1968 to witness the final conference for an Independence Constitution. Mabuza's United Front ran only six candidates in
the 1972 elections, all losing badly. Mabuza's 98 votes
in 1967 increased to 135 in 1972 (out of over 11, 000 in
his constituency).

MABUZA, RICHARD.   The first internationally recognized
   Swazi athlete.   He won a Bronze Medal in the All Africa
   Games of 1973, but he was less successful in the 1972
   Olympics.   He had to withdraw from the 10, 000-meter
   race with an injury, this while leading in his heat.   He
   later came back to place 17th out of 76 runners in the
   Olympic marathon.

MC CORKINDALE, ALEXANDER   (variant: MAC CORKIN-
   DALE).   Scottish-born entrepeneur and pioneer who
   came to South Africa in the 1850's and, a decade later,
   tried to establish a settlement of Scots in the area immediately west of today's border with Swaziland.   The
   land he and the other Scots purchased from the Transvaal President, M. W. Pretorius, was over a million
   acres, as the Boers were happy to have a buffer between themselves and the Zulus and Swazis.   Token
   payment was also made to Swazi King Mswati.   The
   land, called New Scotland, was divided into two blocks:
   Industria, and Roburnia (after Robert Burns).   Roburnia
   includes the present city of Amsterdam (q. v.).   Mc-
   Corkindale also planned a railway across Swaziland to
   Delagoa Bay.   The materials for the railway arrived at
   Delagoa Bay just as he died in 1871 on the island of
   Inyak and the plan folded.   McCorkindale and several
   fellow Scots, including David Forbes, Sr., his niece's
   husband, were the ones to call the country Swaziland,
   after King Mswati II.

MAC DONALD, MALCOLM.   British Secretary of State for
   Dominion Affairs from November, 1935, until January,
   1939, (with one short interval).   His attitude toward the
   transfer of the High Commission Territories to South
   Africa was that transfer was impossible as long as the
   Africans and the British Parliament strongly disapprov-
   ed.   But he also felt that it was his obligation to try to
   cooperate with South Africa on the subject.   Transfer,
   he felt, was both inevitable and probably in the best interests of the Africans in the Territories, but transfer
   probably would not occur for a long time.   The issue
   was especially hot in 1937 when General Hertzog (q. v.)
   had several talks with him on the subject and Parliamentary reaction was especially heated.   Hertzog's lack
   of tact and other mistakes doomed MacDonald's attempts
   at British-South African cooperation.

MC LACHLAN, THOMAS   (variant: MAC LACHLAN).   Along

with his partner, Walter Carter, one of the first prospectors to get a concession from King Mbandzeni. They
had settled at Phophonyane Falls north of present day
Pigg's Peak. The concession was granted in May, 1880,
to prospect north of the Komati River. The word that
they found traces of gold in 1881 got around quickly and
attracted numerous prospectors, including William Pigg
(q. v.).

MADANGALA. Brother of the main wife of King Sobhuza I,
Thandile, and son of the Zulu leader Zwide. He fled
to Sobhuza for protection from the Zulu army and was
granted land in the extreme northern part of Swaziland.
Some of his descendants still live there and speak si-
Swati with a few Zulu variations.

MADLALA, WINSTON. Founder of the short-lived Swaziland
Freedom Party (q. v.) in 1962.

MAFUTENI (variant: MAFUTSENI). A town in central Swaziland located about ten miles east of Manzini on the
main cross-country road, at the spot where this road
meets one of the main roads heading north toward Hhohho.

MAGAGULA CLAN. A Sotho clan which lived near the Black
Mbuluzi River when they were conquered by King Sobhuza I. The clan was noted for its special potion for
rain-making. While some of this medicine remained
with them, King Sobhuza I gave most of it to the Ndlovukazi for her use in time of drought. Several members
of this clan have reached high governmental positions in
independent Swaziland, notably Jonathan Magagula, Permanent Secretary for Power, Works, and Communications.

MAGONGO, TIKHUBA (variant TEKUBA). Important official
during the reign of Mbandzeni, who signed many of the
mineral concessions as a witness. As indvuna of the
royal village, he was responsible for consulting a tangoma or inyanga concerning the illness of the King.
When it was determined by a ceremony that the cause
was the indvuna lenkulu, Sandlane Zwane (q. v.), Magongo was required to have that offiical killed. Magongo
then succeeded to Zwane's position. In this capacity he
spoke in the Swazi National Council against the visiting
Joint Commission of 1889. After Mbandzeni's death,
Magongo's position became insecure. When the Queen

Mother took over in the interim and his death seemed
imminent, Magongo fled to the Barberton area in the
Transvaal.

MAGUDU MOUNTAINS (OR HILLS).   A group of elevations
south of the Pongola River in Zululand.   Early Bembo-
Nguni peoples who ultimately settled in Swaziland under
the leadership of Ngwane III in the 18th century spent
some time near the Magudu.   The Magudu are also
mentioned in a praise song of Sobhuza II, since his
mother descends from Zulus who lived near the Magudu.

MAGUDULELA.   The presumed heir to Mavuso I as leader
of the Bembo-Nguni group destined to become the Swazis.   He did not become king because his mother did
not wish the responsibility of becoming Queen Mother.
Knowing that left-handed men could not become Swazi
kings (by custom), she dipped Magudulela's right hand
into boiling liquid so he would have to become left-
handed and thus disqualified.   Ludvonga I became King
instead.   This was around 1700.

MAHAMBA.   A Swazi town located right at the Swaziland-
South African border in the southwestern part of the
country.   It began as a mission set up by two Wesleyan
missionaries and a number of Basotho evangelists in
1884.   The leader of the Mission was Rev. James Allison.   As a result of an incident among the Swazis involving the Regent Malambule (q. v.), the successful
operation of converting Swazis to Christianity was in-
terrupted as the churchmen and a group of refugees fled
to Natal.   Thus the area was named Mahamba, meaning
"the runaways."   The Mission was reopened there in
1880 by Daniel Msimang, one of the evangelists with
Rev. Allison.   Mahamba might well be the first European settlement in Swaziland.

MAHIYA.   Plural: EMAHIYA.   A loin cloth worn by Swazi
men as part of their traditional clothing.   It is tied on
the right hip.   The custom of wearing them (sometimes
one but often more than one) is reported to have been
copied from the Shangaans of Mozambique.   Young boys
do not wear them.   Girls begin to wear emajobo (q. v.)
over the emahiya, while women add a skin skirt (sidwaba, q. v.).

MAHLANGATSHA.   A community about twelve miles southeast

of Mankayane and the location of a kaolin mine owned
by Kaolin S. D. Ltd.

MAHLANYA. A small Swazi community on the main road between Lobamba and Matsapa, a few miles north of Malkerns. It is in the area of a major irrigation scheme.

MAIZE. Also called mealies. The staple food of most
Swazis, widely grown among peasant farmers for home
or local use. It has usually been necessary to import
some maize from South Africa despite the Ministry of
Agriculture's successful "Grow More Maize" campaign.
It probably was introduced to Swaziland by the Portuguese during the reign of Sobhuza I.

MAKHOSINI. Also called Dlangeni (q. v.).

MAKHWEYANE. A traditional Swazi musical instrument not
unlike a guitar. Similar to ligubu (q. v.).

MALAMBULE. The eldest son of King Sobhuza I, he served
as regent from 1836 until 1840, the period of minority
of Mswati II. He was assisted by a half-brother, Somcuba (q. v.). When Mswati became Ngwenyama, Mala-
bule secretly kept some of the royal cattle for himself.
Mswati found out and Malambule was forced to flee to
southern Swaziland and eventually into Zululand. The
Kunene clan that befriended him en route was attacked
and many of them were killed by Mswati's army even
though the Kunenes had taken refuge among the Wesleyan
missionaries who had just come to Swaziland.

MALAN, DR. DANIEL FRANÇOIS. Prime Minister and Minister of External Affairs of South Africa from 1948 to
November, 1954. During his first years as Prime Minister, Dr. Malan made several statements designed to
pressure the British to transfer the High Commission
Territories to South Africa, but no major diplomatic
discussions on the issue took place.

MALANGENI. The name for the collective body of Abantwana
ba makosi ("children of the kings"). These are district
chiefs from the elder male line of the Nkosi-Dlamini.
Judicial cases of a traditional or tribal nature could be
appealed from the indvuna to these chiefs, and then
to the King.

MALARIA. Once a scourge of the country, especially in the low-lying Lowveld, malaria was brought under control by the Government Malaria Control team in a program begun in 1947. By 1958 it was almost completely eradicated. Continuous monitoring of the population is carried on to prevent a new outbreak.

MALAZA, NIMROD SWELANI. A leader of the Ngwane National Liberatory Congress since the mid-1960's when he was named its Secretary-General. He narrowly missed election to Parliament in the 1967 elections and also failed in 1972.

MALEWU. Leader of a clan of Pedi people living north of Swaziland. In 1864 during the reign of Mswati II, a Swazi impi defeated his clan, killing over three thousand people, according to one report.

MALKERNS. Fifteen miles west of Manzini in the Malkerns Valley, this community is in the center of an important citrus area. It is the site of the country's pineapple industry also, as there are about two thousand acres devoted to it. High quality rice is also grown there. It is the center of the country's largest irrigation scheme, about six thousand acres.

MALOMA. A town in the southeastern part of Swaziland along the main road south to Pongola and at the juncture of the road to Nsoko. High-grade anthracite coal is being mined a little southeast of Maloma, and large reserves of low-grade taconite iron ore exist near the town as well.

MALUNGE, PRINCE. Served under Queen Regent Labotsibeni as assistant regent during the minority of the present King, Sobhuza II. The younger brother of King Bhunu (thereby uncle of Sobhuza), he fathered four children by one of Bhunu's wives, Nukwase (q. v.) in the name of his deceased brother. Nukwase later became Ndlovukazi. As assistant regent, Malunge acted in both advisory and diplomatic capacities; in the latter he led the Deputation of 1907 (q. v.) to London. As advisor he encouraged Labotsibeni to react against the Union of South Africa's Natives Land Act of 1913.

MANGWANENI. A waterfall in central Swaziland. King Sobhuza II is compared to its cold waters in one of Sobhuza's praise songs.

MANKAYANA (variant: MANKAIANA). A town of about six
   hundred inhabitants, mostly Swazi, located south and
   west of the center of Swaziland. It is almost twenty
   miles from Sandlane, Swaziland, and the South African
   border. In a mountain setting in the Highveld, it is
   also a minor marketing and trade center. The name
   means "Little Steps."
      Until the December, 1963, administrative changes,
   Mankayana was also the name of one of the six administrative districts of the country. The District encom-
   passed south-west Swaziland between the Great Usutu
   River and the Assegai River. The town of Mankayana
   was the administrative headquarters of the District.
   Now the area has been included in the rearranged Manzini District.

MANTAMBE RIVER. Starting near the South African border,
   this tributary of the Ingwavuma River flows north and
   east for about twenty miles before it merges with the
   Ingwavuma.

MANTENGA FALLS. A beautiful waterfall about eleven miles
   south of Mbabane.

MANZINI. The name of both a city and a District, it is in
   the very center of the country. Manzini, named after
   a local chief, was one of the six Administrative Districts of the country before the 1963 reorganization. At
   that time the former Mankaiana District was added to it.
   Today the District extends from the western border with
   South Africa well into the center of the country. Among
   the important towns in it are Manzini, Bunya, Mankayana, Malkerns, Luve, Croyden, Mliba, Mafuteni,
   Mhlambanyati, and Sidvokodvo. With an area of 1,570.9
   sq. miles, its population according to the 1966 census
   was 101,277. The city of Manzini (until 1960 named
   Bremersdorp, q.v.) is the administrative headquarters
   of the Manzini District and both the agricultural and industrial center of the country. In addition to typical
   urban offices and stores, it has small factories, a
   maize mill and a rice-drying plant among other enterprises. It is also a major transportation center, only
   five miles from the Matsapa Airport and the Matsapa
   Industrial Estate (q.v.), which is along the railroad line
   to Mozambique, as well as being the center for the
   Road Motor and Transport Services of the South African
   Railways and Harbour Administration. The Manzini
   Urban area had a population of about 6,000 in 1966,

4, 400 of whom were Africans, however the immediate surrounding area had a population of about 10, 000, all but a few hundred of whom were African.

MAPOKO.   Also known as Mapors or Ndzundza.   A small tribe, perhaps of Ndebele stock, who lived north of Swaziland.   They managed to evade the armies of Sobhuza I, but in 1864 an impi of Mswati II defeated them in the Lydenburg district (Transvaal).

MAPUTO RIVER.   The river created by the combining of the Usutu and Pongola Rivers as they unite east of Swaziland at the Mozambique and South African border.   It then flows north to Delagoa Bay, entering the Indian Ocean.

MARITZ, F. I.   A hunter who became involved in the "Little Free State" area with J. J. Ferreira (q. v.).

MARTIN, COL. R. E. R.   An officer of the British Army serving in South Africa, he was chosen in June, 1888 to represent Britain on a four-member boundary commission created to survey and set the boundary between Swaziland and Portuguese Territory.   A year later Sir Hercules Robinson, the High Commissioner, sent Colonel Martin and two others to Swaziland to fulfill a request that someone be sent there to preserve order. These three met with the "White Committee" on July 29, 1889, and the ultimate result was appointment of a Joint Commission (q. v.) to inquire deeper into Swaziland's problems.   Martin was appointed secretary of Britain's four-man team on this commission.   This commission's report led to a Triumvirate Government to govern Swaziland.   Martin was chosen to represent Britain here also.

MARWICK, ALLAN GRAHAM.   A long-time civil servant in Swaziland and later advisor to the Swazi King and Nation, he was born in 1877 in Natal.   He came to Swaziland in 1903 after having served in the Anglo-Boer War.   He was appointed a District Commissioner and served in a variety of civil service positions around the country.   He accompanied the Deputation of 1907 which went to London to complain to Lord Elgin about the land concessions.   He was an interpreter and go-between in this situation, finally disputing bitterly what he felt was a broken promise by Lord Elgin (q. v.).   He served as

Resident Commissioner from 1935 to 1937, after which
he retired and lived in Mbabane until his death in October, 1966. He was an advisor to Swazi Regent Prince
Malunge, and later to King Sobhuza II and the Swazi National Council. His nephew, Sir Brian Marwick (q. v.)
also represented the British in Swaziland.

MARWICK, SIR BRIAN A.   British civil servant whose career
in Swaziland spanned forty years (with lengthy gaps). He
joined the Swaziland Government Service in 1925, serving in varying capacities for nine years.   In 1940 he
published an ethnographic study, The Swazi.   He served
in Swaziland also from 1942 to 1949.   He was appointed
Resident Commissioner for Swaziland, serving from 1957
to 1963.   In that year the post of Resident Commissioner
lapsed and Marwick was appointed to the new post of
Her Majesty's Commissioner for Swaziland.   He retired
to Britain a year later, in May, 1964.   Marwick's last
few years in Swaziland were both hectic and controversial.   Marwick favored a one man-one vote electoral
system which would give power to a young, educated,
non-traditional elite organized in modern political parties.   The Ngwenyama would reign, not rule.   This position brought him into conflict with both the traditional
Swazi elite and the Europeans in Swaziland.   Thus constitutional discussions under his leadership were strife-
ridden and futile.   During the 1963 strikes and disturbances it was Marwick who finally called for London to
send in troops.   In a speech before leaving Swaziland,
Marwick made a final appeal to the King to "stay above
politics, " so that the Kingship would remain while political parties came and went.

MASEKO, MACDONALD MADINGIZWE.   An important political activist in the early 1960's.   A member of the
African National Congress and a businessman in South
Africa, he had been placed under house arrest in Johannesburg.   He escaped to Swaziland and became active
in the Swaziland Progressive Party.   In 1962, however,
he broke with its leader, J. J. Nquku, along with Dr.
Ambrose Zwane and Clement Dumisa Dlamini.   They
eventually called their group the Ngwane National Liberatory Congress, and Maseko was elected Vice President
of it.   The three led a strike of several thousand workers at Ubombo Ranches and Big Bend Sugar in March,
1963, and again in June.   Dlamini and Maseko also led
a peaceful crowd of three thousand through the streets

of Mbabane in June, 1963, and were admitted to see the
Resident Commissioner to register both economic and
political grievances. These activities led to his arrest
and conviction to six months in prison for disturbing
public order and inciting violence. Despite this, he
was a Legislative Council candidate of the NNLC in the
1964 elections, where he lost badly with less than a
thousand votes. When the Joint Council of Swaziland
Political Parties was formed in 1964, Maseko (representing the NNLC) was made Vice President. He continued in this capacity even after he split with Dr.
Zwane in June, 1964. At that time a series of maneuvers by Zwane and N. S. Malaza was successful in suspending Maseko from his position as Vice President and
expelling him from the party. For a while Maseko also
led an Anti-Apartheid Committee to assist political refugees from South Africa. He does not seem to have
been politically active in recent years.

MASOTJA REGIMENT (variant forms: MASOTSHA, EMA-
    SOTSHA). One of the Swazi age regiments (see LI-
    BUTFO). In May, 1941, King Sobhuza selected this
    group of youths (along with the Sikhonyane regiment) to
    form the basis of the Swazi contingent to fight in World
    War II. This company, known as the "1991, " disting-
    uished itself particularly during the battles at Salerno
    and Anzio in Italy. The Masotja Regiment has been
    honored by having its shield, spears, and staff placed
    on both the Swaziland flag and on the national coat of
    arms.

MATSEBULA, JAMES SHADRACK MKHULUNYELWA. Private
    Secretary to King Sobhuza II, and author of eleven books
    in English, siSwati and Zulu, notably A History of Swa-
    ziland. Born in 1918 near Mbabane into a family with
    numerous direct and indirect ties with Swazi royalty, he
    received primary and secondary education in Swaziland.
    He has a B. A. from the University of South Africa. He
    taught from 1941 to 1959, in Swaziland and then as
    Headmaster in the Transvaal. He was one of the
    Ngwenyama's representatives in constitutional discussions
    in the early 1960's. He served as Senior Inspector of
    Schools from 1962 to 1967, when he was appointed the
    Private Secretary of King Sobhuza.

MATSEBULA, SIFUNTI ELKANA. Indvuna of the royal kraal
    at Lozita for perhaps sixty years, and a member of the

Standing Committee of the Swazi National Council in
which he was a vigorous opponent of incorporation into
South Africa.   At the time of his death on December 1,
1965, he was still active with the Mabuza branch of the
Swaziland Progressive Party and was chairman of its
executive committee.   He was also a preacher of the
Christian Apostolic Swaziland Church in Zion.

MATSEBULA CLAN.   One of the most significant Swazi clans
in terms of royal ritual, this clan is one of those called
Bemdzabuko (true Swazi).   The first wife of the new
Ngwenyama must be chosen for him by councillors from
a well-known Matsebula family.   She is called the
"right-hand queen, " and an elaborate ritual is performed
before, during, and after their wedding.   Also after the
original two tinsila (see INSILA) of the Ngwenyama are
allowed to marry, two junior tinsila are chosen; the
"right-hand" one must be from the Matsebula clan.

MATSHAPHA (variants: MATSAPA, MATSAPHA).   A town
four miles west of Manzini on the highway to Mbabane,
it is the site of the major commercial and industrial
center of the country (see MATSHAPHA INDUSTRIAL
ESTATE).   It has the country's only airport, and is
linked by rail with the port at Lourenço Marques one
hundred forty miles away.

MATSHAPHA INDUSTRIAL ESTATE.   Located at Matshapha,
this major industrial center was established in 1965 on
the main highway, five miles from Manzini and twenty
miles from Mbabane.   With both airport and rail lines
adjacent, it has attracted such diverse industry as a
cotton ginnery, a cement grinding and bagging plant, an
abattoir and meat processing plant, and a brewery.
There are several gasoline and oil storage depots also.
Planned and laid out in sites ranging from one-quarter
acre to ten or more acres, it is constantly adding new
industries.   Residential areas and a national school are
located in adjacent Matshapha.

MAUD, SIR JOHN P.   British High Commissioner for southern Africa from March, 1959, until March, 1963. Maud
was both a noted scholar and a civil servant experienced
in the process of decolonization.   He urged Great Britain to invest more heavily in the development of the
High Commission Territories; at the same time he
worked for the evolution of self-government.

MAUDLING, REGINALD. British Secretary of State for Colonies during the 1960's when Swaziland was beginning
constitutional discussions. He received the note from
the European Advisory Council which requested a legislative council, and then authorized the setting up of a
constitutional committee. On different occasions he
sent out Sir Charles Arden-Clarke and Mr. Denis
Stephens to try to help the constitutional committee in
Swaziland. Maudling felt that any legislative body
should assume some power over traditional functions,
even those of the Ngwenyama. He also favored a common voting roll so as to allow non-traditionalist parties
a chance to win seats.

MAVUSO I. A King of the Bembo-Nguni peoples, probably
in the late 17th century. The descendants of his people
became known as the Swazis.

MAWEWE. First-born son of the chief wife of Soshangane
(q. v.) and thus, according to Zulu custom (his people
had broken from the Zulus), the rightful heir to the
Gaza Empire. According to Shangane custom, however,
his brother Mzila (q. v.) was heir. With his brother
banished, however, Mawewe was placed on the throne.
His cruelty as ruler made him unpopular and Mzila led
a successful coup. Mawewe fled to King Mswati II who
sent an army under his top indvuna, Sandlane Zwane
(q. v.). Thus Mawewe was restored as Mzila fled, but
when the Swazis left, Mzila again overthrew Mawewe
who fled to Swaziland, where he lived a number of
years.

MBABANE. Population about 14, 000, the administrative and
judicial capital of Swaziland and headquarters of the
Hhohho District. It is north and west of the center of
the country, roughly twelve miles from the South African
Border. Until 1963 the name Mbabane was also applied
to one of the then six Districts into which the country
was divided for purposes of modern administration. In
December, 1963, a Government Notice (based on an administrative study and approved by the Ngwenyama) de-
creed that the six Districts should be consolidated into
four. The Mbabane District and the Pigg's Peak District were merged into a new Hhohho District. The city
of Mbabane developed near a cattle kraal established by
King Mbandzeni and was named after the local chief at
the time. A Special Commissioner from Great Britain

came to Mbabane and set up administrative headquarters
there in 1902, thus establishing it as a town. A commercial center (as is Manzini), the city's main thoroughfare, Allister Miller Street, consists of a variety
of modern buildings including several banks, modern
shops, embassies, office buildings, hotels, and theaters
for both film and live performances. The city contains
light industry, transportation centers, a variety of
schools and hospitals, and residential areas both within
the boundaries of the city and in its suburbs. It is also
the center for sale of Swazi handicrafts, especially at
the Mbabane Market. Of the 13,803 inhabitants of the
Mbabane Urban Area according to the 1966 census,
11,627 were Africans. It is governed by a town management board.

MBABANE MARKET.   A cooperative marketing area for Swazi
handicraft and other local products.   It was formed in
1950 at the foot of Allister Miller Street.   A fire in
August, 1966 set it back somewhat, but it was rebuilt
and expanded.

MBANDZENI (variant: UMBANDINE).   Also known as:
Dlamini IV.   King of Swaziland, he was born in 1857,
chosen King at the age of seventeen, and ruled five
years until his death in 1889. His mother, Nandzi, had
died several years before he was chosen by Sisile Khumalo (q.v.), mother of the deceased King Ludvonga
(q.v.).   Mbandzeni was installed at Nkanini in June, 1875,
by Sandlane Zwane (q.v.), who helped him rule along
with the King's grandmother Thandile until Mbandzeni
came of age.   Shortly after his coronation, he signed a
reciprocal pact on July 1, 1875, at Ludzidzini with
Boers from the South African Republic.   Later he established his administrative capital at Mbekelweni, near
today's Manzini.   Mbandzeni became involved in an un-
fortunate dispute with the Ndlovukazi, Sisile Khumalo,
which resulted in her being killed while attempting to
escape the country.   In 1879, Mbandzeni sent an impi
of 8,000 men under Mbovane Fakudze to help the British
forces defeat the Bapedi and Sekhukhune (q.v.).   This
won a British promise of independence for the Swazis
forever.   This was seemingly guaranteed by the (Pretoria) Convention of 1881 (q.v.) and the (London) Convention of 1884 (q.v.).   Mbandzeni's greatest significance for Swaziland was in his granting of a tremendous
number of land, mineral, and other concessions to

Whites.   Although he has received much criticism for
this, and is pictured as selling his land for a pittance,
he is quoted as noting that in most of Africa, Whites
took land for nothing, but at least he was making them
pay first.   He also knew that by Swazi custom, such
alienation of land could not be permanent.   He was just
allowing the use of the land, in his mind, and could
take it back when his people needed it.   When relations
with Whites became complicated, he called on Sir Theophilus Shepstone, Sr. , for aid.   He sent his son Theo,
Jr. (q. v.) to 'act as an advisor.   He arrived in February, 1887, just in time to assist Mbandzeni, who re-
luctantly allowed the Europeans to set up a "White
Committee" (q. v.).   At a meeting on May 18, 1887,
Mbandzeni asserted to the Whites that he had just granted leases, not ownership, and that Swazi grazing rights
must still be allowed.   On August 1, 1888, he allowed
the Committee a Charter of Self-Government by the
Europeans in matters only involving them, but nevertheless to be subject to his veto.   It was also during
his reign that the first Swazi Postal Services and telegraph facilities began.   Also, most of Swaziland's
borders were set during his reign, mostly at the loss
of Swazi land.   A series of letters from Mbandzeni
(via Shepstone) brought on the intervention of a Joint
Commission (q. v.) of Boers and Britons under Sir
Francis de Winton (q. v.) in 1889, a few months before
Mbandzeni's death.   In January of that year, the King
dismissed Shepstone as advisor and replaced him with
Allister Miller (q. v.).   Mbandzeni died of jaundice at
the age of thirty-four on October 7, 1889.   He was buried near his brother Ludvonga on Mdimba Mountain.

MBANDZENI NATIONAL CONVENTION (MNC).   A political
group created in July, 1962, by a merger of Clifford
Nkosi's Mbandzeni National Party and Dr. George Msibi's Swaziland National Convention, with Msibi chosen
its leader.   It pledged support for the Ngwenyama and
the Swazi National Council as well as for a one man-
one vote system of democracy.   When the MNC was
invited by the British to send a delegate to the 1963
London Constitutional Conference, Dr. Msibi made the
trip.   He affiliated it there with the ad hoc Allinace of
Political Organizations (q. v.).   Msibi resigned from the
MNC in August, 1963, however, and Clifford Nkosi
tried to continue it, but the organization soon died.

MBANDZENI NATIONAL PARTY.   A small group formed by
   Clifford Nkosi in April, 1962.   It favored a political
   system mixing the best parts of tribal rule and one man-
   one vote democracy.   Shortly after its formation, in
   July, 1962, it merged with Dr. George Msibi's Swaziland National Convention to become the Mbandzeni National Convention (q. v.).

MBEKELWENI (variant: EMBEKELWENI).   The administrative capital established by King Mbandzeni, it was located about six miles from the present city of Manzini.
   In the late 1880's both a postal service and a telegraph
   line connected Mbekelweni and Steynsdorp, South Africa.
   The village became the center of political and economic
   activity under King Mbandzeni, as gold prospectors
   flocked to him to try to get land concessions.

MBHULENI.   An area just to the north of present Swaziland,
   near Carolina, South Africa.   Swazi King Mswati II had
   a military village there from which he attacked Sutu
   peoples.   The whole Mbhuleni valley was lost to South
   Africa as a result of the Alleyne Commission of 1880
   (q. v.) which believed Boer claims that the Mbhuleni
   valley had been sold to some Boer trekkers by the
   Transvaal Government.   The Swazis claimed to still
   occupy the area with homesteads, and even that one of
   Mswati's wives still lived at Mbhuleni.

MBIKIZA.   Also Mbikiza Mngomezulu.   Variant: UMBIGESA.
   A local Swazi chief in the 1880's whose territory was
   bounded by the Lubombo Mountains in the west, the
   Usutu River in the north, and was south of the Ingwavuma River as well.   Attempts by the British to declare the area to be part of Zululand were thwarted by
   evidence that it was truly Swazi territory.   But in 1895,
   when Britain handed the administration of Swaziland to
   the Transvaal Government, Britain quickly declared
   Mbikiza's territory to be part of Zululand, under Natal
   administration.

MBILANENI.   A hilly area in southern Swaziland that is the
   site of royal graves.   Annually cattle are taken there
   and sacrificed to the tribal ancestors.

MBILINI.   Eldest son of King Mswati II, his mother was La
   Makhasiso, chief wife at the royal household at Hhohho.
   He left Swaziland in a furor when his younger brother,

Ludvonga, was named as heir to the throne instead of himself. Mbilini and a group of followers traveled around the perimeter of the country, finally settling in the north of Zululand. Mbilini then led cattle raids across southern Swaziland, especially against the people of Mshiyane. The first was successful, but a second one was not, only angering some Boers. A Boer protest to the British ultimately resulted in a British soldier at Ncaka shooting Mbilini dead in about 1879. His followers then scattered and left Zululand.

MBOKODVO. (Variant of IMBOKODVO, q. v.)

MBONDVO (variant: MBONVO). A hardy shrub that grows in quantity around the capital at Lobamba. During the Ncwala ceremony, boys too young to gather lusekwane (q. v.) collect pieces of the mbondvo for use in the ceremony. It is also used for other purposes of royal ritual, for example, its tough branches are cut into wooden pegs for the Queen Mother's crown, and for the necklace a queen wears while her royal baby is suckling.

MBULUZI RIVER (variant of UMBELUZI RIVER, q. v.)

MBULUZI HOME ECONOMICS TRAINING CENTRE. A school where Domestic Science teachers are trained for all primary and junior secondary schools. Its students are all covered by full Government grants. Domestic Science demonstrators for rural areas also get a year's training here before going to the Swaziland Agricultural College for another year.

MBULUZI LEPER SETTLEMENT. Opened in 1948 near Mbabane by the Nazarene Mission, this center for the care of sufferers from leprosy has treated about seven hundred people in its first quarter of a century.

MDIMBA MOUNTAINS (variant: MDZIMBA MOUNTAINS). A series of elevations south of Mbabane in the Midveld, about halfway to Manzini. Caves in the mountains are the gravesites of some of the Swazi kings. The royal villages are also usually located near the foot of these mountains. The impenetrable nature of these mountains made them natural Swazi strongholds when the Zulus attacked the Swazis, only to give up and go home.

MDLULI CLAN. One of the more important clans in Swazi
   ritual, it is also considered a Bemdzabuko or "true
   Swazi" clan. When a young king is put through the
   ceremony of acquiring tinsila (plural of insila, q. v.),
   one of his first two tinsila is a young boy chosen from
   among the better-known lineages of the Mdluli clan to
   become the king's "right-hand insila. " When the first
   two tinsila have married, they are replaced by a second
   pair of youths; likewise, eventually a third pair may be
   needed. In the third pair, the right-hand insila also
   comes from the Mdluli clan. One of the most prominent members of the clan was Queen Mother Gwamile,
   also known as Labotsibeni.

MDLULI, GWAMILE. Also: LABOTSIBENI. A remarkable
   woman, this Ndlovukazi and Queen Regent dominated
   Swazi politics for over three decades. The daughter of
   Mvelase Mdluli, she was principal wife of King Mbandzeni, who died in 1889. She thus became Ndlovukazi
   when her son, King Bhunu was installed. After his
   death in 1899, she became Queen Regent until the installation of her grandson as King Sobhuza II in December, 1921. She died four years later, to the month.
   Her capital was at Zombodze where she began, among
   her other projects, a National School. Regretting that
   she had not seen her own son, Bhunu, educated, she
   provided for the education of future Swazis, especially
   for her grandson, the future Sobhuza II. She brought
   Robert Grendon, a tutor, from Natal. She created the
   Swazi National Fund (q. v.) for educational purposes and
   saw the Zombodze National School built. She also sent
   Sobhuza to the Lovedale Institution in South Africa for
   three years' advanced education. She had numerous
   diplomatic dealings with Europeans. On the death of her
   husband, she and her Council dealt with the members of
   the Joint Commission in setting up a Provisional Government. She encouraged Swazis to go to South Africa
   to work in the mines and return the money to the Swazi
   nation in order to repurchase Swazi land. In 1900 she
   petitioned Queen Victoria "to take us under your imperial protection and to see that our wrongs are redressed."
   But matters, especially the land question, grew worse
   for the Swazis. Labotsibeni sent a deputation to London
   in 1907, but it failed. Her final hope was Sobhuza's
   law suit in 1922, but it, too, lost, even after appeal to
   the Privy Council, where the case was heard in March,
   1926, three months after her death.

MDLULI, MATSAFENI. The indvuna of King Mswati's administrative headquarters at Hhohho. Mdluli's sister,
Gwamile, was to become a wife of King Mbandzeni and
Ndlovukazi at the time of King Bhunu. Mdluli was one
of the principal advocates of the campaign against the
Bapedi that led to the Swazi defeat at Mosega Kop (see
BATTLE OF MOSEGA KOP). During the battle he dis-
appeared and was thought to be killed, but he returned
home six months later.

MDLULI, SHWAPA. The original right hand insila of the
present Swazi king, Sobhuza II. He died while still in
his twenties.

MDZABUKO. The son of King Mbandzeni and a girl who had
had a promise of marriage from Mbandzeni's deceased
brother Ludvonga. The girl was a daughter of Longa-
libalele, chief of the Hlubi tribe. Mbandzeni had married her against the advice of the Ndlovukazi, Sisile
Khumalo. The young Mdzabuko then received support
from many Swazis as the rightful heir to Ludvonga.
When Mdzabuko died mysteriously, there were rumors
that Mbandzeni had been involved in his death. (see
SISILE KHUMALO for more details.)

METHODISTS. One of the larger Christian denominations in
Swaziland with 8,600 adherents in 1962. Eight thousand
were Africans, 500 Europeans, and 100 Eurafricans.
The Methodists have set up educational institutions and
health facilities, including a hospital at Mahamba. They
were the first to arrive in Swaziland, their leader in
1844 being Rev. James Allison (q.v.).

MEYER, WILLIE. Elected Chairman of the United Swaziland
Association (USA) in March, 1964, during the early
period of Swaziland electoral activity. He was a successful USA candidate for a reserved European seat on
the Legislative Council in 1964. An Afrikaans-speaking
farmer from Southern Swaziland, he retained South
African citizenship also. Thus he was one of the most
vocal advocates of a special place for non-Swazis in
later constitutional arrangements. He participated in
constitutional talks in 1960, and again in 1965-66. He
was correct in his fear that the USA-Imbokodvo alliance
would fall apart as Swazis from weaker political parties
brought their views into Imbokodvo.

MFECANE.   A word used by Nguni speakers meaning a
    crushing of peoples.   (see DIFAQANE.)

MFUKWANE.   The sacred herd, a couple hundred cattle from
    the herd of the Swazi King that have special ritual sig-
    nificance.   They are not used for ploughing or other
    typical activities.   They are specially branded by hav-
    ing the tip of their tail cut off.   They are seldom
    killed, and they are considered to have human feelings.
    Only the King, his mother, and his ritual wife of the
    Matsebula clan are considered strong enough to resist
    the magic in the fat of these cattle.   These three may
    smear themselves with the fat but others coming in con-
    tact with it may go mad.   Dung from the mfukwane is
    smeared on the future Queen Mother in a special cere-
    mony.

MGAZINI (variant: MGWAZINI).   A town in southwestern
    Swaziland, located on the Mankayana-Nhlangano road,
    about four miles from the South African border.   Mga-
    zini is the starting point of a road across the border
    to Kemp, South Africa, a stopping point of the South
    African Railroad.

MHLAMBANYATI.   A town of about 1,400 people, heavily
    European, located a little over ten miles south of
    Mbabane.   It is the Usutu Pulp Company's settlement
    in the Usutu Forest.   Mhlambanyati means literally,
    "Buffalo Crossing. "   In the western part of Swaziland,
    it is roughly twenty miles from the South African border.

MHLATUZANE RIVER.   Rising at Hlatikulu this river flows
    northeasterly about forty miles before joining the Great
    Usutu River four miles south of Phuzamoya.

MHLATUZE RIVER.   A tributary of the Great Usutu River,
    it begins in the south-central portion of Swaziland and
    flows northeasterly until it joins the main river six
    miles west of Big Bend.

MHLUME.   A town of a little over 2,000 people located in
    the northeastern part of the country.   In the Lowveld,
    it is only four miles from the border.   Its name means
    "Good Growth. "   Mhlume was established by the Com-
    monwealth Development Corporation and is the site of
    the Mhlume Sugar Company (q. v.) Estate.   In addition,
    citrus orchards produce well in the area.

MHLUME SUGAR COMAPNY. The second largest sugar producer in Swaziland, after the Ubombo Ranches, Ltd.
(q. v.).   Located at Mhlume in the Lowveld of northeastern Swaziland, it was formed as a partnership between the Commonwealth Development Corporation (q.v.)
and the Sir J. L. Hulett and Sons firm of South Africa.
It has a mill producing about 85, 000 tons of sugar a
year.   It gets water from the CDC irrigation scheme
that pumps it along a forty-two mile long canal from the
Komati River.

MHLUMENI. A border town in Swaziland at the Mozambique
border.   It is about five miles south of the Railway
border-crossing at Umbeluzipoort.   Mhlumeni is on the
most direct route from Siteki to Goba in Mozambique.

MIDDLEVELD.   An area of about 1, 900 square miles cutting
through roughly the middle of Swaziland from the north
border to the south.   With an average altitude of between 2, 000 and 2, 500 ft. , it is well suited for farming, thanks in part to several major irrigation schemes.
It produces maize, cotton, tobacco, pineapple, citrus,
rice and other farm products.   Beef production and
dairying is also found there.   The Middleveld is the
most densely populated part of the country and has been
the site of the capitals of the Swazi nation for two centuries.   The Swazis have no distinct name for it, but
sometimes refer to it as Live or Ngwane; in other
words, the nucleus of the homeland.   The major towns
are Manzini and Nhlangano, as well as the royal villages Lozita and Lobamba.   The Middleveld receives
between 30 and 45 inches of rainfall a year and has a
sub-tropical climate.

MILLER, ALLISTER MITCHELL, SR. A journalist, born in
Scotland in 1865, who came to Swaziland in his early
twenties and made it his permanent home.   Shortly after
arrival, he was appointed Secretary of the "White Committee" (q. v.) and one of the five representatives of
King Mbandzeni on the committee.   He also became
private secretary to the King.   When Theophilus Shepstone, Jr., advisor to the King, angered the King,
Mbandzeni placed Miller in Shepstone's place.   This
lasted only from January, 1889, until October 2, 1889,
shortly before Mbandzeni's death when the Queen Regent
reinstated Shepstone.   It was during Miller's period as
advisor that many of the land monopolies are said to

have been granted. In fact, Miller and John Thorburn
(q. v.) received major concessions and merged them
later as the Swaziland Corporation, Ltd. , which Miller
later managed. During the Boer War, Miller served as
Lieutenant and second in command to David Forbes, Jr.
(q. v.) in the Lubombo Scouts who fought the Boers in
eastern Swaziland. Miller also became the focus of attention when young King Sobhuza II challenged the original partitioning of the country and in 1924 initiated a
lawsuit. The case came to be known as Sobhuza II
versus A. M. Miller and the Swaziland Corporation Limited. Sobhuza lost, but appealed to the Privy Council
in 1926 where he again lost. Miller wrote several
books about the Swazis and their country (see the bibliography). The main thoroughfare of the capital, Mbabane, is named after him. He died in 1951.

MILLET. Also known as "Kaffir corn. " A cereal plant from
India, also called sorghum. It is a common basis for
Swazi meals and equally common in much of southern
Africa. It is a major crop in Swaziland.

MILNER, LORD ALFRED. Born in Bonn, Germany, March
23, 1852, he eventually became an important member
of the British Civil Service. He was appointed Governor of Cape Colony in 1897 and also served as High
Commissioner from 1897 to 1905. In this capacity he
intervened for King Bhunu (q. v.) with the South African
Republic in 1898. He became Governor of the Transvaal (while still High Commissioner) after the Boer War
and served in this capacity which gave him charge of
Swaziland affairs, from June, 1902 until April, 1905.
His main effect on Swaziland at that point was his appointment of a Concessions Commission to investigate
concession claims. It was this commission that eventually led to the Concessions Partition Proclamation (q.
v.). His Swaziland Administration Proclamation of 1904
(q. v.) also had a great effect on the governing of Swaziland. In 1905 he returned to England. From January,
1919 to February, 1921, Milner served as British Colonial Secretary. In this capacity he spoke several
times with both Generals Botha and Smuts about the
possible transfer of the High Commission Territories
to South Africa. His telegram to the High Commissioner, Lord Buxton (q. v.), in 1919 indicated that he felt
the transfer was inevitable, and that Swaziland should
be the first to be transferred, although he did express

some concern for fair treatment of the Africans.

MINERAL CONCESSION AREAS PROCLAMATION OF 1927.
A proclamation issued as a result of a commission's
study that showed that many mineral concessions were
dormant, as little effort had been made to prospect the
areas. The options given by the proclamation were:
surrendering the concession to the Government, paying
an undeveloped minerals tax, allowing the Government
to supervise prospecting or mining by others, and en-
gaging in adequate prospecting by the concession holder
himself.

MJINDINI. The name of one of the military villages of King
Mswati II, its site was near the present town of Barberton in the Transvaal province of South Africa.

MKATSHWA. A Nguni clan that is classed among the Ema-
fikamuva (q. v.) or "late-comers" in Swaziland. The
mother of King Sobhuza II was born into this clan, and
thus the term is sometimes used in his praise poems.

MKHULUMNQANDE (variant: MKHULUMNCHNATI). The
supreme being or creator in Swazi tradition. After
shaping the earth and placing upon it flora and fauna
and people, he returned to where he came from, never
to return. He occasionally sends a messenger, Mlentengamunye (q. v.). Extremely rare occurrences (e. g.,
a child born with teeth) are attributed to Mkhulumnqande if it is felt that other spirits could not have
caused it. Regular sacrifices are not made to him nor
is he worshipped. Some missionaries have tried to re-
late him in some ways to their Almighty, Unkulunkulu.

MKONDO RIVER (variants: MKONDVO, UMKONDO). Rising
about thirty miles west of Piet Retief in the Transvaal,
this river enters Swaziland north of Mahamba in the
southwestern part of the country. It flows northeasterly,
picking up the Ndlozane and Mozane Rivers as tributaries before it joins the Great Usutu River south of Sidvokodvo. The Mkondo River is also known as the
Assegai River.

MLAWULA. An important town for transportation in northeastern Swaziland. It is three miles from the main
cross-Swaziland highway; it is along the Mlawula River
just before it joins the Umbeluzi River to go through

the gorge to Goba in Mozambique; and it is the last
stop of the Swaziland Railway before it enters Mozambique eight miles away.   It is also just a few miles
from a rich agricultural area.

MLAWULA RIVER.   A tributary of the Umbeluzi, it rises
    just outside Siteki in the Lubombo Mountains and flows
    north, around the town of Mlawula and joins the Umbe-
    luzi two miles east of the town.

MLENTENGAMUNYE.   A messenger sent to earth on occa-
    sion by the supreme being, Mkhulumnqande (q. v.).   His
    appearances seem to fit no particular pattern, nor do
    they occur just in Swaziland.   People do not try to ap-
    proach him, but as word spreads, the people perform
    any of several customary practices reserved for such
    an occasion.   Since he appears to have done little ex-
    cept show up, there seems to be no reason for his
    arrival to be feared.

MLIBA.   A crossroads community in north-central Swaziland,
    roughly 2, 100 feet above sea-level.   It is a cotton-
    growing region.

MLILWANE GAME SANCTUARY.   The major game reserve
    in Swaziland, originally located eleven miles south of
    Mbabane.   Begun by Terence Reilly in 1960 on his
    family's 1, 100 acres, it was partly stocked and opened
    in 1964.   The South African Wild Life Foundation
    bought and donated an adjacent 2, 800 acres and the
    Anglo-American Corporation added 350 more acres. An
    addition of 5, 400 acres in 1971 brings it even closer to
    Mbabane.   Down in the Ezulwini Valley, it is set among
    mountains, one called Mlilwane ("little fire") because its
    iron content attracts lightning.   The elephants and big
    cats are about the only major African animals missing.
    Reilly, now the Chief Warden, is also adding reptiles,
    birds, and even native flora.   The sanctuary also has
    a rest camp and is the site of the Gilbert Reynolds
    Memorial Garden, including over 230 species of aloe.

MLUMATI RIVER.   Another name for the Lomati River,
    (q. v.).

MNUMZANA (variant of UMNUMZANA, q. v.).

MONA.   The name given in infancy to the son and heir of

King Bhunu. When Mona was installed as the present
King in December, 1921, he took the name Sobhuza II.

MOODIE'S GOLD FIELD. Along with the De Kaap Gold Field
(q. v.), it was located near Barberton just to the northwest of Swaziland and attracted many miners to the
Eastern Transvaal-Swaziland area. It was named after
George Pigot Moodie, Surveyor-General of the Transvaal from 1881 to 1884, whose personal mining concession contained gold of tremendous worth. Both the
Moodie and De Kaap Gold Fields were responsible for
attracting concession hunters into Swaziland where they
also found gold in quantity.

MORGAN, DAVID L. Resident Commissioner for Swaziland
from 1951 to 1956.

MORGAN. A unit of measurement used to measure land,
and commonly used in Swaziland. A morgen is approximately 2. 11 acres.

MORSE, PROFESSOR CHANDLER. Chairman of an Economic
Survey Mission (q. v.) which toured the High Commission Territories from September 12 to December 17,
1959. The Report was filed on March 1, 1960.

MOSEGA KOP see BATTLE OF MOSEGA KOP

MOTSA, NGOLOTSHENI. The first "left-hand insila" of the
current reigning monarch, Sobhuza II.

MOTSA CLAN. One of the more significant of the clans in
Swazi ritual. Of Sotho origin (specifically, Bapedi), it
is classified Emakhandzambili, meaning those clans
found ahead by Sobhuza I as he took over central Swaziland. In the Swazi ritual involving tinsila (singular:
insila, q. v.), a youth from the Motsa clan becomes the
new Ngwenyama's first "left-hand insila. " Also the
Swazi nation provides the Ngwenyama with his first two
queens, one of whom, called "the left-hand queen, "
must be from the Motsa clan. She is the second to be
married.

MOTSHANE (Variant: MOTJANE). A small community along
the main road from Oshoek to Mbabane in western Swaziland. About five miles from the South African border,
Motshane is at the junction of the Mbabane road with

the gravelled road leading north to Forbes Reef and
Pigg's Peak.

MOZAMBIQUE.   Scheduled to become an independent country
     in June, 1975, this large territory, sometimes referred
     to as Portuguese East Africa, shares sixty miles of
     Swaziland's eastern border.   Swaziland's railway runs
     through Mozambique to the port of Lourenço Marques.
     Portugal had considered Mozambique to be an overseas
     province.   Revolutions in both Mozambique and Portu-
     gal have led to the impending change of status.   Entry
     points by road from Swaziland are by way of Loma-
     hasha and Goba Fronteira, both in northeast Swazi-
     land.

MOZANE RIVER.   A minor tributary of the Mkondo River,
     it starts seven miles southeast of Mankayane, flows
     south, and joins the Mkondo ten miles northwest of
     Hlatikulu.

MPAKA.   A community located twelve miles east of Siteki in
     the Lowveld.   It is not only on the main trans-Swazi-
     land highway, but is also one of the few stopping points
     along the Swaziland Railway route.   Trains stop at
     Mpaka to load coal both for export to Mozambique and
     Kenya and also for use by the railway.   Mpaka is the
     site of the coal mine run by the Anglo-American Corp-
     oration of South Africa.

MPANDE (variants: PANDA, UMPANDA).   Zulu king, and
     brother of Dingane whom he succeeded after a series of
     conflicts and a battle at Magongo in 1840.   South African
     Commandant-General Pretorius installed Mpande as King
     of the Zulus.   In the mid 1850's his impis perpetrated
     a series of raids on the Swazis, the most notable cul-
     minating in the Battle of Lubuya (q. v.).   Finally King
     Mswati persuaded Sir Theophilus Shepstone to put
     pressure on Mpande, and the raids stopped.   Mpande
     died in 1872.

MSHIYANE.   A grandson of King Sobhuza I, Mshiyane was
     chief of a group of Swazis living at Mgazini in the Man-
     kayane district in the 1870's.   They were the victims
     of several attacks by the dissident son of Mswati II,
     Mbilini (q. v.).   To escape renewed attack, Mshiyane led
     his people to a new area, near Ermelo in what is now
     South Africa.

MSIBI, DR. GEORGE.   A medical doctor and an active par-
ticipant in Swazi national politics for over a decade.
Even before finishing his education in India and Japan,
he had been contacted by Dr. Allen Nxumalo and others
about their National Convention Party.   Upon his return
to Swaziland in 1961, he was given its leadership and
soon merged it with the Mbandzeni National Party to
form the Mbandzeni National Convention (MNC), with
Msibi its leader.   In 1963 he was chosen by the British
to represent the MNC at the London Constitutional Conference, where he affiliated it with the Joint Council of
Swaziland Political Parties.   While his political stand
favored a modern democracy, he also consistently supported the Swazi King and the Swazi National Council.
Meanwhile, Msibi resigned from the MNC in August,
1963, and a year later was an active member of the
traditionalist Imbokodvo National Movement and an aide
to its leader, Makhosini Dlamini.   Msibi soon became
the Secretary General of Imbokodvo and, by July, 1965,
was also its treasurer.   In August, 1965, an appointed
member of the Legislative Council, Msibi then was
appointed by the British Commissioner, Sir Francis
Loyd, to the new Constitutional Committee.   For several
years Dr. Msibi was out of politics, partly as a result
of a conflict of interest charge that made headlines.   In
the 1970's, however, he has again become active, in
business as well as politics.   In 1972 he was appointed
to the Senate by the new Parliament, and in 1973 he
was appointed by the King to the Royal Constitutional
Commission.

MSUNDUZA TOWNSHIP.   A rapidly expanding suburb of Mbabane, and the site of the residences of many of the
Swazis working in and around Mbabane.   Originally a
rather dingy collection of squatter huts, it has seen
much recent development and has been the center of
attention by both the Government and private developers
interested in improving the conditions there.   Some of
the opposition groups also find political support there.

MSWATI I.   One of the earlier Bembo-Nguni leaders subsequent to Dlamini I.   It is estimated that he was Ngwenyama in the vicinity of 1600 A. D.

MSWATI II.   Also known as Mavuso II.   Born in approximately 1820 to King Sobhuza I by his wife Thandile, he
became the heir upon his father's death in 1836.   He

gained the reputation as having been "the greatest of the
Swazi fighting kings, " and his name, in a form cor-
rupted by Europeans, became the name for the country
--Swazi-land. Mswati was the first Swazi King to in-
vite missionaries to his country (see REV. JAMES
ALLISON). Nevertheless, he drew fame and fear from
his large-scale military raids, especially among the
Sotho groups north of Swaziland in what is today the
Transvaal. One writer called him "the Chaka of the
north. " He maintained several regiments at his royal
residence at Hhohho and several at the Ndlovukazi's
royal residence at Ludzidzini. He also set up military
villages (complete with chieftains, indvuna, and regiments) at Mekemeke, Mjindini, and Mbhuleni. His
armies met the Zulus at the Battle of Lubuya (q. v.),
but generally he avoided this contact, appealing successfully to Sir Theophilus Shepstone (q. v.) for help in
stopping Zulu raids. Mswati was also noted for sending regiments to settle internal disputes among the
people within the area he claimed to control, for example, those involving the descendants of Ndawonde
Shabalala and Soshangane. On the other hand, he sent
armies after two of his own relatives, Malambule and
Somcuba. Nevertheless, it is Mswati who is credited
with unifying the Swazi nation as it is today, including
the addition of new clans. He died at Hhohho in 1868,
and was buried near his father on the royal burying
hill at Mbilaneni.

MTFANENKOSI. A "prince, " also, a "child of a king
    (Nkosi). " The term is also extended to a son of a son
    of a king. A prince automatically is a member of the
    libandla (q. v.), and helps to determine upon the succes-
    sion to the kingship and whether or not the nation goes
    to war. Frequently, the mature prince will be as-
    signed land away from the capital which he will govern,
    both so that he may serve as a local representative of
    the Nkosi and in order to lessen the temptation for such
    a close relative to attempt an overthrow. Nevertheless,
    he is available for consultation and for attendance at
    important events.

MTINDEKWA RIVER (variant: MTINDZEKWA). Beginning
    near the transterritorial highway ten miles west of
    Siteki, it flows south through cattle-raising areas to
    join the Great Usutu River seven miles northwest of
    Big Bend.

MTSETFWA, MANDANDA (variant: MTETWA). Indvuna at
Zombodze and one of the more respected councillors of
the Swazi nation during the first half of the twentieth
century. He accompanied the young King Sobhuza II on
his trip to London in 1923.

MUNTFU. Variant of umuntu (q. v.).

MURPHY, JAMES SPRINGH. A member of both the 1967
and 1972 Parliaments as a result of being appointed to
them by King Sobhuza II. From an old Swaziland
family, he attended school in Mbabane. He served for
many years on the European Advisory Council as well
as on other important advisory or supervisory boards.
He is also a Justice of the Peace.

MZAMOSE. The first child of Thandile (Lazidze) and sister
of the man who was to be known as King Mswati II. As
such she had very high status in the nation and her advice was important in choosing her brother's successor.

MZILA. Eldest son of Soshangane (q. v.) and according to
Shangane custom the rightful heir to leadership of the
Gaza Empire after his father's death. Having been
banished by his father and having fled to Spelonken in
the Eastern Transvaal, his brother Mawewe was declared chief. Playing on the dissatisfaction of his
people with his brother's rule, he led a faction in de-
posing Mawewe. When the Swazis supported the de-
posed chief, however, Mzila was forced to flee. The
Swazis soon left, however, and Mzila returned with
Portuguese aid to retake the throne. Preferring the
British to the Portuguese, he turned to Sir Theophilus
Shepstone (q. v.) for diplomatic aid and to inquire about
trade. But Shepstone and the British declined to get
involved in Portugal's sphere of influence.

MZIMPOFU RIVER. This tributary of the Great Usutu River
begins two miles north of Helehele near Manzini and
flows to the southeast to join the Usutu two miles south
of Phuzamoya. The name means "Eland water. "

-N-

NABOMNTFWANA. Literally "Mother of the Child, " it is a
title given to the woman who will be the future Queen

Mother of the newly designated heir to the Swazi kingship. Upon the death of the previous Ngwenyama (q. v.),
the hut of the Nabomntfwana is removed by night to a
location a short distance from the old capital. Three
years later, after the mourning period, she and the
young Umntfwana (q. v.) move into a new homestead, the
beginnings of the new capital. She remains Nabomntfwana until the Umntfwana celebrates his first recognized
marriage, at which point she becomes the Ndlovukazi
(q. v.).

NATAL. The smallest of the four provinces of the Republic
of South Africa, covering the southeastern portion of the
country. It is separated from the southern border of
Swaziland by just a few miles of the Transvaal province.
Natal is adjacent to Swaziland along the latter's southeastern border, in the area known as Ngwavuma (q. v.).

NATIONAL CONVENTION PARTY   see SWAZILAND
NATIONAL CONVENTION

NATIONAL TREASURY PROCLAMATION.   A proclamation of
1950 by which the Swazi National Treasury was established. The High Commissioner was empowered by it to
decide the proportion of the native tax allocated to this
fund and arrange for audits when necessary. The
Ngwenyama also was granted power to regulate the constitution and conduct of the Treasury and how its funds
should be expended.

NATIVE ADMINISTRATION PROCLAMATION OF 1944.   Enacted in October, 1944, the subject of such a proclamation had been discussed for four years between British
and Swazi officials. The Swazis maintained that the
British proposal (which ultimately became the 1944 Proclamation) infringed too severely on Swazi rights in the
area of native law and custom, rights guaranteed by the
Order in Council of 1903 (q. v.). Swazis specifically
objected to provisions giving the Resident Commissioner
powers regarding appointment and dismissal of chiefs,
powers previously assumed only by the Ngwenyama-in-
Council. While it was enacted, the controversial Proclamation of 1944 was never really implemented, and
because of the Swazi objections, it was superseded by
the Native Administration Proclamation of 1950 (q. v.).

NATIVE ADMINISTRATION PROCLAMATION OF 1950. A re-

vised and modified version of the Native Administration
Proclamation of 1944. It was enacted because the 1944
Act had been unacceptable to the Swazis and unwork-
able. The Proclamation prescribed the powers and
functions of the Native Authorities recognized by the
British government. It especially related to crime pre-
vention, the enforcement of order, and the collection of
taxes, but also recognized the traditional authority in
native customs and laws. A change from the 1944 Proclamation made the Ngwenyama-in-Libandhla the authority for any orders (rather than the colonial government), while still being subject to the approval of the
Resident Commissioner.

NATIVE AUTHORITY. A term used by the British throughout their African territories to designate generally all
the African leaders (at whatever level) whose official
power and functions were recognized by the British
Government. Their names, powers, and functions are
specifically noted and recorded, especially those powers
or functions which are owed to the British administration or which are supervised by it. While such a Native
Administration arrangement was enacted for Swaziland
in 1944, it did not become effective until the Native Administration Proclamation of 1950 (q. v.).

NATIVE COURTS PROCLAMATION. A proclamation of 1950
establishing the authority of Swazi native courts as
recognized by the British government. It recognized
virtually all authority over native courts to be in the
hands of the Ngwenyama, subject to approval by the Resident Commissioner. Also in rare instances the Resident Commissioner could intrude if the Ngwenyama
failed to act, but only with due respect for native law
and custom. Also, district commissioners would have
power only in criminal, not civil, cases. This proclamation granted much more judicial control to the Swazis
than Britain had granted to other African territories.

NATIVE RECRUITING CORPORATION. The South African
corporation that recruits laborers for the gold mines.
It is regulated by the African Labour Proclamation
(q. v.). The number of Swazis being recruited each
year has stabilized at about five to six thousand. In
1962 it was 8, 800 men, but the expanding Swaziland
economy is absorbing more Swazis every year.

NAZARENE CHURCH.   One of the significant Christian denominations in Swaziland.   Of the 6, 000 or so members
in 1968, virtually all were Africans.   The Church sponsors educational and health institutions in the country,
notably Nazarene College (a primary school), and the
Mbuluzi Leper Hospital (q. v.) near Mbabane, the Raleigh
Fitkin Memorial Hospital (q. v.), and the Manzini-Naza-
rene Teacher Training College, as well as the Nazarene
Bible College at Siteki for the training of missionaries.
The first Nazarene missionaries, Rev. and Mrs. H. F.
Schmelzenbach came from the United States to Pigg's
Peak in 1910.   Dr. and Mrs. David Hynd (q. v.) ar-
rived in 1925.

NCWALA (variant: INCWALA).   An annual ceremony held
in December and January which is the most sacred of
all Swazi ceremonies.   While it is called the Feast of
the First Fruits of the year, its significance for Kingship and the Nation goes much deeper, emphasizing
both unity and power.   It begins at the new moon of the
month preceding Ncwala month (the timing is geared
heavily to astrology), when special officials are sent
off to the ocean and to certain rivers to obtain water.
Their return marks the beginning of the Little Ncwala
ceremony.   The night of the full moon of the following
month marks the beginning of the main Ncwala over a
period of six days.   The first three days involve activity by the young men and the emabutfo of the Royal
Villages, Lobamba and Lozita.   They collect certain
kinds of branches and shrub to be used in building a
special enclosure in the siboya for the Ngwenyama.
Special rituals and songs are performed.   The fourth
day is the most important one.   Warriors come in full
war dress and a hundred guests arrive (including Europeans) to observe.   After a series of rituals, the
Ngwenyama and other Nkosi Dlamini dance into the enclosure. All guests leave as the participants begin a long
ritual of dances and songs, leading to the Ngwenyama ultimately tasting the first fruits of the year (and thus allowing
his subjects to use their new crops). The rituals of the day
have included several indicating the "magical" strength of
the King, and the unity of the Swazi people against outsid-
ers. The fifth day is one of seclusion in which the Royal
Family smears itself with fat from the sacred herd, mfukwane (q. v.). The sixth day involves more rituals, especially involving dance-songs around a specially-built fire.
Rain--the blessing of the ancestors--is expected to fall
and put it out that day. Usually it does.

NDLOVUKAZI (variant: INDLOVUKATI). Literally "The
Lady Elephant," the Swazi term used to denote the
Queen Mother of the nation. Her importance derives
heavily from the fact that upon death of the Ngwenyama,
the heir is designated on the basis of the position of
the mother in relation to the deceased Ngwenyama and
the other wives. The clan she is from will also be a
factor in choosing the new Queen Mother and her son
as Ngwenyama. Under rare circumstances the Ndlovukazi will not be the actual mother of the youth designated as heir. If a Ngwenyama lives a long life, such
as Sobhuza II, he will probably outlive one or even
several Queen Mothers. In this case, another of his
father's wives or even one of his own wives may be
designated Ndlovukazi. Historically, the Ngwenyama
and Ndlovukazi have been co-holders of power, and of
importance in ritual. A long-reigning and educated
monarch such as Sobhuza II has become dominant in the
country, however, despite the privileged position in
ritual that the present Ndlovukazi still shares. The
traditional influence of the Ndlovukazi is seen in several
ways: she rules the Royal Village, the capital, while
the Ngwenyama sets up a secondary Royal Village some
distance away. She presides over the second highest
court in the nation, she and her counselors are important advisors to the Ngwenyama, she is custodian of the
nation's sacred objects. Of course, she is a member
of both the liqoqo (q. v.) and libandhla (q. v.).

NDLOZANE RIVER. A tributary of the Mkondo River, it begins a few miles into the Transvaal from where it
drifts south and east to join the Mkondo ten miles west
of Hlatikulu, cutting its way through an impressive
gorge.

NDUNA. Variant of Induna, itself a variant of Indvuna (q.v.).

NDVUNGUNYE, KING (variants: NDUNGUNYE, NDUN-
GUANYA, NDVUNGUNGE). Also known as Zikodze.
The son of King Ngwane III, who died in about 1780,
Ndvungunye ruled the Swazis until he was struck by
lightning in about 1815 and died. His mother, laMnd-
zebele or laKubheka, had her residence at (old) Lo-
bamba, while the King's administrative capital was at
Shiselweni. A strong ruler, he began an embryonic
Swazi army and used it to secure his father's conquests
and absorb additional tribes. Likewise, his son and

successor, Sobhuza I, increased the prestige of the ruling Dlaminis.

NDWANDWA, PRINCE (variant: NDWANDWE). A half-
brother of King Mswati II, and a son of File, a subsidiary co-wife of Mswati's mother, Lazidze. Ndwandwa
and Lazidze served as regents during the minority of
Mswati's heir, Ludvonga. In this capacity, Ndwandwa
met Bishop Thomas Wilkinson (q. v.) when he visited
Swaziland in 1871. When Ludvonga died the next year,
Ndwandwa was accused of murder and of seeking power
for himself. The Swazi council then ordered Prince
Ndwandwa clubbed to death and also the people of his
home, except for his heir and his mother. This was
done.

NDWANDWE TRIBE. A group of Bembo-Nguni people closely
related to the royal Dlamini clan of Swaziland. Split-
ting in the sixteenth century from the group later to be
called Swazis, they moved south of the Pongola River
and settled between the Pongola and Umfolozi Rivers.
In the early nineteenth century they became strong under
their great leader Zidze (q. v.), also known as Zwide.
Hoping for an alliance with them, King Sobhuza I requested one of Zidze's daughters as his wife and mother
of his heir. When Thandile was thus chosen, she became known as Lazidze, and later became famous as
mother of King Mswati II. The Shangane people of Mozambique split away from the Ndwandwe and became a
distinct group in the first third of the nineteenth century.

NENGWASE. One of the sisters of King Sobhuza II.

NEW SCOTLAND. A name referring to an area just to the
west of Swaziland's present boundaries. It was occupied
by a number of Scottish immigrants (see ALEXANDER
MCCORKINDALE) at a time when the area was still
under the sovereignty of Swazi kings, in the 1880's.
Despite agreements between the settlers and the Swazis,
the area was absorbed into the South African Republic
(Transvaal) in 1893.

NGONI. Although they are referred to by one author as a
branch of the Swazis that moved away, other evidence
is that they, like the Swazis, are of Nguni (q. v.) origin
but otherwise unrelated. Two groups of Ngoni led by
different leaders fled north from the Zulus in the 1820's

during the Mfecane. (see DIFAQANE.) One group
clashed with the Shangane (q. v.) and ended up in Tanzania. The other group also fled past Swaziland and
settled in Malawi.

NGONINI. A citrus and lumber-producing area in the extreme northern part of Swaziland, about five miles from
the South African border. It is the site of a major irrigation scheme along the Lomati River that flows
through the area. There is also a small airstrip in
the vicinity.

NGUBANE, JORDAN. One of the original founders of the
Swaziland Democratic Party on March 2, 1962. A
South African, he had been a Vice-President of the
Liberal Party there and was also active in the African
National Congress. When he was banned under the
South African Suppression of Communism Act, he fled
to Swaziland, where he helped to organize the moderate
and multi-racial SDP.

NGUNI. One of the principal ethno-linguistic groups of Bantu
peoples in Southern Africa. They migrated south from
the area north of the Limpopo River in the fifteenth
century along with the Sutu peoples (q. v.). The Nguni
tended to stay east of the Drakensberg Mountains, near-
er the Coast, while the Sutus stayed to the west. The
Swazis are the main Northern Nguni peoples, while the
Xhosa and the Zulus (and their defectors, the Ndebele)
are among the prominent Southern Nguni peoples.

NGWANE I. An early leader of the Bembo-Nguni peoples,
and a predecessor of Dlamini I (q. v.).

NGWANE II. One of the earlier rulers of the Dlamini branch
of the Bembo-Nguni peoples, later called the Swazis.
He ruled possibly during the early seventeenth century,
although dates of early Swazi rulers are very much in
doubt. A successor to Mswati I, he preceded Dlamini
II as ruler.

NGWANE III. One of the most important of the early Swazi
rulers, settling his people in the area now called Swaziland during the mid-eighteenth century. The terms
kaNgwane (land of Ngwane) and bakaNgwane (people of
Ngwane) which are still applied to Swaziland today refer
back to Ngwane III. Bringing his people northwest from

the Pongola River, he built his tribal capital at a place
he called Zombodze.   His administrative center he
named Hhohho.   He then expanded his following by con-
quering and absorbing nearby clans.   He died around
1780, and was buried on a hill called Mbilaneni, now
an important burial place of kings.

NGWANE IV.   Another title of King Sobhuza I (q. v.).

NGWANE V.   Another title of King Bhunu.

NGWANE NATIONAL LIBERATORY CONGRESS (NNLC).   The
    outgrowth of a series of splits in the Swaziland Pro-
    gressive Party (SPP) in 1961 and 1962, this party was
    created by Dr. Ambrose Zwane (q. v.) who gave it this
    name in April, 1963.   It was previously referred to by
    many as "SPP (Zwane). "   The NNLC ultimately became
    the only truly successful opposition party in Swaziland.
    Its success in the 1972 elections, however, may lead to
    its being declared illegal.   As of 1963 it advocated a
    democratic Swaziland under a one man-one vote system.
    It should be a multi-racial state, Pan-Africanist, so-
    cialist, and under the rule of law.   It opposed tribalism
    and colonialism, and favored free and compulsory edu-
    cation.   Trade unions would be encouraged.   The NNLC
    was well organized at first and had a large following,
    led by its President, Dr. Ambrose Zwane, and its
    Secretary-General, (Clement) Dumisa Dlamini.   When
    Dlamini had legal troubles, Arthur Khoza and Macdonald
    Maseko became key leaders.   The NNLC supported some
    of the labor unrest of 1962 and 1963, and many of its
    leaders were on trial just before the 1964 elections.   It
    contested the elections with greater success than the
    parties other than Imbokodvo (q. v.).   It then began to
    oppose the three-man constituency arrangement under
    the Constitution, since it seemed to prevent opposition
    parties from success.   It came close to winning some
    seats in 1967 despite the defection of Maseko, Khoza
    and several others in 1966 and despite the three-man
    constituencies.   It received 20 per cent of the votes.
    Ultimately it did succeed in getting Zwane, B. T.
    Ngwenya, and Mageja Masilela elected in 1972, despite
    another party split in 1971 that removed several other
    key leaders of the NNLC, especially K. T. Samketi
    (q. v.) and Abbey Msibi.   These men formed their own
    wing of the party, also called the NNLC, but were very
    unsuccessful in the 1972 elections.   Since the conclusion

of the incidents involving B. T. Ngwenya (q. v.) and the
voiding of the Constitution, Dr. Zwane has been under
government detention.

NGWANE PARK.   A very large township bordering Manzini.
Its original plans were for 645 residential plots, church
sites and business and domestic industry.   It has been
expanded since its inception in the mid-1960's.

NGWANE WONKE.   "All Swaziland, " a council which, in past
years, has been called when there was danger of im-
pending war.   All men of the country were eligible to
attend and speak, and women were allowed to attend and
listen.   The Ngwenyama and Ndlovukazi would both be
present.   These assemblies were rare.

NGWAVUMA (variant: INGWAVUMA).   An area adjacent to
Swaziland, east of its southern part.   Descendants of
the Bembo-Nguni (q. v.) still live there and some of
them continued to pay allegiance to the Swazi King
throughout the nineteenth century.   Although earlier
boundary commissions acknowledged the status quo, on
April 27, 1895 Britain issued a proclamation making
the area a part of Zululand.   Today it is part of the
Republic of South Africa.
        There is also a town called Ingwavuma located at
the Swaziland border just inside the Republic of South
Africa.   It is an administrative center and has a population of about four hundred.   King Bhunu (q. v.) fled
there during his conflict with the South African Republic
in 1898.

NGWEMPISI RIVER.   Rising in the Transvaal about thirty
miles west of Swaziland, it enters the country about
twelve miles south of Sandlane and, following a very
crooked path, flows south of Mankayane until it joins
the Great Usutu River near the center of the country.

NGWENYA.   The second tallest mountain in Swaziland at
6, 002 feet.   The word means "crocodile. "   Located
near the border in northwest Swaziland, it is part of a
range referred to as the Ngwenya Mountains.   Part of
this area is Bomvu Ridge, which is being mined heavily
for iron ore.   (See also SWAZILAND IRON ORE DE-
VELOPMENT CO. LTD.)

NGWENYA, BHEKINDLELA THOMAS.   An active but rela-

tively obscure member of the Ngwane National Liberatory Congress (NNLC), Ngwenya became a pivotal force
in Swaziland's constitutional crisis of 1973. By receiving 4,583 votes in the Mpumalanga constituency in 1972
elections, Ngwenya and two other members of the NNLC
became the first elected opposition members in the
Swaziland Parliament. Several weeks later the government declared Ngwenya a prohibited immigrant (and
therefore not qualified for Parliament) because he was
illegally in Swaziland. Despite his having lived most of
his life as a farmer in Swaziland, as Immigration Tribunal declared in January, 1973 that Ngwenya was born
in Ntonga, near Piet Retief, South Africa, rather than
in Nsalitshe, Swaziland, as he claimed. In September,
1972, the High Court agreed with his appeal to set aside
the "prohibited immigrant" status, noting his long record of life in Swaziland and previously uncontested voting several times. It also accepted evidence that he
was born at Nsalitshe. When Ngwenya tried to take his
seat in the House of Assembly in October, the Government members boycotted the session and it adjourned
for lack of a quorum. In November, an Act was passed
creating a special Immigration Tribunal. It was this
Tribunal that found Ngwenya to have been born in South
Africa. During the hearings his lawyers withdrew from
the case after an unusual legal ruling, and his witnesses
were never called. The Swaziland Court of Appeal then
declared in March that the Act creating the Immigration
Tribunal was unconstitutional. The next month the constitution was declared "unsuitable" by King Sobhuza II
and thus void. In May the Tribunal was reestablished
and all previous decisions (only the one declaring
Ngwenya to be illegally in Swaziland) were declared to
be operative.

NGWENYAMA (also INGWENYAMA). Literally, "The Lion,"
   the traditional name given to the King of Swaziland.
   (See KING OF SWAZILAND for references to his position under the modern Constitutions and in the period
   since Independence.) The Ngwenyama is more than just
   the leading political figure, the monarch. He physically
   represents the nation in all its vitality. He is to be
   kept from any association with death. As ruler, he
   shares power with the Ndlovukazi to whom he owes his
   own choice as Ngwenyama. Nevertheless, his ruling
   power is greater than hers. He presides over the highest court, controls the age regiments (as seen during

his 1973 takeover of power), has the power to distribute
Swazi land, and is the nation's leader in rituals, especially the Ncwala (q. v.).   The Ngwenyama is always
chosen from the children of the wives of the previous
Ngwenyama; thus he will always be a member of the
ruling Nkosi Dlamini clan.   He is never the first son
of the Ngwenyama, and he is chosen specifically because
the councillors decided that his mother was to be the
Ndlovukazi.   His closest associates are two tinsila
(singular insila, q. v.) who are ritual brothers who are
intended to protect him from evil, both physical and of
the spirit world.   He is also guided in his actions by
the Swazi National Council (q. v.).

NHLAMBELO.   A sacred enclosure or sanctuary found in the
upper end of the cattle enclosure in the royal village.
It is used particularly during the Ncwala ceremony for
a variety of ritual purposes, especially those involving
the King where he is doctored with special medicines.
In ordinary times, however, calves of the royal herd
are kept in it overnight.

NHLANGANO.   Formerly Goedgegun, it is an agricultural
center and has a population of some 1, 700, of which
about 1, 400 are Africans.   In the southwestern corner
of the country, it is about eight miles from the South
African border and the Swazi town of Mahamba.   It is
the administrative headquarters of the Shiselweni District and also the headquarters of the Swaziland Tobacco Co-operative.   A sawmill processes local timber.
It is also the site of the Evelyn Baring School, a board-
ing school which takes students through to matriculation.

NHLAPHO, MLAMBO.   A chief of the Nhlapho clan during
the nineteenth century.   When he died, there was a fight
over succession between his sons, Mhlangala and Bashele.   King Mswati II intervened with soldiers on the
side of Bashele, who was losing.   Mhlangala was killed
and Bashele installed as chief.

NKAMBULE, DANILE.   The indvuna at the tribal capital
called Lobamba during the reign of King Ndvungunye,
circa 1800.

NKAMBULE, NYEZI.   The senior indvuna of the royal village
called Zulwini, during the reign of King Sobhuza I
around 1825.

NKAMBULE, TIBATI.   Also known as Madvolomafisha.   One
  of the co-wives of Nandzi, the mother of King Mbandzeni, Tibati was elevated to the role of Ndlovukazi to
  replace Sisile Khumalo (q. v.) when King Mbandzeni
  found it necessary to have her sought out and killed.
  This was around 1877.

NKAMBULE CLAN.   One of the clans referred to as Emafi-
  kamuva (q. v.) or late-comers, the Nkambule people
  seem to be originally of Sotho origin.   Yet they have
  made a place for themselves in important Swazi ritual.
  When the original tinsila (singular insila, q. v.) of an
  Ngwenyama are allowed to marry, they are replaced by
  two more young men, one of whom must be from the
  Nkambule clan.   The Nkambule insila is called "the
  left-hand insila. "   Members of the clan were also in
  the important post of indvuna for early Swazi kings.

NKANINI (variant: ENKANINI).   The nation's capital (home
  of the Ndlovukazi) during the reign of King Mbandzeni.
  It was the home of the ill-fated Sisile Khumalo (q. v.).
  The present capital, Lobamba, stands on the same site
  formerly occupied by Nkanini.

NKOSI (variant: INKOSI).   Generally this term means
  "ruler, " but it often is used to mean more specifically
  King, or sometimes, Chief.   Its most frequent use is
  in reference to the King of Swaziland, the Ngwenyama,
  (q. v.), but it is also used for the Queen Mother, the
  Ndlovukazi (q. v.), who is considered a twin ruler.

NKOSI, CLIFFORD.   A law clerk for a firm of South African
  lawyers, he returned to Swaziland in the early 1960's
  and formed the Mbandzeni National Party in April, 1962.
  His platform seemed to encourage a traditional tribal
  form of government that would somehow use the one
  man-one vote principle.   Some writers suspect him of
  pro-South African leanings, perhaps with a Bantustan in
  mind.   Nevertheless, he merged his party several
  months later with that of Dr. George Msibi (q. v.) and
  thus he became Secretary-General of the Mbandzeni National Convention (MNC).   A year later, when Msibi resigned from the MNC, Nkosi became its President. The
  small party soon died, however, never contesting the
  1964 elections.

NKOSI II.   One of the earlier rulers of the Dlamini branch

of the Bembo-Nguni people, later known as Swazis. He
succeeded Dlamini II and preceded Mavuso I, according
to the most authoritative Swazi Royal Genealogical Table
available. This was probably sometime in the mid to
late seventeenth century.

NKOSI DLAMINI. The ruling clan of Swaziland, the Royal
House. The sibongo or clan name Dlamini (variant:
Dhlamini) is actually the name of the clan which rules
Swaziland. The prefix Nkosi (q. v.) is used as a royal
sibongo and is added as an acknowledgement that this
clan produces royalty. Nkosi is also used as a sibongo
by several other Swazi clans which are actually subdi-
visions of the Dlamini clan. For example, the Nkosi
Ginindza and the Nkosi Mamba, among others, were
created in order to allow the King to marry a woman
who otherwise would have been of his own clan, a
Dlamini.

NKUNDLA. Plural: Tinkundla. A rural district council established by the Ngwenyama to serve as a disseminator
of orders and instructions. Twenty-nine were established throughout the country when they were organized
in 1956. Each nkundla consists of the local chiefs under
an appointed chairman. They have provided an important connection between the government and the people,
especially in promoting rural development work. Where
the chiefs see these councils as a threat to their traditional authority, however, the effectiveness of the
nkundla has been lessened. In 1972 Prince Masitsela
Dlamini, Minister of Local Administration, announced
that the tinkundla would become meeting points for the
purpose of adult education.

NOBKUBULWANE. A female deity who seems to be able to
send sickness to human beings, according to Swazi tradition. She may be appeased by the offering of pots of
beer or sour porridge which are taken to a hillside for
her. She may then remove the sickness. There do
not appear to be any connections between Nobkubulwane
and other Swazi deities such as Mkhulumnqande or
Mlentengamunye (q. v.).

NOMAHASHA. A town on the Mozambique side of the border,
across from Lomahasha, Swaziland (q. v.).

NORTH LANCASHIRE LOYAL REGIMENT. The First Bat-

talion of this British regiment arrived in Swaziland in
July, 1963, replacing the Gordon Highlanders who had
come to quell disturbances two months earlier.   They
saw no real action; however, they were very helpful in
cordoning off several sections of the country which had
been severely affected by an outbreak of hoof and mouth
disease in 1964 and 1965.   The last of this regiment
left in July, 1965, being replaced by the Gloucestershire
Regiment.

NQUKU, JOHN JUNE.   Important educator, journalist, and
political leader in Swaziland.   Born of Zulu parents in
Pietermaritzburg, South Africa, in 1899, he was trained
as a teacher and served as a school principal in South
Africa from 1920 to 1929.   In January, 1930 he was
the first African to be appointed Inspector of Schools in
Swaziland.   He also became active in the Swaziland
Progressive Association (q. v.), of which he became
President in 1945.   In 1934 he became founder and editor of Izwi Lama Swazi, a vernacular newspaper, which
was eventually taken over by the Bantu Press.   In 1955
he founded and edited The Swazilander.   In 1940 he resigned as Inspector and, supported by King Sobhuza,
became a member of the Swazi National Council, with
duties in the areas of both education and religion.   In
1944 he became secretary-general of a merged religious
group called the United Christian Church of Africa.   His
religious activities continued into the 1970's as he has
been active with the Swaziland Council of Churches.   In
1960 he transformed the Swaziland Progressive Association into the Swaziland Progressive Party (q. v.), re-
maining as President.   It urged a one man-one vote
democracy.   The SPP quickly became active in the
stimulating Pan-African climate of the early 1960's.   He
traveled frequently to Ghana and around the world.   But
his leadership in Swaziland, described variously as
"firm" and "dictatorial, " led to numerous splinter factions (see DR. AMBROSE ZWANE and OBED MABUZA),
especially in 1961 and 1962.   Nquku had been invited to
be on the constitutional committee of 1960-61, but was
expelled from it on May 18, 1961, for having expressed
a dissent to the committee's majority of traditionalists
and Europeans.   He continued to fight for a democratic
constitution despite his greatly diminished following after
the 1961 and 1962 SPP splits.   The British invited
Nquku (over Dr. Zwane and Mabuza) to the 1963 London
constitutional conference.   Nquku and his diminished

SPP put up candidates in the 1964, 1967, and 1972
elections, but received minimal support from the voters.
In February, 1972 he retired as the SPP President.

NSIBANDE, MASENJANA.   The indvuna at Zombodze, the
tribal capital under King Ngwane III during the latter
half of the eighteenth century.

NSOKO.   A town in southeastern Swaziland, about three miles
west of the South African border at Ingwavumapoort. It
is on the main road south from Big Bend to Lavumisa.
It is in the area of an irrigation scheme which supports
a sugar crop.

NTUNGWA-NGUNI CLANS.   The use of this term is not clear
in the several Swazi histories where it is found, indicating only that Swazis encountered these people in Swaziland in early times.   One ethnologist makes the term
Ntungwa synonymous with Nguni, in the context of "true
Nguni" rather than conquered clans which have been absorbed.   The awkwardness is that Swazis are themselves Nguni people, and thus presumbaly also Ntungwa.

NUKWASE, QUEEN MOTHER.   An aunt of the present King,
Sobhuza II, she replaced her deceased sister Lomawa
as Queen Mother in 1938.   She served in this capacity
as Ndlovukazi until her death in 1956 (another scholar
reports 1958).   Nukwase was still a child when King
Bhunu, husband of her full sister, Lomawa Nxumalo,
died.   Nevertheless, she was made a co-wife of Lomawa
and she bore two sons and two daughters by Bhunu's
brother Malunge (q. v.) in the name of Bhunu.

NXUMALO, ALBERT WINSTON MTHWALO MGCOBEYA.   A
long-time associate of J. J. Nquku in the latter's
branch of the Swaziland Progressive Party.   For about
ten years since the 1962-63 splits within the SPP, he
has been its Secretary-General, a strong and vocal right
arm for Nquku.   He is occasionally identified as Mgcobeya Nxumalo, but more often as A. W. M. Nxumalo,
not to be confused with Austin W. (A. W.) Nxumalo of
the Swaziland United Front.   He was an unsuccessful
candidate for the House of Assembly in 1964, 1967 and
1972.

NXUMALO, DR. ALLEN MKHAWULO.   Major political and
governmental leader in the 1960's, he is the son of Ben-

jamin Nxumalo (q. v.), who was an uncle and close advisor to King Sobhuza II.   He went from his education
at the Swazi National School on to Fort Hare College
and then to Johannesburg where he received his medical
degree in 1957.   During that period he spent several
years working in Johannesburg and was also very active
in the African National Congress Youth League.   He also
taught for several years before earning his M. D. degree.
He returned to Swaziland where he entered the medical
branch of the civil service.   In 1960 he and others organized the Mbandzeni National Convention, the leadership of which he soon turned over to Dr. G. Msibi
(q. v.).   In March, 1962, Simon Nxumalo and others
formed the Swaziland Democratic Party, a moderate,
multi-racial group designed to compete with the more
radical SPP.   Simon Nxumalo was President of the SDP
until December 4, 1963, when he stepped down in favor
of the Vice-President, Dr. Nxumalo, who had joined in
February, 1963.   The doctor's office served as a good
base for a leader to stay in touch with his party.   Dr.
Nxumalo stressed that Swaziland needed a constitutional
monarchy, with a non-partisan King, and completely
separate from either extreme, Communism or Apartheid.
A member of the 1963 Constitutional Commission, he
split from the side of the traditionalists at the London
Conference because of their support of a 50-50 legislature with the Europeans.   When the Imbokodvo Party
split from the Europeans in 1965, however (after Dr.
Nxumalo and his party lost badly in the 1964 elections),
Nxumalo merged his party with Imbokodvo in April,
1965.   In 1967 he received almost 9, 000 votes in being
elected to the House of Assembly as an Imbokodvo
member.   He was then appointed Minister for Health
and Education.   In 1972 he did not run for office but
was appointed to the Senate by the Ngwenyama.   He
then became Minister of Works, Power, and Communications.

NXUMALO, AUSTIN W.   Close associate of Obed Mabuza
    (q. v.) in the latter's branch of the Swaziland Progres-
    sive Party since the split from J. J. Nquku in 1963.
    When Mabuza was instrumental in organizing the Swazi-
    land United Front in 1964, Nxumalo became its organiz-
    ing Secretary and later its Secretary-General, a position
    he has maintained.   He should not be confused with Al-
    bert W. M. (A. W. M.) Nxumalo.   In 1962 he was
    elected the first chairman of the Swaziland Pulp and

Timber Workers Union, the first of its kind to be registered in Swaziland.

NXUMALO, BENJAMIN. An uncle of King Sobhuza II and an
important counselor to him, as well as Secretary to the
Swazi nation, during the young King's early reign especially. He accompanied Sobhuza on the 1922-1923
trip to London concerning the land question. He was a
founder of the Swaziland Progressive Association in 1929
and its President until he died in 1942. In that year he
also attended a conference in the United States representing his Church, the African Methodist Episcopal
Church. Two of his sisters, Lomawa and Nukwase,
were successively Swazi Queen Mothers, and his son,
Dr. Allen Nxumalo (q. v.), became both a medical doctor
and one of the more prominent political and governmental figures of modern Swazi history.

NXUMALO, LOMAWA see LOMAWA, QUEEN MOTHER

NXUMALO, SIMON SISHAYI. Also, Sishayi Simon Ndwandwe.
An important political and governmental leader in Swaziland in the 1960's and 1970's. Born in 1936 at Nkam-
beni in Swaziland's Lowveld, he was one of many children of an important chief. Educated near his home, he
eventually earned his Junior Certificate and taught primary school from 1954 to 1958. After a brief stay in
Johannesburg, he returned to business activity in Swaziland in 1960. In 1961 he helped to found the Sebenta
National Institute (q. v.), an adult literacy organization,
which he helped run for many years. He worked with
Vincent Rozwadowski (q. v.) and others to form the Swaziland Democratic Party (q. v.), officially announcing it
on March 2, 1962. He was its President until December 4, 1963, when he stepped down to Secretary-General
in order to work on branch organization throughout the
country. Dr. Allen Nxumalo (q. v.) became President.
During 1963 Simon Nxumalo represented the SDP at the
London Constitutional Conference where he, with the
assistance of other members of the Alliance of Political
Organizations which he founded and led there, helped
create a constitutional dead-lock. He was only twenty-
seven at the time. He urged that two-thirds of the
Legislative Council should be elected by universal adult
suffrage, one man-one vote. On October 4, 1964, he
resigned from the SDP and joined with the supporters
of the Imbokodvo Party (after having been defeated

decisively in the 1964 elections). He was soon named
head of the Swazi National Voluntary Service and
traveled around Africa as the representative of King
Sobhuza. He laid the groundwork for Pan-African ac-
ceptance of Imbokodvo. He has since traveled the world
often in his governmental positions. Easily elected to
the House of Assembly in both 1967 and 1972, he was
appointed Assistant Minister of Finance, Commerce and
Industry in 1967. He later became Minister of Commerce, Industry and Mines, and is currently Minister
of Industry, Mines and Tourism. He is the author of
several books (see the Bibliography).

NYETANE RIVER. Beginning in the Lubombo Mountains just
west of Siteki, it flows south to become a tributary of
the Great Usutu River four miles east of Big Bend.

-O-

OLIFANTS RIVER. A Transvaal River about 150 miles north
and west of Swaziland. It is claimed that the Swazi King
Mswatı granted all land between the Crocodile and Olifants Rivers to the Lydenburg Republic of the Boers in
1846. This land was never regained. (See SOMCUBA.)

ORDER-IN-COUNCIL, JUNE 25, 1903. A British Order-in-
Council which was the formal basis for the British
claim to rule Swaziland from 1903 until 1968. Claiming that their defeat of Swaziland's former "rulers, "
the South African Republic, in the Boer War gave them
the right to rule, the British gave the Governor of the
Transvaal the power to exercise all governing powers.
It provided limited recognition of traditional laws and
Swazi Chiefs. Most judicial powers were also assumed
by Great Britain, except in some civil cases. The
legislative power of the libandhla was also preempted.

ORDER-IN-COUNCIL, DECEMBER, 1906. A British Order-
in-Council simultaneous to the granting of self-government to the Transvaal. It removed Swaziland from the
jurisdiction of the Governor of the Transvaal and placed
it under the British High Commissioner for South Africa.
It was a necessary administrative formality that allowed
Great Britain to retain control over the country.

ORGANIZATION OF AFRICA UNITY (OAU). Founded in May,

1963, this organization consists of all independent African states except the Republic of South Africa and nominally-independent Rhodesia. Swaziland joined shortly after its 1968 day of independence. Prior to that, both the dominant party, Imbokodvo, and the various opposition parties in Swaziland competed for both assistance and recognition from the OAU and its leading member states. While originally supporting the opposition parties, with whom they were more compatible ideologically, many leaders, especially Ghana's Nkrumah, were impressed by the big electoral success of Imbokodvo.

OSHOEK. A small but important Swazi border town, as it is on one of the main roads between Johannesburg and Mbabane. Its location near the iron mines on Bomvu Ridge and the terminus of the Swaziland Railway at Kadake, both a few miles away, add to its significance.

OXFAM. The Oxford Committee for Famine Relief, an English philanthropic organization that has spent large amounts of money around the world to aid the needy. It has engaged in several major projects in Swaziland.

-P-

PAN-AFRICANIST CONGRESS (PAC). A political organization of Africans founded in the Republic of South Africa in March, 1959. Its membership, led by President Robert Sobukwe, and National Secretary Potlako Leballo, had split away from the African National Congress. It especially opposed ANC alliances with political movements of other racial groups, but also emphasized a goal of creating a socialistic democracy. On April 8, 1960, both the PAC and ANC were declared "unlawful organizations." Many of its leaders and members were arrested, but some made their way out of South Africa, often using Swaziland as either a home or an escape route.

PARALLEL RULE. Also referred to as "Dual Rule." A system by which a colonial power allows the continuance of traditional rule by native leaders in the majority of governmental affairs, while nevertheless maintaining its separate authority pattern over the people through its own administrators. Despite complaints by the Swazis that their King had been reduced to the status of a Par-

amount Chief, Great Britain seemed to pursue by de-
fault a system of Parallel Rule until Acts of 1950 altered this, producing a more classic pattern of Indirect
Rule (q. v.). Because of Parallel Rule, however, the
Swazi King maintained power and status that leaders in
other parts of Africa had lost.

PARAMOUNT CHIEF. A term used often by colonial officials
to indicate the highest chief in a given tribal group, despite other terms used by the Africans which would have
indicated the term "King" might have been more appropriate. Since a King is normally independent; a Paramount Chief, it was assumed, lacked full freedom of
action because recognition of his status came through
the colonial officials. In the case of Swaziland, a British Order-in-Council of June 25, 1903, interposed British rights of rule and lowered the Ngwenyama to the
status of Paramount Chief.

PARLIAMENT. Under the 1967 and Independence Constitutions, it was the law-making arm of Government, consisting of the Senate (q. v.) and the House of Assembly
(q. v.), each with equal status except in relation to
financial matters. Bills passed through both Houses
and assented to by the King became law. Parliament
did not have the power to pass laws dealing with Swazi
law and custom except by permission of the Swazi National Council (q. v.). Each Parliament was to last
normally for about five years. In April, 1973 Parliament was dissolved by the King.

PEAK TIMBERS LTD. Pioneers in pine afforestation, this
wholly owned subsidiary of the Anglo-American Corporation began planting in northwestern Swaziland near
Pigg's Peak in the late 1940's. Owning over 75, 000
acres in the area, it has successfully produced large
quantities of timber each year. At the end of 1962,
Peak Timbers was hit by the short strikes by trade
union activists that had also hit Usutu Pulp Company
earlier in the year.

PEDI see BAPEDI

PHUZUMOYA. A Swazi community in the Central Lowveld
on the Mzimpofu River two miles north of its junction
with the Great Usutu River. Its principal significance
is its location along the Swaziland Railway and the fact

that it is the only loading stop for the products of southeastern Swaziland. At Phuzumoya the train heads due
north. Cattle, citrus, and sugar are among the main
products of the area.

PIET RETIEF. A South African town of about 10, 000 people
in the eastern Transvaal, about eleven miles west of the
Swaziland border. Located along a railroad line, it
connects with Hlatikulu through the South African Railways and Harbours bus service, thus giving Swazis access to work in the farming regions of the Transvaal
and the mines at Johannesburg. Founded about 1884
and named after the Voortrekker leader, it is in a farming area that was considered part of Swaziland at one
time when it claimed independence as "The Little Free
State" (q. v.). Many Swazis both live and work in the
area.

PIGG, WILLIAM. An early prospector in Swaziland who discovered gold on March 26, 1884, near the town now
called Pigg's Peak. This led to the founding of the
Pigg's Peak Mine, the richest source of gold in the history of Swaziland mining.

PIGG'S PEAK. A town of about 2, 000 people, mostly of
Swazi origin in the northwestern part of Swaziland. It is
located about ten miles by road east of the South African
border and the Swazi town of Havelock. It is in the
middle of a very scenic area, with rivers and waterfalls especially attractive. Ten miles away are located
excellent examples of Bushman rock paintings at Nsangwini Shelter.
     Until the administrative changes of December, 1963,
Pigg's Peak was also the name of the northern-most of
the six administrative districts of Swaziland. It en-
compassed everything in Swaziland north of the Komati
River. This area has, since 1963, been added to the
old Mbabane District to become the Hhohho District.

PIGG'S PEAK MINE. Located at Pigg's Peak in the northwestern part of Swaziland, the mine, named after William Pigg who discovered the reef in 1884, became a
major producer of wealth and employment. The Mine
employed four hundred people at one time and was developed down to eight hundred feet below the summit of
Pigg's Peak. Production was stopped during the First
World War and only started periodically after that. It

was reopened between 1941 and 1951.

PIKE, SIR PHILIP ERNEST.   Chief Justice of Swaziland and
   presiding officer of the High Court from 1970 until his
   retirement in December, 1972.

PIM REPORT.   Sir Alan Pim was sent to Swaziland in 1931
   (and in subsequent years to Bechuanaland and Basutoland) to investigate its financial and economic position.
   His report, published in 1932, bitterly criticized the
   Administration's neglect of education and social services
   as well as lack of concern for the development of mining, agriculture, and animal husbandry.   Pim's report
   produced some immediate change of policy, especially
   regarding grants-in-aid, but these were of minimal size
   and significance until the 1940's when the Colonial Development and Welfare fund began to take increasing interest in Swaziland.

PIUS XII COLLEGE   see   UNIVERSITY OF BOTSWANA,
   LESOTHO, and SWAZILAND

THE PLACE OF BURNING.   The much-used translation of
   "Shiselweni" (q. v.), the name given to the place which
   the Swazis consider to be the birthplace of their nation.

POLICE.   Formed first in 1907, the Swaziland Police Force
   has a strength of about seven hundred.   It has headquarters at Mbabane, and there are district headquarters
   at Manzini, Siteki, Nhlangano and Mbabane.   There are
   other police stations and police posts around the country.
   A radio network links the various locations.

PONGOLA.   A South African town about six miles south of
   the Swaziland border on the north side of the Pongola
   River.   The Swazis feel that this area belongs to them
   and was unjustly given to South Africa in boundary
   agreements arranged by the British.   Many Swazis live
   and work in the area.

PONGOLA RIVER.   Starting in the Drakensberg Mountains
   south and west of Piet Retief, South Africa, it almost
   parallels the southern border of Swaziland as the river
   forms the boundary between the Transvaal and Natal
   provinces.   After passing through the Lubombo Mountains, it flows north where it joins the Usutu River to
   form the Maputo River, then emptying into Delagoa Bay.

The Swazis feel that the Pongola was the natural southern boundary of Swaziland, and that they were cheated
out of this land by the British in 1895.

PRETORIA CONVENTION OF 1881   see   CONVENTION OF
1881

PRETORIUS, MARTHINUS WESSEL.   First President of the
South African Republic in 1857.   Serving several terms
as President, he added to the Territory of the Republic
through consolidation of other areas, such as Lydenberg
(q. v.).   In the 1860's he sold over a million acres of
land just west of Swaziland (and claimed by the Swazis)
to Alexander McCorkindale (q. v.) and his Scottish settlers in order to provide a buffer between his people
and the Swazis and Zulus.

PRIME MINISTER.   Except for the King himself, the princi-
pal administrative and policy-making official of the
country under the 1967 and Independence Constitutions.
He is appointed by the King as the individual command-
ing the support of the majority of the members of the
House of Assembly.   He is assisted by a Deputy Prime
Minister and a Cabinet.   The first Prime Minister of
Swaziland is Prince Makhosini Dlamini.

PROTECTED STATE AGREEMENT.   An agreement between
King Sobhuza II and the British Government signed on
April 24, 1967, at Lobamba.   It established Swaziland
as an officially protected state, and the new self-government constitution went into effect.   That constitution
provided that the kingdom of Swaziland would become independent by December 31, 1969, at the latest.

PROTECTORATE.   A political and administrative term with
very inadequate specific meaning, it is sometimes applied to Swaziland, and is specifically used in the term
"Bechuanaland Protectorate. "   While it seems to apply
formally when a group of people actually petition a
power for protection (not the case in Swaziland in 1903),
there seems to be a de facto condition under which it is
also deemed applicable by some.   It is this assumption
of the power of protector by Great Britain that is used
to justify the term's application to Swaziland and other
territories.   In the case of Swaziland, the Ngwenyama
would have been happy in 1906 to accept the status of
"Protected State" if it meant complete internal autonomy

for Swaziland. The British High Commissioner was not willing to accept this, however, as he was concerned that the Swazis would cancel the land and mineral concessions to Europeans. (See CONCESSIONS PARTITIONS PROCLAMATION OF 1907.)

PROTOCOL OF 1898. Considered an amendment to the Third Swaziland Convention (q. v.), this was an agreement between Great Britain and the South African Republic in Pretoria on October 5, 1898. Motivated by the trial of King Bhunu (q. v.), it took all matters concerning serious crime (felonies, in effect) away from the jurisdiction of Swazi courts, even if the crimes only involved Swazis. This reduced the Swazi King to a position as Paramount Chief, as he would now be subject to the Europeans' laws and courts.

THE PROVISIONAL GOVERNMENT. Also referred to as The Triumvirate Government, it became the official Government of Swaziland as a result of the report of the Joint Commission (q. v.) and the First Swaziland Convention (q. v.) of 1890. Theophilus Shepstone, Jr. represented the Swazi nation and was Chairman. Col. R. E. R. Martin represented Great Britain, and D. J. Esselen represented the South African Republic. It made its headquarters at Albert Bremer's Hotel which it bought with the condition that the town to be built should be called Bremersdorp. A civil administration was built up and judges, justices of the peace, and police were appointed. Taxes were levied on all Europeans in the country, and deficits were to be shared by the British and Transvaal Governments. The courts approved most of the concessions granted by the Swazi Kings. Nevertheless, the Transvaal Boers were not satisfied and drew up a Second Swaziland Convention, 1893, and a Third Swaziland Convention, 1894. These, despite Swazi protests, had the approval of Great Britain and went into effect in February, 1895, when the Provisional Government was replaced by a commissioner, Johannes Krogh, representing the Government of the South African Republic.

THE PUBLIC SERVICE COMMISSION. Until June, 1973 a commission of from three to five members which, subject to certain limitations, had the power of appointment, dismissal, and disciplinary control of those persons who are to hold or act in any offices in the public service. Excluded from this were certain lower members of the Police Force and Prisons Service. Also the Prime Minister could appoint some officials (including permanent secretaries and diplomatic representatives) after consulting with the Public Service Commission. This Commission consisted of a chairman and from two to four other members who were all appointed by the King on the advice of the Judicial Service Commission, which had to consult with the Prime Minister. An active politician was disqualified from membership. In June, 1973, it was announced that a King's Order-in-Council replaced this board with a new Civil Service Board, the powers of which were "modified and qualified."

-Q-

QUEEN MOTHER see NDLOVUKAZI

-R-

RALEIGH FITKIN MEMORIAL HOSPITAL. The largest hospital in the country with over 250 beds, it is located at Manzini and run by the Nazarene Church mission. Its doctors make regular visits to the Mbuluzi Leper Settlement as well as to seventeen clinics in the northern half of Swaziland which are staffed by nurses trained at the hospital.

RAMSDEN, WILLIAM ARTHUR. Attorney-General of Swaziland (and thereby a non-voting member of the House of Assembly) from April, 1967 until he retired in December, 1971. Born August 6, 1926 in England, he came to South Africa in 1935. He was educated at the University of Witwatersrand, and has a B.A., LL.B. and Q.C. He was Registrar of the Court of Appeal for the three High Commission Territories and Registrar of the High Court of Basutoland and Judicial Commissioner for Basutoland from 1955 to 1961. He was Crown Counsel for Swaziland from 1963 to 1967 before becoming Attorney-General.

RAND. The major unit of currency in the common currency area shared until 1974 by South Africa, Lesotho, Botswana, and Swaziland. It is subdivided into one hundred cents. Exchange rates vary, but traditionally the Rand was equal to about half a pound sterling and about $1.40 American currency. Swaziland converted to this decimal currency on February 14, 1961. In March, 1974, the Swazi Government announced that it would replace the Rand with new currency, the Emalangeni (q. v.).

RECONSTITUTED EUROPEAN ADVISORY COUNCIL (REAC). A body of Europeans created by a Government Proclamation in 1949, replacing the previous European Advisory Council (q. v.). Its membership consisted of ten elected members chosen by Europeans throughout Swaziland, plus seven non-voting Government officials. Its purpose was to advise the Resident Commissioner concerning matters affecting European residents, and any matter referred to it by the Resident Commissioner. It met at least twice a year, and was partly guided by a Standing Committee. The body was always conservative by nature, and especially represented the pro-South African sympathies and connections of most Europeans in Swaziland. Led by Mr. Carl Todd, chairman of the elected members, it became a very vocal group and attacked the colonial administration on a wide range of subjects. It was especially vehement in resisting British attempts to institute a one man-one vote constitutional arrangement. It was the REAC that took first steps toward a Legislative Council by proposing in January, 1960 to the British Secretary of State that a multi-racial council be organized. Half should be elected by the Europeans, and half by the equally conservative Swazi National Council. This would effectively shut out new political parties. Members of the REAC continued to participate in the constitutional discussions (until the Legislative Council replaced it in 1964), usually in alliance with King Sobhuza and Swazi traditionalists and against the British position and the new political parties. REAC members eventually formed the United Swaziland Association, successfully winning significant representation in the Legislative Council but less than its desired 50 per cent.

THE REED DANCE see UMHLANGA

REFUGEES. Particularly a problem in the early 1960's after the Sharpeville incident in South Africa, when numerous political figures fled to Swaziland. (See AFRICAN NATIONAL CONGRESS and PAN-AFRICANIST CONGRESS.) Among the most prominent were Jordan Ngubane and

Dennis Brutus. The former became active in the Swaziland Democratic Party, perhaps one reason why the
SDP was one of the few political groups in Swaziland to
proffer aid to refugees despite South African objections.
A few other groups, some church-related, tried to help
refugees, some of whom were refugees from Mozambique. A Swaziland Refugee Committee, under Mr.
Seperepere tried to organize support from other politi-
cians, but both Dr. Allan Nxumalo and Dr. Ambrose
Zwane backed away. Subsequent government action
forced most of the refugees to leave the country, often
into probable capture. Almost the only "refugees" still in
Swaziland are a number of South African Liberals, such
as former Swaziland Minister of Finance, Leopold
Lovell, who have found the Swazi political climate more
to their liking.

REILLY, TERENCE E. A farmer at Mlilwane and the son
    of a former tin-miner, he developed in the 1960's a
    game sanctuary there. The King has also placed the
    Ehlane Game Reserve in the Lowveld under Reilly's
    care as Chief Warden.

"REINDEER REFERENDUM". A referendum held by the
    Swazi National Council on January 19, 1964. The vote
    was planned to show the British that Swazis supported
    the Ngwenyama's position on constitutional arrangements
    (basically a 50-50 sharing of power between Swazi tra-
    ditionalists and Europeans) instead of the imposed Brit-
    ish constitution calling for regular electoral politics.
    Held despite British refusals to sanction it or aid in it,
    the election resulted in overwhelming support of the
    Ngwenyama. There were only 162 votes against the
    King out of a total of 124,380 cast. Some attribute this
    margin to the fact that the largely illiterate voters were
    given the choice of voting for a lion (traditionally a
    symbol of the Swazi King) or a reindeer, a strange-
    looking animal totally alien to the Swazis. Support for
    the King from Carl Todd and the European Advisory
    Council resulted in only eight European votes against
    King Sobhuza's position. It is probable that the King's
    success in this referendum convinced Sobhuza and the
    Swazi National Council to form a traditionalist party
    (the Imbokodvo) to compete in the 1964 elections.

REPUBLIC OF SOUTH AFRICA. The dominant country in the
    southern portion of Africa, coming into existence origi-

nally as the Union of South Africa (q. v.) on May 31,
1910.   A referendum of October 5, 1960 was favorable
to its conversion from a monarchy (under the Queen of
England) within the British Commonwealth to a Republic
outside the British Commonwealth on May 31, 1961.
Since its inception in 1910, it has inevitably had a
major influence on Swaziland, in part because it is adjacent to more than eighty percent of Swaziland's borders.   Among its relations with Swaziland of particular
significance are: South Africa provides many Swazis
with a major source of income through work on its
farms and in its mines; the issue of Incorporation into
South Africa (q. v.); the South African Customs Union
(q. v.); South African businessmen have found Swaziland
a lucrative field for investment (among the most prominent has been the Anglo-American Corporation of South
Africa); and Swaziland has been a convenient country
for some South Africans to use for at least temporary
political refuge.   In addition, some notable South Africans have taken up residence in Swaziland.   Finally,
King Sobhuza has had numerous dealings with South
African lawyers and economists who have assisted him
and his government.

RESIDENT COMMISSIONER.   The title given to the principal
British administrative official in Swaziland.   The title
was changed from Special Commissioner by Sir Alfred
Milner in a 1904 proclamation, but it was not implemented until Lord Selborne issued a proclamation on
February 22, 1907, providing for the appointment of the
first Resident Commissioner.   This was F. Enraght-
Moony, who had been Special Commissioner.   Although
the Head of Government in Swaziland, the Resident Commissioner was subject to instructions from the British
High Commissioner stationed in South Africa.   The post
of Resident Commissioner was abolished when the 1963
Constitution took effect on January 7, 1964, replacing
it with a new position, Her Majesty's Commissioner for
Swaziland.

RIPON, LORD.   British colonial secretary, 1892-1895.   In
1892 he chose not to advocate annexation of Swaziland,
which would have led to a confrontation with the South
African Republic.   But he also refused to accept incorporation of Swaziland into the Republic.   The Third Swaziland Convention (1894) which he agreed to, transferred administration of Swaziland to the Republic, but

with certain guarantees for the Swazis. This was after
he rejected the request of a deputation of Swazis in
November, 1894, who wanted Queen Victoria to establish Swaziland as a British Protectorate.

RITUAL MURDER. A practice found in various parts of
southern Africa (and indeed around the world) by which
people are killed and parts of their bodies used for
ritual purposes. While not part of Swazi tradition,
some instances of it have been uncovered in Swaziland
and the participants found guilty and executed. Some
writers have made it seem more common than it actually is. It seems to take two specific forms: rituals
for the purpose of fertilizing the crops and increasing
the yield, and rituals for making medicines to increase
the power and influence of an individual. The problem
has resurfaced in recent years and has been both vig-
orously prosecuted and denounced by everyone from
King Sobhuza down through the line of authorities. The
King called a special meeting of the Swazi nation on
June 20, 1974 to denounce the increase in Ritual Murders.

ROBINSON, SIR HERCULES. British-born colonial official
who served as Governor of the Cape Colony from 1880
to 1889, and again from 1895 to 1897. He served si-
multaneously as High Commissioner for South Africa.
In this capacity he was reluctant to commit Great Britain to positive action of aid for the Swazis, especially
refusing King Mbandzeni twice when he sought aid. In
1888, however, he did recommend to the British Secretary of State that he appoint a joint commission (with
the South African Republic) to look into the affairs of
Swaziland, which was having trouble with the Boers.

ROCK PAINTINGS. At least twenty examples of primitive
rock paintings are known to exist in Swaziland, over a
half of them within a fifteen-mile radius of Mbabane.
They are very similar to Bushman art found in other
parts of Africa, and thus most are attributed to the
Bushmen (q. v.). They depict battle scenes, hunting
parties and dances in addition to animals. The best
preserved are in the Komati valley near the Nsangwini
royal residence, but others are at Malutha, Ekuthandeni,
Nkaba, Ntungula, near Gege, near Lobamba, and along
the banks of the Mpetsane. One not necessarily of
Bushman origin is high on the Lubombo escarpment

overlooking the Ehlane game reserve.

ROMA. A town in west-central Lesotho which is the site of
the main campus of the University of Botswana,
Lesotho and Swaziland.

ROMAN CATHOLIC CHURCH. One of the larger Christian
denominations in Swaziland. A 1962 survey showed
8, 500 Catholics, of whom 7, 600 were African, 600 European and 300 Eurafrican. It sponsors educational institutions and hospitals in different parts of the country.
Roman Catholic missionaries first arrived in 1914.

ROMAN-DUTCH LAW. The common law of Swaziland and of
the Republic of South Africa. It is based on the 17th
century law of the Netherlands, which is built on a
foundation of Roman Law (particularly Justinian's Corpus
Juris). It was modified by men such as Hugo Grotius.
Its principles of land ownership provide for absolute
ownership of land, as contrasted to the English theory
that all land is held by the Crown.

ROYAL CONSTITUTIONAL COMMISSION, 1973-1974. First
planned in May, 1973 but finally appointed by the
Ngwenyama, Sobhuza II, in September, 1973, the Commission was required to hear opinions throughout Swaziland concerning the fundamental principles on which a
new Constitution should be based. Both the further instructions from King Sobhuza and the membership of the
Commission insured that the ultimate recommendations
would place increased emphasis on traditional Swazi
political elites and structures, while maintaining some
"modern" principles of constitutional law. The Commission also visited other African states, notably Zam-
bia, Tanzania, Kenya, and Malawi, in order to examine
their constitutional arrangements. The membership of
the Commission was: Senator Polycarp Dlamini, Senator George Msibi, Prince Sifuba Dlamini, Councillor
Ndleleni Gwebu, Councillor Makobha Gumedze, Mr. J.
F. Troughton, and Mr. R. P. Stephens, Mr. David
Cohen, the Attorney General, was named Professional
Advisor, and Mr. Arthur Khoza became the Commission's Secretary.

ROYAL IRISH FUSILIERS. The last of the British troops to
be stationed in Swaziland on rotation after the June,
1963, labor unrest. They arrived in April, 1966, and

were transferred the same November.

ROYAL PIONEER CORPS.   A British unit in World War II
consisting of warriors from the African colonies.   Four
thousand Swazis enlisted and served in it throughout
North Africa, Sicily, Italy, and the Middle East, especially distinguishing themselves at the famous landings
at Salerno and Anzio.

ROZWADOWSKI, VICEK (VINCENT) J.   A founder and an
active member of the executive council of the Swaziland
Democratic Party (SDP), he was chosen Second Vice-
President in December, 1963.   However, he was expelled from the party at a party congress in October,
1964.   He emigrated from Poland as a young man in
1939, serving in the French underground until 1945,
earning the Croix de Guerre and the title of Major.
Losing his family land (his family was of minor nobility)
to the Communists, he became a rancher in South
Africa.   Upset by the growth of Apartheid, he and his
South African wife came to Swaziland and became dairy
farmers near Mbabane.   He soon became President of
the Sebenta Society (now the Sebenta National Institute,
q. v.), which concentrates on adult literacy.   He later
joined with Sebenta associates Simon Nxumalo and Jordan
Ngubane in forming the Swaziland Democratic Party on
March 2, 1962, creating a moderate, multi-racial party.
His moderate position did not win him friends in Swaziland's European community, and he was defeated in the
1964 Legislative Council elections by almost four to one
in campaigning for a "reserved White" seat.   He has
been strongly anti-Communist, and perhaps his financial
support of the SDP was motivated by fear of reported
Communist support of the Swaziland Progressive Party
(SPP).   His later expulsion from the SDP was for having acted independently of the party leadership on several important issues.

RURAL LAND DEVELOPMENT BOARD.   The conservation
authority of the Swazi National Council, this Board is
appointed by the Ngwenyama.   Its duty is to approve
land use schemes and resettlement schemes, and has
wide control over land use on Swazi national land.   It
has been successful in conserving both land and water.

RYAN, S. T.   Discoverer of tin in the Mbabane River just
south of the city of Mbabane in 1892.   (See TIN.)

-S-

SAMBANE (also: SAMBANE NYAWO; variant: ZAMBAAN).
The chief during the late nineteenth century of the
Nyawo clan occupying the territory just east of the Lubombo Mountains and north and west of the Pongola
River.   Sambane and his people paid allegiance to the
Swazi kings and the territory was considered part of
Swaziland.   Despite testimony and evidence indicating it
was Swazi territory, the British declared Sambane's
territory to be part of Zululand and thus under Natal
administration.   This occurred in 1895 when Britain was
handing over the administration of the rest of Swaziland
to the Transvaal Government.

SAMKETI, KINGSWAY THULASIZA.   A major Swazi political
activist for over a decade in the 1960's and 1970's.
Active in the Swaziland Progressive Party in the early
1960's, he was a supporter of its leader, J. J. Nquku,
until August, 1962, when he combined with O. M. Mabuza and B. M. Simelane to oust Nquku.   As the SPP
splintered in several directions, Samketi was President
of one fragment for several months.   He eventually
joined with Dr. Ambrose Zwane in the NNLC and became its Vice-President.   He worked closely with Zwane
for many years, gaining publicity when the two tried to
block the beginning of the 1967 constitutional conference
in London with a "lay-in" across the steps of Marlbor-
rough House.   While he was unsuccessful running for
the House of Assembly in 1967, he came closer than
any other opposition candidate to winning a seat.   His
3,553 votes were only 143 votes too few.   In August,
1971, Samketi led a move to oust Zwane from party
leadership and created a faction called the Qhuzasha
Movement or the NNLC (Samketi).   Under the latter
title it competed in the 1972 elections, but all its candidates were overwhelmingly defeated, while Zwane's
faction won three seats.   Samketi is now a farmer in
Vuvulane.

SANDLANE.   A Swazi town located at the South African border in west-central Swaziland, about two miles south of
where the Great Usutu River enters the country.

SANDYS, DUNCAN.   British Secretary of State for Commonwealth Relations and Colonial Affairs from 1960 to late
1964, a period of great importance for the constitution

of Swaziland. When the London Conference in February, 1963 ended in a stalemate between Swazi traditional forces and political parties, Sandys decided to impose his own "solution. " In May he dictated what has since been called "Sandys' Constitution, " and it became the basis for the 1964 Government and Legislative Council. It provided for a compromise arrangement whereby the traditionalists and parties might share membership in the Legislative Council, along with some White seats.   This was not the result, however, as the traditionalists and Whites won all the seats.   Sandys' compromise was not popular with any of the contending forces.

SCANDINAVIAN PROTESTANTS.   There are three churches sponsored by this religious denomination in Swaziland. Of its 6, 800 members in 1962, all but two hundred were Africans.   Missionary representatives of the Scandinavian Alliance first arrived in 1893.

SCHREINER, OLIVER DENIS.   Judge of the Swaziland Court of Appeal for twelve years and President of it for three years until he retired in November, 1973.

SCUTT, JOAN.   A missionary teacher at Nqabaneni Mission School and Secretary of the Swaziland Conference of Churches.   She has written several books on Swaziland, especially a history of the country for use in primary schools.

SEBENTA NATIONAL INSTITUTE.   Founded as the Sebenta Society about 1960 by Simon Nxumalo, Nell Green, and Vincent Rozwadowski, it is an adult education program aimed at developing literacy among the Swazis.   Its success has been recognized in recent years by support from official sources both in Swaziland and around the world.

SECOND SWAZILAND CONVENTION.   An agreement between Great Britain and the South African Republic, dated November 13, 1893.   The failure of the Provisional Government (q. v.) to satisfy both the Boers and the British led to a meeting between the British High Commissioner and the President of the Republic in April, 1893 at Colesburg in the Cape.   Their discussions led to this agreement, also called the Convention of 1893. It provided that the South African Republic would be

allowed to take all rights of jurisdiction, administration,
and protection over Swaziland (but without absorbing it
into the Republic), if only it could get the Queen Regent,
Gwamile Mdluli, to sign the necessary proclamation.
Swazi traditional law and grazing rights would still be
allowed the Swazis. Not only did the Queen Regent re-
fuse, but she sent a delegation of Swazis to London in
1894 to protest that Queen Victoria was handing the
Swazis over to the Boers after previous guarantees of
independence. While the deputation was not successful
in winning its protest, there was a Third Swaziland
Convention which, in effect, made this one inoperative.

SEKHUKHUNE (variants: SEKUKUNI, SIKUKUNI). Chief of
the Bapedi, succeeding his son, Sekwate (q. v.), in September, 1861. In addition to confronting the Boers on
numerous occasions, he was a thorn in the side of the
Swazis, as he protected a number of Swazi refugees
(including a son of King Sobhuza I) from King Mswati.
The Swazis lost a major battle at Mosega Kop (see
BATTLE OF MOSEGA KOP) where a number of princes
were killed. Sekhukhune spent the next several years
fighting or resisting the Boers and the British as his
empire alternately expanded and contracted. Finally,
in 1879, the Swazis retaliated by sending several emabutfo in the form of an 8, 000 man impi under the command of Mbovane Fakudze (q. v.). Combined with the
2, 000 European troops of Sir Garnet Wolseley they beat
the Bapedi on November 28, 1879, and captured Sekhukhune who was sent to Pretoria on December 9. He was
set free in 1881 but was murdered by his half-brother
Mampoer in August, 1882.

SEKWATE (variant: SEKWATI). Son of Tulare, a leader of
the Bapedi people, he was responsible for rallying the
remnants of the group in the 1820's, after they were
devastated by Mzilikazi and the Ndebeles. Solidifying
his position, he set up a mountain defense against the
Zulus, Swazis, and Ndebeles. Sekwate was less successful against the Boers in the late 1840's and the
Swazi under Mswati in the late 1850's, both times suffering temporary defeats. Sekwate was forced to acknowledge Mswati's authority, but later he retook the
Bapedi land. Sekwate died September 20, 1861, and
was succeeded by his son, Sekhukhune (q. v.).

SELBORNE, LORD. Governor of the Transvaal and High

Commissioner for South Africa from 1905 to 1910. His
role in Swaziland's history involves two events. First,
it was his chore to struggle through the concessions
problem. He issued the Concessions Partition Proclamation of 1907 (q. v.) and appointed George Grey as
Special Commissioner to divide the land. Other actions
involving Crown Lands and mineral concessions also
took place during his five-year term. Equally important, however, was his role in the potential transfer of
the High Commission Territories to South Africa. On
this subject his opinions vacillated. While originally
assuming their transfer would soon occur, his admira-
tion of the Basuto National Council (but simultaneous
horror at Swazi traditional rulers) convinced him that
transfer should only occur if extreme conditions pro-
tecting the peoples of the Territories were written into
the Draft Constitution by which Great Britain would
allow South African independence. Otherwise he feared
an absorption attempt and certain war after independence.
Later he was converted to the idea that transfer should
not take place until much later, but that the three Territories should still be safeguarded by a list of conditions and Schedule of Transfer in the Constitution for
the time when the transfer would occur.

SELLSTROOM, A. A leader of the Swaziland Eurafrican
community, he was active in the Eurafrican Welfare
Association and chosen as its representative at the London Constitutional Conference of 1963. There he added
his support to the Alliance of Political Organizations
(q. v.). Still active politically in the 1970's, he has
been a member of Dr. Ambrose Zwane's NNLC.

SEME, DR. PIXLEY KA IZAKA. A South African Zulu who,
as a young lawyer in 1912, was a founder and moving
force behind the African National Congress (q. v.). Involved in a newspaper venture for a while, he received
financial support from the Swazi Queen Regent Labotsibeni. Later, in the 1920's, he was a legal advisor
to King Sobhuza II in his case concerning land concessions. In 1922-23 he accompanied Sobhuza and his
party to London in their appeal to the British Government. In 1926 he carried the case (Sobhuza II versus
A. M. Miller and the Swaziland Corporation Limited)
to the Privy Council, where the decision again went
against the Swazis.

THE SENATE.   The smaller of the two houses of Parliament
(q. v.) under the 1967 and Independence Constitutions.
It consisted of twelve members, six elected by the
House of Assembly and six nominated by the King.   The
Senate had power to initiate legislation on any matters
other than finance, taxation, and Swazi law and custom.
It had a President as presiding officer.

SENCABAPHI, PRINCESS.   A sister of King Sobhuza II and
widow of Dinane, Chief of the Ndwandwe.   She attended
Lovedale School in South Africa with Sobhuza.   Upon returning home she was told that an aunt, Tonga Tonga,
had died shortly after arriving at the village of her new
husband, Dinane.   A substitute wife was needed, and
Sencabaphi agreed to become the substitute.   Being very
close to Sobhuza, she did it for the sake of the kingship, she said.   She bore Dinane two daughters and no
sons.   When he died there was a major problem in the
lack of a satisfactory male heir.   Sencabaphi eventually
returned to live at Lobamba.

SEPEREPERE.   A South African refugee in Swaziland in the
early 1960's who, as a member of the Swaziland Refugee Committee, took an active part in founding the
Anti-Apartheid Committee in 1963 and was elected its
chairman.   Although it originally had the support of
Swazi political parties and South Africa's banned ANC,
it broke up quickly due to internal dissension and some
harassment by the Swaziland Administration.   In 1964
Seperepere was caught in South Africa while trying to
go from Swaziland to Bechuanaland, and the South African Government sentenced him to a year in prison for
trying to leave the country without a passport.

SHABALALA, NDAWONDE.   A chief of a clan living along
the Mkondo River in the Drakensberg Mountains in the
mid-nineteenth century.   Upon his death there was a
succession dispute between two of his sons, Madlangampisi and Sibankwa.   The former lost in a battle and fled
to the Swazi King Mswati II for aid.   Mswati's army
killed Sibankwa, and Madlangampisi became chief, after
paying allegiance to the Swazi King.

SHANGANE (variant: SHANGAAN).   A group of Africans belonging to the Ndwandwe clan who fled Zululand in 1821
to dominate the Gaza Empire in southern Mozambique
near the Limpopo River for most of the rest of the

century. Named after their great leader Soshangane
(q. v.), they survived battles with Chaka's Zulus in 1828
and with the Swazis, and eventually conquered the Shona
and Tonga peoples. Their empire finally collapsed at
the hands of the Portuguese in the 1890's, by which time
even the Tongas (q. v.) were referred to as Shangane.

SHE-ELEPHANT. A term respectfully applied to the Ndlovukazi, (q. v.), indicative of her importance to her people.

SHE MINE. Located about four miles west of Forbes Reef,
near the South African border, this mine was active between 1960 and 1966.

SHEBA'S BREASTS. Twin peaks located high above the
Ezulwini Valley south of Mbabane.

SHEPSTONE, SIR THEOPHILUS. South African statesman,
born in England in 1817. Well-liked and respected by
the Africans, he was contacted by the Swazis for help
against marauding Zulus in the 1850's. Shepstone
quickly put pressure on Zulu King Mpande and the raids
on Mswati's country stopped. When Mbandzeni sent to
Shepstone for help against the concessionaires in 1886,
he sent his son, Theophilus ("Offy") Shepstone, Jr.
(q. v.), instead. The senior Shepstone died in 1893.

SHEPSTONE, THEOPHILUS, JR. ("OFFY"). The eldest son
of Sir Theophilus Shepstone (q. v.), and a member of
the Bar at Pietermaritzburg. He was appointed Resident Advisor to the Swazi King, Mbandzeni, when the
King tried to get Sir Theophilus to appoint an advisor.
He held the position from December, 1886 to July, 1893.
His position was also that of Agent of the Swazi nation
and included powers to act in all matters concerning
white people in Swaziland. Problems with concessionaires were in fact the reason Mbandzeni sent for help.
His first fight was with members of the "White Committee" (q. v.), who were divided for and against him.
Especially opposed were the friends of John Thorburn
(q. v.), who had been an advisor to the King before
Shepstone. They were finally successful in having the
King dismiss him in January, 1889, replacing him with
Allister Miller (q. v.) until the Ndlovukazi reappointed
Shepstone shortly before the King's death in October of
the same year. Among his other activities, Shepstone
represented Swaziland on a boundary commission in 1888

and continued to negotiate with European officials over
the Transvaal-Swaziland-Mozambique borders. He also
represented the Swazis in dealing with the Joint Commission (q. v.) in 1889. When the result was the formation of the Triumvirate Government (q. v.), Shepstone
was named the representative of the Swazis and its
chairman.

SHIBA, MDINBANE. The indvuna of Hhohho, the administrative center of the country, during the reign of King
Ngwane III in the mid to late eighteenth century.

SHISELWENI (variant: ESHISELWINI). Literally: "The
Place of Burning." The village founded by King Ndvungunye as his administrative capital. His son, Sobhuza
I, also used it as his royal residence until there was a
threat of attack by the Ndwandwe leader Zwide, who destroyed the vacated royal residence by fire. Nevertheless, Shiselweni is considered to be the birthplace of
the Swazi nation, and those clans with Sobhuza at Shiselweni are known as "true Swazis" or Bemdzabuko.

SHISELWENI DISTRICT. Covering 1, 844 square miles, it is
the southernmost district of the four making up the
country. Shiselweni spans Swaziland from west to east.
It has a population of about 100, 000, only a small part
of which could be called urbanized. Its main towns are
Hlatikulu, Nhlangano (formerly Goedgegun), Lavumisa
(formerly Gollel) and Hluti.

SIBACA. A Swazi dance of no ceremonial significance, common in the country since the 1930's. Encouraged by
King Sobhuza who was once active in it himself, there
is annual competition between teams of distinctively
dressed Sibaca dancers. The King himself is the judge.

SIBANDZE, MBHABHA (variants: MBABA, UNBAPA). An
"indvuna lenkulu" (q. v.), he succeeded Tikhuba Magongo
(q. v.) in that position. He served under King Bhunu
(Ngwane V). The King ordered him killed at the royal
residence at Zombodze on April 9, 1898. One source
indicated that the young King was jealous of his power
as advisor to the Ndlovukazi who was dominant at this
time. Another source indicates that Mbhabha was accused of witchcraft against the King by sending the leg
of a sacrificial animal to some Sutu hiding in the
mountains. The second explanation appears to have

been a charge used to cover for the truth of the first
explanation. Regardless, the death of Sibandze pro-
voked an incident involving King Bhunu (q. v.).

SIBAYA.   An enclosure for cattle that is one of the three key
structures of a Swazi homestead (see also INDLUNKULU
and LILAWU).   It is circular and built of strong logs
and flexible branches.   In addition to containing the cattle (highly valued possessions in the Swazi tradition),
the sibaya has special areas designed to contain the
grain crops, thus representing the totality of the community's wealth and livelihood.   Only men and children
are allowed to enter it except in rare instances.   It is
also the site of some rituals, such as part of the Incwala at the capital, also marriage rites, puberty rites,
and ancestor rites.   It is also often the site of the
meeting of the important council, the liqoqo (q. v.).

SIBONGO.   "Clan. "   The most significant means of ethnic
grouping and differentiation among the Swazi.   The
sibongo group ("clan") is the furthest extension of kinship, as people with the same sibongo (clan praise
name, e. g. Dlamini, Maseko, Sukati, Zwane, etc.) are
considered to be related through their fathers in a patrilineal system.   Even children whose mothers are not
legally married acquire this clan name (surname) which
continues as their identification.   Women do not lose
their sibongo upon marriage but can not pass it on to
their children.   Subdivision of clans occurred often, and
some lists show close to a hundred different sibongo,
only thirty-five of which are considered "true Swazi"
(see BEMDZABUKO).   A number of lineages in which
descent can be traced over many generations are to be
found in each clan.   Ties between these lineages may
not be obvious except through their sibongo which they
bear in common.   A number of social and political relationships are established through one's sibongo identification.   For example, only a king can marry within
his clan; also some clans have specific ritual ties with
the King, supplying his first two wives, or his tinsila,
or filling other specific needs.   Two centuries or so
ago, all Swazi clans were of equal importance, but this
evolved into a hereditary monarchy.   People bearing the
same sibongo usually feel a special relationship with
and even responsibility toward one another.   This is
helped by the fact that people with the same sibongo
will tend to dominate a village or even a whole section

of the country, sometimes even having distinctive customs and superstitions. The Nkosi Dlamini is the royal clan and is preeminent in the country, and others have a recognized rank of some greater or lesser importance. One's sibongo does not automatically extend or limit one's ability to achieve within the society.

SICUNUSA. A community three miles east of the South African border in the southwestern part of Swaziland, it is the site of a pyrophyllite mine being worked by Swaziland Industries Ltd.

SIDVOKODVO. A town of about nine hundred people in central Swaziland about fifteen miles south of Manzini, and the largest town between Manzini and Hlatikulu much further south. The Swaziland Railway runs through the community, which is in an area good for both cotton and cattle-raising.

SIDVWASHINI. The site of one of the military villages set up by King Mswati II during the mid-nineteenth century. It was located near the present town of Hectorspruit in South Africa.

SIDWABA. A skin skirt that is basic to the traditional dress of the Swazi woman.

SIDZIYA. A skin apron traditionally worn over the sidwaba (q. v.) by Swazi women. Modern Swazi women have usually replaced it with European style clothes. The Swazi bride (makoti) traditionally wore her sidziya in one position before bearing a child, and in another position after becoming a mother.

SIKULU (variant: SIKHULU; plural: TIKULU). A hereditary chief who rules over a sive (principality), the first (lowest) local unit which has a ruler officially recognized by the central authorities. His hereditary position is subject to ratification by the King and his accountability to the King is presumed. He is the head of the area in law, land, and ritual. He presides over cases and sanctions fines and other punishments. He has the power to accept new subjects and grant them land, and to evict subjects from land. The power of a sikulu derives from the number of people owing him allegiance. Subjects are free to withdraw from his area and transfer their allegiance.

SIMELANE, BENJAMIN M.   One of the officers of the Swaziland Progressive Party during the early 1960's.   Originally a supporter of its leader, J. J. Nquku, during
several attempts by Dr. Ambrose Zwane to replace him,
Simelane finally joined with O. M. Mabusa and K. T.
Samketi in August, 1962, to suspend Nquku from office.
Simelane was then chosen its President.   When Nquku
returned from Europe he refused to accept the ouster.
A meeting called by Simelane and Samketi to resolve
the situation on September 30, 1962 failed from lack of
adequate attendance.   Eventually Simelane returned to
support Nquku and stayed with him for several more
years, but by 1967 he was an unsuccessful parliamentary
candidate for the Swaziland United Front.   In 1972 he
also lost, this time on Dr. Zwane's NNLC slate.

SINOKOTI.   A skin cloak of antelope skin or cattle hide worn
by Swazi men and women to cover their upper torso
when the weather is either cold or damp.   It differs
from a siphuku only in that the latter is made from
goat skin.

SIPOFANENI (variant: SIPHOFANENI).   A small community
about twenty-five miles southeast of Manzini.   It takes
on added importance from its location alongside both the
Swaziland Railway and the Great Usutu River.   It is
also the site of a thermal mineral spring, the only one
in the eastern part of the country.

SISWATI.   The language of the Swazi Nation.   In many ways
it is very close to isiZulu and other languages of Nguni
people.   It is at minimum a distinct dialect, if not a
distinct language.

SITEKI.   The only major town on the Lubombo escarpment,
its population is about 1,400.   Literally meaning "the
place of marriage," it was known as Stegi (q. v.) until
shortly after independence.   It is the administrative
headquarters of the Lubombo District.   For those tra-
veling by road to Mozambique, it is a convenient stopping point on the route to the frontier at Goba, only 15
to 20 miles away by road.   Siteki is two thousand feet
above sea level and is settled in among beautiful scen-
ery.   While the town's population is not very large, the
surrounding area more than equals the town itself.
There is a hospital there at the Good Shepherd Roman
Catholic Mission.   North of Siteki, overlooking the

Ehlane game reserve, are some unusual rock paintings
by Sotho clans, but possibly of earlier origin. There
is also an airfield.

SITOBELA. A crossroads community in south-central Swaziland. Four miles north of it at Pentouyz is one of
Swaziland's tin mines, no longer in production. It is
in a good cotton-producing area.

SIVE. A principality, the lowest local unit which has a leader or headman who is recognized by the central authorities. The leader may be a sikulu (chief) or umtfwanenkosi (prince).

SIYINQABA. A siSwati word meaning "We are the Fortress."
It is on the Swaziland Coat of Arms established at the
time of Independence.

SMUTS, JAN CHRISTIAN. Prime Minister of South Africa
from 1919 until 1924, and again from 1939 until 1948.
In his first period as Prime Minister, Smuts showed
great interest in having Swaziland transferred to South
African sovereignty. He was even prepared to promise
a railway to encourage support from Europeans in Swaziland. His electoral defeat in 1924 cut this short. Just
a month after taking office in 1939 Smuts again moved
with a request for the transfer of Swaziland and possibly Bechuanaland to South African control. In late October, Smuts' friend and representative, Col. Deneys
Reitz, had a conference in England with Anthony Eden
(q. v.), who informed him that transfer during the war
would be impossible. After the war, Smuts indicated
in 1946 that the High Commission Territories were an
"indivisible part of South Africa" and that his government would try to get them under its administrative
control. But he was in no hurry, and in 1948 he lost
his office.

SOBHUZA I, KING. Also bore the title Ngwane IV; also
known as Somhlolo. The son and heir of King Ndvungunye, who died in 1815. Sobhuza's mother was Somn-
jalose Simelane. Soon after becoming king in 1815, he
continued his father's military activities. With discretion, however, he avoided confrontation with Zwide (q.
v.) and the Ndwandwes by moving his capital north.
The clans with Sobhuza at this time were called "true
Swazis" or Bemdzabuko. They settled in the Lusutfu

River Valley at Nqabaneni. With the aid of the Maseko
tribe he moved further north to the foot of the Mdimba
Mountains, near Lozithehlezi today. Many more clans
were absorbed in this area and Sobhuza's following grew
dramatically. He built his capital there around 1820
and called it Lobamba (not the same as the present capital also called Lobamba), where the Ndlovukazi ruled.
She was named Lojiba (q. v.). He built other major
villages at Zulwini and Langeni. Sobhuza's military
campaigns continued in the north, especially against the
Pedi and as far north as the upper Komati River. To
the south, however, he used European-type diplomacy,
requesting a daughter of Zwide for his bride and future
queen. His selection, Thandile, also known as Lazidze,
became mother of the great Swazi King, Mswati II.
Maize was introduced to Swaziland as a result of successful dealings between Sobhuza and the Portuguese in
Mozambique. Sobhuza was also said to have been invited by Chaka to visit him in Zululand. The visit was
another diplomatic success. Sobhuza died in 1836 in
his administrative residence at Langeni.

SOBHUZA II, KING. Also called Mona, Mahogoza, and
Nkhotfotjeni. Ngwenyama of Swaziland from December
22, 1921, until the present. He was born on July 22,
1899, only five months before his father, King Bhunu,
died. His mother was Lomawa Nxumalo. Soon after
his father's death, Sobhuza was named king-designate.
The National School at Zombodze was ordered built by
his grandmother, Labotsibeni, to assure his education,
one that would not be controlled by missionaries. She
also brought Robert Grendon, a Eurafrican from Natal,
to serve as his tutor. Sobhuza and several other Swazi
youths were sent to Lovedale Institute in the Ciskei for
secondary education. Sobhuza attended there from 1916
to 1918 when he was brought home to begin preparation
for kingship. During his minority, Labotsibeni served
as Regent and her son, Prince Malunge, assisted her.
Immediately after becoming Ngwenyama on December
22, 1921, Sobhuza began an effort to get Swazi land returned to the Swazis. In December, 1922, he sailed
with a group of advisers to London to claim that Swazi
land had been illegally taken from them by the British.
In January, 1923, they met King George V and his Secretary of State for the Colonies, but the Swazi pleas
were rejected. Sobhuza's test case in 1924, heard by
the Special Court of Swaziland, was also dismissed by

the Court, but he appealed it to the Privy Council in
March, 1926. Again the courts found against Sobhuza.
In the early days of the Second World War, Sobhuza
pledged and sent an impi of Swazis to aid England and
her allies. In 1941 he also petitioned King George VI
for land, and a native land settlement scheme resulted.
In March, 1947, Sobhuza welcomed King George VI and
his Queen and daughters to Swaziland, and in 1953 he
attended the coronation of Queen Elizabeth II in London.
From 1944 until independence, King Sobhuza and his
council constantly fought Great Britain to get proper
recognition of the Swazi King in colonial administrative
proclamations.   The King was successful in 1950 when
the Swaziland Native Administration Proclamation was
issued.   Also, despite some setbacks during the constitutional negotiations of the early 1960's, the position of
the King was satisfactorily outlined in the Independence
Constitution. Sobhuza was very active, often through
his aides, during the period of constitution making.
When the Sandys' Constitution of 1963 proved unsatisfac-
tory, he took the advice of his legal advisors and called
a special election, the "reindeer referendum" (q. v.) to
demonstrate his influence among the Swazis.   Successful in this first "modern" political action, he was responsible for the formation of the Imbokodvo National
Movement in 1964 and for Prince Makhosini Dlamini being chosen its leader.   Sobhuza also cooperated heavily
with European settlers during this period in order successfully to fend off the challenge of other political
parties.   Eventually, he dropped the alliance with Europeans and worked to integrate Swazi party members into
Imbokodvo.   In March, 1973 he called together a Swaziland Army from among some veterans and youth.   The
next month he issued a proclamation suspending the Independence Constitution and declared that the country
would be ruled by the King in Council until a new Constitution could be drawn up.   He appointed the Royal
Constitutional Commission in September, 1973 for that
purpose.   A strong and intelligent leader despite his
advancing age, he has many wives and many children,
one of the latter to eventually become his successor.

SOMCUBA.   A son of King Sobhuza I, he assisted his half-
brother Malambule, who served as regent during the
minority of another half-brother, Mswati II.   This was
from 1836 to 1840.   A few years later, after Malambule (q. v.) was forced to flee the country after an attack

by Mswati, Somcuba fled north and received protection
from the Bapedi (q. v.). Eventually, however, his
homestead was found by Mswati's men; it was attacked
and burned. He was killed and all but one of his children were returned to Swaziland. South African Boers
laid claim to a large part of today's Transvaal Province
by claiming that Somcuba signed a treaty granting it in
July, 1846. This would not be legal, however, as Somcuba was then a fugitive from Mswati, not an official
representative.

SOMHLOLO.   Another name of King Sobhuza I.

SOMTJALOSE (variants: SOMTSHALOSE, SOMJELUSE).
Mother of King Sobhuza I, she assisted Malambule and
Somcuba in running the country from 1836 to 1840 while
her grandson, Mswati II, was still in his minority. She
also gained a reputation for having been something of a
restraining influence on King Sobhuza during his reign,
setting a precedent for future Ndlovukazis. Her clan,
Simelane, received land in southern Swaziland in order
to allow them to escape the attacks of the Zulus. This
was done out of respect for Somtjalose, then the Ndlovukazi.

SONNENBERG'S RETREAT.   An early name for the town
which grew up to be the present day city of Mbabane,
the capital.

SOSHANGANE.   Leader of a group of Ndwandwe clansmen
who escaped from Chaka and Zululand in 1821. His
followers became known as Shangane (q. v.) and they
were to control the Gaza Empire until the 1890's. He
conquered the Tonga and Shona and fought off raids by
the Swazis of King Mswati and the Zulus. His people
lived north and east of the Swazis, but when he died
(in 1845 or 1859 according to two contradictory sources),
King Mswati ordered his men to intervene in the succession dispute between Soshangane's sons, Mzila and
Mawewe (q. v.). Swazi success was short-lived. While
Soshangane left a large empire, he had made enemies
of the conquered and was never able to make them into
a nation.

SOTHO (also SUTU).   A sub-category of the Bantu-speaking
peoples of Africa. Several million Sotho live in Southern Africa. They are divided into the Southern Sotho

(many of whom reside in Lesotho, q. v.), the Western
Sotho, also called Tswana (many of whom reside in
Botswana, q. v.), and the Northern Sotho, especially the
Bapedi (q. v.).   Most of the Northern Sotho live in the
Transvaal near Swaziland, and some of them on occasion in the past have been under the authority of Swazi
kings. In today's Swaziland, it has been estimated that
about thirty percent of the "Swazis" are of Sotho origin
rather than the Nguni origin of the founding Dlamini
clan.

SOUTH AFRICA see REPUBLIC OF SOUTH AFRICA,
    SOUTH AFRICAN REPUBLIC and UNION OF SOUTH
    AFRICA.   Occasionally the term is used in a broad
    sense, however, to include everything south of the Lim-
    popo River, in which case it would include Swaziland
    within its meaning.

SOUTH AFRICA ACT.   Also known as the Act of Union.   The
    basis for the existence of the Republic of South Africa
    today, it was formally passed by the British Parlia-
    ment in 1909, and went into effect as the document es-
    tablishing South Africa's independence on May 31, 1910.
    A draft version of this Act was drawn up by a South
    African National Convention in 1898 before it was sent
    on to the British Parliament.   The Act of Union made
    provision for a future incorporation of the High Com-
    mission Territories and Rhodesia.   Although such in-
    corporation did not take place, both the framers of the
    Act and the British Government clearly anticipated it,
    under the condition that the consent of the inhabitants
    would be sought prior to such action.   (See also IN-
    CORPORATION INTO SOUTH AFRICA.)

SOUTH AFRICAN RAILWAYS AND HARBOURS ROAD MOTOR
    SERVICE.   A decision in the summer of 1927 by the
    Railway Board of South African Railways and Harbours
    dramatically increased Swaziland's communication and
    transportation facilities with South Africa.   It introduced
    bus service on roads linking Manzini (then Bremers-
    dorp) and Mbabane to the railroad at Breyten.   Also it
    linked Manzini with another rail terminus at Gollel (now
    Lavumisa), and linked Hlatikulu with Piet Retief.   It
    gave a tremendous boost to the Swazis' ability to travel
    and it increased mail service and the amount of supplies
    reaching the country.   British Colonial Secretary Amery
    saw to it that the money needed to improve the dirt

roads for this purpose was available.   Service to other
railheads at Komatipoort and Hectorspruit has since
been added.

SOUTH AFRICAN REPUBLIC.   A state that existed in southern Africa, coterminous with what is today called the
Transvaal (q. v.), from 1860 until its defeat at the hands
of the British in 1902 during the Boer War (q. v.).   It
actually was a union of several Voortrekker republics
that had been set up in the middle of the nineteenth
century.   Although a single constitution for the republics had been adopted in 1855, it was somewhat ignored.
Modifications of the constitution in 1858 made it satisfactory to all but one of the republics, and it, the
Lydenburg Republic (q. v.), joined in 1860.   The South
African Republic, its leaders and its citizens, inter-
acted with Swaziland constantly from 1860 until the Boer
War.   In the 1870's and 1880's, its citizens acquired
numerous land and mineral rights concessions, especially from King Mbandzeni.   Once residing in Swaziland
they quarreled both among themselves and with the
British, and finally got permission to form a "White
Committee" (q. v.) for self-government.   The Republic
and Great Britain began to vie for dominance in Swaziland, especially since the Republic's leaders saw control of Swaziland as a potential way of breaking the Republic's land-locked status.   A long series of agreements between Great Britain and the Republic (with the
Swazis as impotent observers) finally gave control of
Swaziland to the Republic in 1894.   The Republic governed Swaziland for five years until the outbreak of the
Anglo-Boer War.

SOUTH AFRICAN WAR.   Another name for the Anglo-Boer
War (q. v.).

SOUTHERN AFRICAN CUSTOMS UNION.   Also known as the
Common Customs Area, it consists of the Republic of
South Africa, South-West Africa (Namibia), Botswana,
Lesotho, and Swaziland.   Visitors entering Swaziland
from South Africa meet no customs formalities.   Originally agreed to by South Africa and the United Kingdom
(on behalf of the High Commission Territories) in 1910,
it provided for South African currency to be legal
tender, and that the area be treated as a single entity
for customs regulations and restrictions.   Tariffs were
set by South Africa and fixed proportions of revenue

were distributed to the three Territories. In 1965-66
there was a revision of the figures and Swaziland was
granted a higher percentage of revenue (0. 53033 percent) than it had received earlier. A new agreement,
signed in December, 1969, and effective on March 1,
1970, provided a revised, self-adjusting formula for
revenue distribution, and the funds distributed in the
first year tripled. The dramatic increase for Swaziland
balanced its budget for 1970-71 and should do so for
some years to come. The agreement also provides for
establishment of a Customs Union Commission for con-
sultation on a number of important topics of mutual economic interest.

STANDARD BANK OF SOUTH AFRICA LTD. One of the three
    banking institutions in Swaziland, it has branches in
    Mbabane, Manzini and Big Bend, plus about ten agencies
    in other locations. Its main office is in London.

STANDING COMMITTEE OF THE SWAZILAND NATIONAL
    COUNCIL (LIBANDHLA 'NCANE). The Swazi National
    Council (or Libandhla laka Ngwane) is a large and un-
    wieldy group that meets about once a year for a period
    of several weeks. Since more frequent decisions of na-
    tional importance must be made, King Sobhuza II devised
    a more practical body, the standing committee of the
    Libandhla. This is not identical with the Liqoqo, as
    several writers imply. It consists of a chairman, the
    treasurer of the Swazi National Treasury, the secretary
    of the nation, and representatives from the country's
    administrative districts, all paid from the Swazi National
    Treasury. This committee meets weekly, or more often
    if necessary, to deal with matters of importance to the
    Swazi nation. The committee is appointed by the King
    in Council. Sometimes called the Libandhla 'ncane, or
    "Little Council, " it often is expanded beyond its original
    size by additional royal appointees, usually Swazis with
    special expertise in economic, legal, or technological
    matters.

STANLEY, SIR HERBERT J. High Commissioner for Basuto-
    land, Bechuanaland and Swaziland, and High Commis-
    sioner for the United Kingdom in South Africa from
    April 6, 1931, until January 6, 1935. He was the first
    High Commissioner who was not simultaneously Governor
    General of South Africa. Stanley was completely opposed
    to any possibility of the High Commission Territories be-

Stegi

158

ing transferred to South African control.

STEGI. The name of the easternmost of the six districts of Swaziland before they were merged into four in December, 1963. At that time the name of the Stegi District was changed to Lubombo while the District was otherwise kept intact. Meanwhile the town serving as the administrative headquarters continued to have the name Stegi until it was changed shortly after independence to Siteki (q. v.).

STEINACHER, LUDWIG. A Bulgarian who fought in Swaziland for the British during the Anglo-Boer War. He and forty men successfully blew up a bridge between Malelane and Komatipoort in June, 1900, wrecking a Boer supply train. After other incidents he was promoted to major, and was allowed to recruit fifty horsemen, who became known as "Steinacher's Horse." Using Lomahosha as his base, he and his men raided a number of settlements including Hhohho and, in March, 1901, Bremersdorp. After looting the village his men stayed there until a commando of Boers beat them four months later, burning Bremersdorp to the ground. Steinacher had not been in Bremersdorp during the attack, however, and he escaped to the Lubombo Mountains where his troop was eventually increased to six hundred men and he was promoted to Lieutenant-Colonel.

STEPHENS, ROBERT PORRITT. Swaziland's Minister of Finance since June, 1972. Born in the Cape Province in 1905, he has a B. A. from the University of Cape Town and another from Oxford. After serving in World War II, he started Peak Timbers in 1947 and was chairman of the company until he retired in February, 1968. He was an outspoken member of The European Advisory Council in the 1950's and 1960's, took part in the constitutional talks that began in November, 1960, and, as a member of the United Swaziland Association, was elected to the Legislative Council in 1964. His nearly 9, 000 votes tripled the number received by his opponent, Vincent Rozwadowski (q. v.). In 1966 he was again appointed to the constitutional committee, and was subsequently appointed by King Sobhuza II to the House of Assembly. This appointment was renewed in May, 1972, and, in the new House, he was made Minister of Finance. In 1973 the King appointed him to the

Royal Constitutional Commission (q. v.).

STEPHENSON, SIR HUGH. High Commissioner for Basutoland, Bechuanaland, and Swaziland, and High Commissioner for the United Kingdom in South Africa from
June, 1963 until October of that year when the first
post was replaced by a new position, Her Majesty's
Commissioner. Sir Brian Marwick assumed this title.
Stephenson visited Swaziland in July and toured the
country. He had been responsible for ordering British
troops to be sent to Swaziland the previous month to
restore order after a series of labor strikes and civil
demonstrations.

STERN, MICHAEL A. A young Englishman who founded
Waterford School (q. v.) in Mbabane in 1962. He resigned as its Headmaster in September, 1973, after
building this progressive school from nothing to an internationally recognized center for liberal education.
It was renamed Waterford-KaMhlaba by King Sobhuza
in 1967. Stern has been appointed an executive of
Drum Publications.

STRAND, LAURA. A Norwegian missionary of the Free
Evangelical Assemblies church, she came to Swaziland
in 1909 and served until June, 1971. She died in Norway on December 16, 1971 at the age of 93. She was
the first missionary of her church in the country and
saw her work spread far from its mission and school
at New Haven, Hlatikulu. Her work received recognition from many, including the monarchs of Norway and
England.

STRIKES. Labor unrest leading to work stoppages. While
such stoppages have occurred in several industries periodically over the last ten years, 1963 was the year of
widespread unrest. Led in part by members of the
Ngwane National Liberatory Congress, such as Dumisa
Dlamini, Macdonald Maseko and Dr. Ambrose Zwane,
there were six major disruptions in barely three and a
half months. Five thousand workers at many of Swaziland's largest employers were involved. The key dates
and locations were: February 28 (railway construction), March 18-28 (Ubombo Ranches), March 29-April
6 (Peak Timbers), May 20-June 17 (Havelock Mine),
June 10-15 (Mbabane urban area), June 12-20 (Ubombo
Ranches). Numerous arrests were made, especially

Sugar   160

after British troops were brought into the country in
June.   The convicted were mostly leaders of the NNLC.

SUGAR.   Swaziland's most valuable single agricultural export
is sugar.   Grown especially around Big Bend and
Mhlume, its production has increased from 6, 200 tons
in the 1958-59 season to about 200, 000 tons today.
Irrigation is needed for both large estates, the Ubombo
Ranches Ltd. (q. v.) and the Mhlume Sugar Company
(q. v.).   In addition a large number of smaller land-
holders also grow sugar.   Until 1965, most of the sugar
cane was marketed through the South African Sugar
Association.   But the Swaziland Sugar Association now
has a large overseas quota as a signatory to the Commonwealth Sugar Agreement.   The industry has a labor
force of about 10, 000.

SUKATI, JOHN BRIGHTWELL MFUNDZA.   Deputy Prime
Minister of Swaziland from June, 1967 until July, 1971.
Born at Ezabeni in the Manzini District in 1915, he was
educated at the Swazi National Schools.   He was appointed senior indvuna of the Swazi regiments in World
War II by King Sobhuza in 1940, thus serving in an
important liaison role between the Swazis and the European military leaders.   His bravery and leadership at
the Anzio beach landing is often noted, and he became
a sergeant-major.   In 1964 he was elected by the Swazi
National Council to the first Legislative Council.   Two
years later he was chosen as one of eight members of
Imbokodvo on the constitutional committee.   After serving as Deputy Prime Minister for four years, he was
appointed Minister for Power, Works, and Communications in 1971 (he had been elected to Parliament in
1967).   Sukati did not compete in the 1972 elections,
and was named chairman of the Road Transportation
Board.

SUKATI, S. T. MSINDAZWE.   A distinguished Swazi diplo-
mat and trusted representative of King Sobhuza II. Born
in Ezabeni royal village, June 11, 1910, he received a
B. A. from the University of South Africa in 1940, the
second Swazi to obtain such a degree.   Four years
later the King made him senior liaison officer between
the King and the Swazi National Council and the British
administrators.   He served in this capacity for two
decades.   He participated in all constitutional discussions leading to the first Legislative Council, where he

served as clerk. In 1967 he was appointed Speaker of
the House of Assembly, and the next year received an
honorary L. L. D. from the University of Botswana, Lesotho, and Swaziland. In 1968 he was also appointed
Swazi ambassador to the United States and High Commissioner for Swaziland in Canada, posts he held for
five years. He returned to Swaziland in October, 1973,
and was appointed Chairman of the National Industrial
Development Corporation of Swaziland.

SUTU see SOTHO

SWAZI NATION. In siSwati, variously written as amaNgwane
or amaSwazi or in the form Bantu bakwa Ngwane (the
people of Ngwane) or merely bakwa Ngwane. In each
case the identification is with King Ngwane III, the ruler
of these peoples in the mid-eighteenth century. The
term later included all the peoples absorbed by the
Swazi leaders since Ngwane III. Allegiance to the reigning Swazi Ngwenyama and Ndlovukazi would be important
evidence of membership in the Swazi nation today.

SWAZI NATIONAL CHURCH. A religious group founded in
1939 at the suggestion of King Sobhuza II. At this time
separatist churches and Zionist churches were flourish-
ing in Swaziland and missionary churches were at a
standstill. In 1944 the church, again at Sobhuza's suggestion, changed its name to the United Church of Africa in order to attract other than Swazis. The secretary of the church was a close associate of Sobhuza,
J. J. Nquku (q. v.), who years later founded the first
Swazi political party.

SWAZI NATIONAL COUNCIL (also SWAZILAND NATIONAL
COUNCIL (SNC). Also known as the Libandhla (q. v.)
or libandhla laka Ngwane (council of the Ngwane nation).
It is a general council representing the nation in advis-
ing the King. It usually meets only once a year, however, and is thus represented by a Standing Committee
of the Swaziland National Council (q. v.) which has
offices at the tribal capital, Lobamba. References to
the Swazi National Council often refer merely to the
Standing Committee. While responsible for traditional
Swazi concerns, the Council has taken great interest in
modern politics through its creation of the Imbokodvo
National Movement.

SWAZI NATIONAL FUND.   A fund started in 1911 by the
Queen Regent, Labotsibeni, and continued to the present.   Originally it was set up to provide funds to edu-
cate the young King-to-be, the Regent's grandson, along
with the sons of chiefs and councillors, but is now used
for the education of any Swazi child chosen by the Government, trustee of the fund.   Originally every Swazi
taxpayer contributed two shillings a year.   In 1957 the
Swazis raised the tax to five shillings a year.

SWAZI NATIONAL ROYAL CLUB.   An organization of Swazis
living in South Africa, especially in or near Johannesburg, dedicated to continuing their ties with their King
and their country despite their absence.   It was founded
in 1931 by King Sobhuza himself as he visited the house
he kept up in Sophiatown (a district within Johannesburg that was torn down in the 1960's).   Sobhuza's house
was made the Club's center, and a relative of the King
placed in charge of this meeting place for Swazis.
Supposedly representing fifteen thousand Swazis in 1963,
the Club approved a resolution supporting the King's
desire to sever all ties with Britain.

SWAZI NATIONAL SCHOOLS.   The two principal schools supported by the Swazi National Fund are located at Zombodze and Matsapha.   The Zombodze school is an ele-
mentary school founded in 1906 with Government aid
upon the urging of the Regent, Queen Labotsibeni.   The
National Fund provided additional support when it was
created in 1911.   A school was begun at Matsapha in
1931 to continue education at the secondary level.   In
1971 the Government of Sweden promised a grant of one
million Rand to the schools.

SWAZI NATIONAL TREASURY.   Established by the National
Treasury Proclamation of 1950, the national Treasury
was to receive its funds from court fines, fees, and
head taxes.   The Ngwenyama-in-Libandhla was granted
power to regulate the constitution and conduct of the
Treasury and how its funds should be expended.   After
1950 the Swazi National Fund (q. v.) was administered
through the Treasury.   Funds from this Treasury, it
was anticipated, would be used for purposes of the Swazi nation, as distinct from the Government of Swaziland.

SWAZILAND ADMINISTRATION PROCLAMATION NUMBER 3.
A proclamation issued in 1904 by Sir Alfred Milner,

Governor of the Transvaal.   It definitely eliminated the
criminal jurisdiction of the Swazi King and placed limits
on his civil jurisdiction.   As amended by Proclamation
No. 4 of 1907 it applied the laws of the Transvaal to
Swaziland.   The title of the British representative in
Swaziland was changed from Special Commissioner to
Resident Commissioner (q. v.).

SWAZILAND AGRICULTURE COLLEGE AND UNIVERSITY
     CENTRE (SACUC).   Located in west-central Swaziland
     at Luyengo, this institution, which is associated with
     the University of Botswana, Lesotho, and Swaziland
     (which is in Lesotho), was opened in 1966.   Costing
     R600, 000 to build, it was financed heavily by the United
     Kingdom Freedom from Hunger Campaign and by Oxfam.
     It has both a three-year university diploma course and
     a short course center.   While it stresses agriculture
     and forestry courses, it also offers work in home eco-
     nomics and a variety of management and economics
     areas.

SWAZILAND BROADCASTING SERVICE.   Opened in April,
     1966, with studios in Mbabane, it was the only Swazi
     radio station until 1972.   Run by the government on a
     semi-commercial basis, it is on the air for seven hours
     a day on its ten-kilowatt medium-wave transmitter.   Its
     first director was Ian Aers, (q. v.).

SWAZILAND CONSTITUTIONAL COMMITTEE.   Initiated by
     the British in November, 1960, the work of the com-
     mittee ultimately ended in a stalemate at the London
     Constitutional Conference (q. v.) on February 12, 1963.
     The ten Swazis on the committee were Prince Makho-
     sini Dlamini, Prince Lutho, Polycarp Dlamini, S. T. M.
     Sukati, J. S. Matsebula, A. K. Hlophe, D. Lukhele,
     J. J. Nquku, Obed Mabuza, and Dr. Ambrose Zwane.
     Among the twelve Europeans were Dr. David Hynd,
     C. F. Todd, R. P. Stephens, Willie Meyer and H. D.
     G. Fitzpatrick.   Thus seven of the ten Swazis were
     oriented toward traditional values.   While Nquku, Zwane
     and Mabuza were members of the Swazi National Coun-
     cil, they were also active in the Swaziland Progressive
     Party.   Most of the Europeans were closely identified
     with the Reconstituted European Advisory Council which
     had proposed constitutional advance in January, 1960.
     The constitutional committee quickly broke into three
     factions--the traditionalists and the Europeans each

wanted constitutional provisions to protect their interests, while the three SPP members wanted a one man-
one. vote election without reserved parliamentary seats
for Europeans.   Nquku was expelled from the committee when his political speeches were called "disruptive"
on May 18, 1961, and Dr. Zwane and O. M. Mabuza
soon resigned also.   The committee then developed proposals for a 50-50 split in the Legislature between traditionalists and Europeans, with no direct elections
among the Swazis.   The Resident Commissioner and
other Government officials strongly opposed such an
arrangement.   The eventual conference in London in
January and February, 1963 was stalemated as political
party members and Colonial officials opposed the traditionalists and Europeans.   Eventually the Colonial
Secretary, Duncan Sandys, imposed a "compromise"
constitution.

SWAZILAND CREDIT AND SAVINGS BANK.   A statutory body
managed by a publicly-appointed board, it opened in
1965.   Its head office is in Mbabane and it has branches
in Manzini, Pigg's Peak, and Nhlangano, and an agency
at the Usutu Mill Site.   It operates through the Swaziland Post Office for its savings department.   While it
encourages rural Swazis to develop the banking habit,
its other goal is to help provide credit for developing
agriculture and low-cost housing.

SWAZILAND CROWN LANDS AND MINERAL ORDER-IN-
COUNCIL.   Three Orders-in-Council issued by Great
Britain in 1907, 1908, and 1910 and supplemented by
Proclamations in 1911 and 1912.   They made clear that
all lands not reserved for the exclusive use of Swazis
nor held by concessionaires would be treated as Crown
Lands and thus were available for grant or lease from
the High Commissioner.   Also, they affirmed that all
expired mineral concessions reverted to the British
Crown, not to the Swazi nation.

SWAZILAND DEMOCRATIC PARTY (SDP).   An active and influential political party from the announcement of its
formation on March 2, 1962.   Its first president was
Simon Nxumalo who, along with former South Africans
Jordan Ngubane and Vincent Rozwadowski, was among
its principal founders.   Its program was moderate,
non-racial, and anti-Pan-African.   It favored a one man-
one vote plan six months after its founding, having first

proposed a qualified franchise. It favored making the
Ngwenyama a constitutional monarch, and expressed opposition when it appeared that he had ties with the South
African Government. At the 1963 London constitutional
conference, Simon Nxumalo, the SDP representative, led
a party coalition, the Alliance of Political Organizations
(q. v.). At that same conference Dr. Allen Nxumalo
joined with the SDP. On December 4, 1963, Dr. Nxumalo was chosen party President while Simon Nxumalo,
a distant cousin, became Secretary General, a job more
suited to his ability to travel the country with greater
freedom than the doctor's practice would allow. Thus
Allen became the spokesman and Simon became the party
organizer. Sipho Dlamini and Rozwadowski became
Vice-Presidents. The big issue of 1963, labor unrest,
saw the SDP as generally opposed to the NNLC-spon-
sored strikes. The SDP ran eight candidates in the 1964
election and was very unsuccessful, receiving a total of
1, 271 votes, 1. 4 per cent of those cast. Simon Nxumalo left the party on October 1, 1964, in order to
work for national unity, he said. A party conference
that month saw a split develop as two important members, Rozwadowski and Dr. V. S. Leibrandt were expelled. Finally, Dr. Nxumalo announced on April 22,
1965, that the SDP was joining the Imbokodvo. Both
Nxumalos soon became influential in it.

SWAZILAND ELECTRICITY BOARD. A statutory body which
supplies electricity to most of the country's urban, industrial or major agricultural areas. Its main power
station is at Edwaleni (q. v.), but another recent hydro-
electric station is at Magaduza.

SWAZILAND FREEDOM PARTY. A short-lived political party
formed in May, 1962 by Winston Madlala. It opposed
the concept of sharing power equally between Europeans
and Swazis, and put forth a constitutional proposal much
like the ultimate "Sandys' Constitution. " Madlala called
for a legislature composed of eight elected Swazis, eight
Swazis appointed by the Ngwenyama, and eight Europeans
elected by Europeans. This compromise arrangement
(which included four British officials also) was opposed
by all groups in 1962, as it would be again in 1963 when
Sandys imposed a similar plan.

SWAZILAND INDEPENDENT FRONT (SIF). A political association formed on April 2, 1964 to compete in that year's

Swaziland elections.   Its steering committee consisted
of Frank Corbett, Peter Braun, C. J. van Heerden,
and Dr. R. J. Lockhart.   It decided to run candidates
only for the four European Roll seats, its candidates
being Corbett, van Heerden, Lockhart, and G. T. Bertram.   This moderate party of Europeans was designed
to counter the United Swaziland Association (q. v.), and
its policy was to promote Swaziland as a non-racial
country with full majority (Swazi) rule.   It opposed Bantustan status within South Africa.   In the election its
most successful candidate was Bertram with 607 votes,
several hundred short of victory.

SWAZILAND INDUSTRIAL TRAINING INSTITUTE.   Begun in
1946 as the Mbabane Trade School, the Institute changed
its name in mid-1974 to the College of Technology.   It
has evolved into a two-year course for such jobs as
carpenters, plumbers, mechanics, and electricians. But
it also offers knowledge in technical drawing, sciences,
and mathematics to about 270 students.   It also gives
tests for people who have gained experience in trades
outside the College to judge their level of development.

SWAZILAND IRON ORE DEVELOPMENT CO. LTD.   Formed
by the Anglo-American Corporation and the British industrial combine of Guest, Keen, and Nettlefolds in
1957, this company has developed the Swaziland iron
deposits at Ngwenya.   It was given minimum authorized
capital of £3 million, of which £500,000 was subscribed
by the Colonial Development Corporation.   In September, 1961, the company signed an agreement with major
Japanese steel producers to buy its ore over a ten-year
period.

SWAZILAND IRRIGATION SCHEME.   A Commonwealth Development Corporation (CDC) engineering project which
provides water via a 42-mile canal for the Mhlume
Sugar Company, also a CDC subsidiary.   The barrage
is across the Komati River a little east of Balegane,
but the actual headquarters is at Tshaneni.

SWAZILAND MINING PROCLAMATION.   A Government Proclamation of 1958 that amended and consolidated previous
laws concerning mineral rights in Swaziland.   In an
attempt to stimulate prospecting on concessions, it imposed a tax on all holdings, with a rebate allowed if
activity was taking place.   To avoid the tax, conces-

sionaires could hand their concession back to the Government. This resulted in almost doubling the percentage of the country in which mineral rights were in Government hands. At independence this 87 per cent of the country's mineral rights came under the supervision of the King of Swaziland.

SWAZILAND NATIONAL CONVENTION. A political movement formed in 1960 by Dr. Allen Nxumalo and some other Swazi intellectuals with the approval of King Sobhuza. The King saw this as a moderate reaction against the Swaziland Progressive Party. When Dr. George Msibi returned from study in India in 1961, Nxumalo encouraged Msibi to take over its leadership. The movement favored a non-racial system under a constitutional monarchy with strong support for traditionalism. In May, 1962 Msibi merged this group with the Mbandzeni National Party to become the Mbandzeni National Convention (q. v.).

SWAZILAND ORDER-IN-COUNCIL. Promulgated on December 20, 1963, this Order-in-Council gave the force of law to the Constitution (so-called "Sandys' Constitution") imposed by the British Government on Swaziland. It provided for an eight-member Executive Council (three official members and five appointed), and a Legislative Council composed of official members plus twenty-four elected members. Eight would be Swazis chosen by the traditional methods (King-in-Council), eight would be persons elected on a national roll, and eight would be Europeans, four of whom would be elected on a national roll and four by Europeans only. The same Order-in-Council also conceded certain mineral rights to the Ngwenyama in Crown mineral areas.

SWAZILAND PROGRESSIVE ASSOCIATION (SPA). Founded in January, 1929 by Benjamin Nxumalo (q. v.) with the assistance of the Resident Commissioner, T. A. Dickson, and the encouragement of the Ngwenyama, Sobhuza II. It was to be a social and intellectual discussion group for educated Swazis. Some of its members were employed by the Government. While the group generally supported the side of the Swazi nation, some chiefs and other traditionalists were suspicious of the young intellectuals. Thus in the mid-1930's it became affiliated with the Swazi National Council, with the approval of both King Sobhuza and the Administration. While its

membership was probably never over a hundred, it took
policy stands on issues such as taxation and labor conditions.   A dispute in 1939 between Swazi and non-
Swazi members caused a split.   In 1945 a close friend
of King Sobhuza, J. J. Nquku (q. v.) became its president and editor of Ngwane, its newspaper.   He began to
politicize the group in the mid-1950's, and eventually
changed it into the country's first political party, the
Swaziland Progressive Party, on July 30, 1960.

SWAZILAND PROGRESSIVE PARTY (SPP).   The earliest of
the political parties of Swaziland.   It was founded on
July 30, 1960, at Kwaluseni when the Swaziland Progressive Association (q. v.), under its president J. J.
Nquku, transformed itself into a political party. Despite
warnings from traditionalists that parties only caused
dissension, the SPP quickly grew in membership and
activity under Nquku and his Secretary-General, Dr.
Ambrose Zwane.   The party favored a non-racial society, run by a government elected under a one man-
one vote franchise.   It opposed incorporation by South
Africa, and supported Pan-Africanism and socialism.
Nquku made frequent trips to Ghana and other African
capitals, as well as to the United Nations to plead Swaziland's cause.   Three members of the SPP, Nquku,
Zwane, and Obed Mabuza, were appointed to the 1961
constitution committee by the British.   Their activities
in favor of a one man-one vote system quickly got
Nquku ousted, and the other two resigned.   The SPP
then sought the aid of Professor Denis Cowen (q. v.), an
expert on constitutional law, who drew up a plan for
Swaziland which quickly became the party program. Although rejected by all but the SPP, it proved to be very
similar to the Independence Constitution.   A series of
splits began within the SPP from late 1961 until 1963.
The major causes were personality disagreements among
the various party leaders.   Many accused Nquku of one-
man rule of the party, and claimed that his frequent
foreign trips were self-serving.   Zwane made an attempt
to take over SPP leadership in July, 1961, but failed.
Finally he broke away, claiming to head the true SPP,
on February 14, 1962.   He declared himself President
of what was soon called SPP (Zwane), and the SPP
Youth League leader C. Dumisa Dlamini became his
Secretary-General.   Confusion existed for a year until
Zwane renamed his faction the Ngwane National Liberatory Congress in April, 1963.   A further split in August,

1962 saw Obed Mabuza, Benjamin Simelane and K. T.
Samketi (all party officers) forming a new version of
the SPP.   For a time there were four SPP groups,
each identified by the party initials followed parenthetic-
ally by the name of the leader.   SPP (Mabuza) lasted
for several years until it lost its name within the Swaziland United Front which was to be dominated by Mabuza.   Samketi later joined Zwane, and Simelane returned to Nquku for a while.   Despite his minimal support by late 1962, Nquku was invited by the British to
the 1963 London constitutional conference to represent
the SPP.   Zwane and the others were furious that they
were not invited.   For the next several years Nquku
and his new Secretary-General, Albert W. M. Nxumalo,
kept the semblance of a party organization and kept
themselves in the public eye through letters to the news-
papers.   The party itself had minimal success.   In the
1964 elections, the seven candidates of the SPP (Nquku)
received about half of one per cent of the votes cast,
only a total of 589.   Nquku received 56 votes.   At the
same election, the SPP (Mabuza) received about half the
total of Nquku's faction and Mabuza got 34 votes.   In the
1967 elections, SPP (Nquku), now the only party using
that name, nominated seven candidates for the twenty-
four seats.   This time Nquku got only 37 votes and his
candidates totaled 0.1 per cent of the national vote. Despite Nquku's minimal leadership, the party continued
to exist and ran four candidates in 1972 elections. They
totaled 541 votes between them.   By this time Albert
W. M. Nxumalo was the party's main spokesman, and
he announced in March, 1972 that Nquku had retired as
the party's leader.

SWAZILAND PROGRESSIVE PARTY (NQUKU).   A designation
used for a time in the early 1960's to distinguish the
faction of the SPP led by its founder, J. J. Nquku (q.v.)
from those separatist factions led by Dr. Zwane, K. T.
Samketi, B. M. Simelane, and Obed Mabuza.

SWAZILAND PROGRESSIVE PARTY (ZWANE).   A designation
used in the early 1960's to distinguish the faction of the
SPP led by Dr. Ambrose Zwane from those led by J. J.
Nquku, K. T. Samketi, B. M. Simelane and O. M.
Mabuza.   The term ceased to be used when Dr. Zwane
reorganized his faction under the name Ngwane National
Liberatory Congress in April, 1963.

SWAZILAND RAILWAY. A 137-mile line from Kadake near
the iron deposits at Ngwenya in the northwest to the
port of Lourenço Marques in Mozambique. Using a
very indirect route for the benefit of the whole
country, it loops south past the Matsapa Industrial
Estate and through Sidvokodvo, following the Great Usutu
River eastward to Phuzumoya where it heads north again
to Mlawula. It leaves the country at Umbeluzipoort.
The £8 million was financed by the Colonial Development Corporation, the South African Mutual Life Assur-
ance Corp., and the Anglo-American Corporation. It
was opened November 5, 1964 by the King at Kadake.
None of it would have been possible without the guarantee of the traffic of iron ore from the huge mine at
Ngwenya to the port. Eighty per cent of the traffic is
iron ore.

SWAZILAND REFUGEE COMMITTEE. A group formed in
Swaziland in the early 1960's and especially active at
that time. It was designed to look after the interests
of the numerous refugees, especially from South Africa
but also from Mozambique, who had found their way into
Swaziland. Mr. Seperepere was one of its active leaders at that time. The Committee's main problem was
to get the Swaziland Government to grant asylum and
permission to reside in Swaziland without undue restrictions. Many of the early refugees had left the country
by 1965.

SWAZILAND STUDENT UNION. Founded in 1960 by Timothy
Zwane (q. v.), a student at Pius XII College in Basutoland, this well-organized body of Swazi secondary and
university students adopted political positions on several
occasions in the early 1960's. Stating opposition to a
purely traditional system, they favored a one man-one
vote system and a political platform recognizing the
representative quality of the Swaziland Progressive
Party. It called on the Constitutional Committee in
1961 to propose a non-racial state with full adult suffrage, and with the Ngwenyama as a constitutional monarch over a legislature with an elected majority.

SWAZILAND SURFACE RIGHTS PROCLAMATION. A Government Proclamation of 1910 by the British which set
rules to govern the settlement of conflicts between rival
concession holders, one of whom held mineral rights
and the other surface rights for the same land.

SWAZILAND TOBACCO CO-OPERATIVE COMPANY LTD.
The company that markets all tobacco produced in Swaziland. It has offices, a factory and a store at Nhlangano. While tobacco is not among the biggest money-makers of Swaziland's economy, it is long-established and has prospered under this cooperative organization. It was formed in 1931 with aid from the British-sponsored Land and Agricultural Loan Fund in Swaziland. The Co-operative was formed as a result of marketing pressures from South Africa.

SWAZILAND UNITED FRONT. A political group formed in 1965, changing its name from the Joint Council of Swaziland Political Parties (q. v.) which had been formed in 1964. Its basic support came from Obed Mabuza's branch of the SPP and the supporters of Macdonald Maseko from the NNLC. In 1967 it added the members of the Umvikeli wabantu National Movement (q. v.) to its rolls. Never a large party, it has been vocal, especially through its President, Mabuza, and Secretary-General, Austin W. Nxumalo. It has been fighting for single-member constituencies, one man-one vote, and pledges racial cooperation. Two of its candidates in the 1967 election were Europeans. None of its candidates in either 1967 or 1972 have had much success. Several attempts at cooperation with Dr. Zwane's NNLC have proven to be futile.

THE SWAZILANDER. A political newspaper founded in 1955 by John June Nquku (q. v.), who also became its first editor.

SWEARS, C. J. Partner of Alex Forbes who, in November, 1884, discovered the gold-bearing reef to be named Forbes Reef. In July, 1887, he was elected chairman of a "White Committee" (q. v.) of concession holders, storekeepers, and other Europeans.

-T-

TAMBANKULU. A major sugar-producing area in northeast Swaziland, roughly fifteen miles from the Mozambique border.

TANGOMA. A diviner or ritual specialist who specializes in the use of spirits to determine the cause and cure of

illness.   The most powerful and respected of special-
ists, the tangoma often finds that the ill person is possessed by some wandering spirit.   Thus the tangoma
resorts to expulsion or exorcism as the cure.   On the
other hand, diviners themselves are considered to be
possessed by friendly spirits.   (See INYANGA.)

TEMBE.   A group of Bantu people living near the sea south
of Delagoa Bay.   Of Nguni origin, they are closely
aligned to the Bembo-Nguni (q. v.) who lived in the same
area for several centuries.   The Dlamini (royal clan of
Swaziland) are still called "baka Tembe" (those of
Tembe).   In either case the word Tembe derives from
the Tembe River which flows in that area near the pre-
sent-day city of Lourenço Marques.   The Swazis
claimed much of the land east of the Lubombo Mountains near the Tembe River during the boundary demar-
cations of the nineteenth century, but it was denied to
them by the Europeans.

THANDILE, QUEEN MOTHER.   Also: LA ZIDZE (q. v.).

THIRD SWAZILAND CONVENTION.   Also: The Convention
of 1894.   An agreement between Britain and the South
African Republic signed on December 10, 1894.   This
document (following the futile deputation of Swazis to
London after the Second Swaziland Convention) reestablished most of the provisions of the Second Convention,
making Swaziland a protectorate of the South African
Republic even if the Swazis failed to accept it.   The
Swazis refused to sign it.   It had a variety of provisions: Swazi traditions could continue if "civilized,"
the Swazi King could retain political powers, the Republic would not build a railway through Swaziland unless
the British approved, no taxes would be levied on Swazis for three years, British interests in Swaziland
would be recognized, and more.   The Boer Government
began its administration of the country in February,
1895, with Johannes Krogh appointed special commissioner.   This Convention was modified by the Protocol
of 1898 (q. v.).

THOMAS, J. H.   British secretary of state for Dominion
affairs from June, 1930 until November, 1935.   He
opposed the transfer of the High Commission Territories to South Africa, on the grounds that the Africans
themselves were opposed to it.   He successfully nego-

tiated an agreement with General Hertzog in 1935 which
secured a long postponement of the whole question of
the transfer of Swaziland to South Africa until conditions
were more favorable.   Thomas could not foresee any
time when conditions would be more favorable, however,
and did not expect such transfer to be approved by the
Swazis.

THOMSON, GEORGE.   British Commonwealth Secretary in
    1968.   He officially presented the constitutional instru-
    ments embodying the Independence of Swaziland to King
    Sobhuza II at noon on Friday, September 6, 1968, at
    Lobamba.

THORBURN, JOHN.   One of the early White settlers in Swa-
    ziland.   His store and hotel were only half a mile from
    King Mbandzeni's Royal Kraal at Mbekelweni (near Man-
    zini).   He was very popular with the King, a fact that
    made it easy for him to acquire a number of important
    mining concessions from him.   The last was on July
    26, 1889, the Unalloted Lands Concession (q. v.), when
    the King was virtually on his death bed and all other
    official duties had been suspended.   In 1895 Thorburn
    and Allister Miller went to England and merged their
    concessions into the Swaziland Corporation Ltd. , of
    which Miller later became manager.   Thorburn was
    elected one of the first members of the "White Commit-
    tee" in 1887, and in fact the Committee met at his
    store.

THWALA CLAN.   Variant spelling of Twala.   An important
    Swazi clan, one of those called Bemdzabuko or "true
    Swazi. "   The Motsa clan and the Thwala are considered
    to be interrelated sub-clans and intermarriage is pro-
    hibited.   The Thwala are honored in ritual by supplying
    a left-hand insila (q. v.) to the Ngwenyama.   This oc-
    curs, however, only after the first two sets of tinsila
    are married.

TIKHONDZI.   Lieges of the Swazi King.   The term is
    applied to those people who were immigrants to Swazi-
    land, partly as the result of warfare which disrupted
    some of the Bantu kingdoms of southern Africa.   King
    Mswati was especially responsible for accepting some
    of these groups which he settled in sparsely populated
    parts of the country, some under their own leaders and
    others under his appointees.   (See LABAFIK'EMUVA.)

These people have been integrated into modern Swaziland in spite of their origins, but their clan names
(sibongo) point them out as immigrants.

TIKULU. Plural of Sikulu (q. v.). Variant spelling is tik-
hulu.

THE TIMES OF SWAZILAND. The principal newspaper in
Swaziland, publishing weekly with a circulation of about
8, 500 copies. It was established in 1897 and published
until October, 1899, when its press was smashed by
the administration of the South African Republic (q. v.)
as it fled the country. It reappeared on October 16,
1903, but ceased publication again on January 30, 1909.
It came back to stay on November 12, 1931. It is published in English.

TIN. A major source of revenue for Swaziland for the first
half of the twentieth century, the deposits are now
pretty well depleted. It was first discovered in the
form of cassiterite in 1892 in the Mbabane River south of
the present Mbabane Market by Mr. S. T. Ryan. It
also was produced in mines elsewhere in the Ezulwini
Valley as well as along the Ngwempisi River and near
Sitobela. Produced steadily for fifty years, the tin produced from 1900 to 1950 was worth over £2 million. It
contributed almost 95 per cent of the mineral value
produced in Swaziland between the First and Second
World Wars.

TINDVUNA. Plural of Indvuna (q. v.).

TINJOBO. Tassels made of feathers from the lisakabuli and
ligwalagwala birds. They are symbolic of the King
since they can be used only by him. Three tinjobo are
displayed on the staff and shield which are on the flag
of Swaziland.

TINKUNDLA. Plural of Nkundla (q. v.).

TINSILA. Plural of Insila (q. v.).

TINVANGA. Plural of Inyanga (q. v.).

TOBACCO see SWAZILAND TOBACCO COOPERATIVE
COMPANY LTD.

TODD, CARL FREDERICK. A member of the Swazi Senate,
he has been the most important leader of the European
community in Swaziland in the period immediately before
and after independence. Born in Durban, South Africa,
on May 13, 1903, he did not receive a college degree
but he eventually became a partner in a Johannesburg
law firm. He bought his first land in Swaziland in 1938,
and since then has lived part of each year at his Siteki
home and part of the year near Johannesburg. He has
extensive sugar and ranching acres now in Swaziland,
but is also on the boards of an estimated thirty to fifty
South African companies. He served on the European
Advisory Council from 1948 to 1964 when the Legislative
Council was organized, and was chairman of the EAC
for five years. As a member of the Constitutional
Committee appointed in 1960, he favored a "50-50"
Constitution, giving equal weight to Europeans and Swazi
traditionalists. As principal organizer of the United
Swaziland Association, he worked hard for a long interim in which European interests would have strong
representation in new constitutional arrangements.
Nevertheless, during elections for the Legislative Council in 1964, he did not run on the USA ticket. Instead
he was chosen to run by the King's party, Imbokodvo,
as its first white member. This symbolized the close
USA-Imbokodvo partnership at the time. During his
term on the Legislative Council he was chosen to the
self-government constitutional committee and was in
charge of the Portfolio of Agriculture and Mines. After
the 1967 parliamentary elections he was appointed to a
seat in the Senate by King Sobhuza II, whom he has
served as an adviser for many years. He was reappointed to the Senate in May, 1972. Mr. Todd has
been a supporter of the King and traditional Swazi political system for a long time, feeling that a British type
system of Parliamentary government is not suitable for
African countries.

TOMLINSON COMMISSION REPORT. The report issued by
the Commission on the Socio-Economic Development of
the Bantu Areas, under the Chairmanship of Professor
F. R. Tomlinson of the University of Pretoria. The
committee was appointed in 1951, and in 1955 produced
a report in seventeen volumes, with 63 detailed maps.
It proposed the establishment of a number of African
areas based on the existing native reserves. While
these "Bantustans" would have a degree of self-govern-

ment, economic ties with South Africa would be sub-
stantial, ensuring their amiability. The maps showed
that the three High Commission Territories would be
included as Bantustans under this proposal. The report
also stated that the three areas should be incorporated
into South Africa as soon as possible.

TONGA (variant: THONGA). A group of Africans traditionally living along and near the Indian Ocean in the
area of Mozambique today and slightly south. North
or east of the Nguni peoples (of whom the Swazis are
one), they carried on trade for centuries over wide
areas. Preferring small communities, they never created an empire. Thus they were constantly vulnerable
to attack from the Zulus and the Shangane, among
others. Although the Shangane conquered them in the
1830's to the point that the Tonga were even referred
to as Shangane, the Tonga rose against the Shangane
and threw them off in the 1890's. Tongaland became
important to the Swazis in the 1890's as the South African Republic wished control over Swaziland in major
part because Swaziland could give the Republic access
to Tongaland, which in turn gave the Republic an ocean
outlet with even a potential port at Kosi Bay. A railroad would be built along this route. Britain ended this
thinking by annexing Tongaland in 1897.

TRADE UNIONS. The Swaziland Trade Union and Trade Disputes Proclamation of 1942 gave Swazis the right to
unionize. Yet it was twenty years later before the first
true industrial trade union began. Despite the mining
and lumber camp strikes of 1962 and 1963 and the encouragement of the Whitson Report (q. v.), there were
only ten registered workers' unions by 1971. Paid-up
membership was estimated at under five thousand in
total. The 1942 Law was revised and amended considerably in 1966. There is also a Federation of Swaziland Employers.

TRANSVAAL. Literally, "across the Vaal (River)." The
second largest of the provinces of the Republic of South
Africa. It is the territory adjacent to Swaziland on all
but the eastern border of Swaziland. The province
evolved from the South African Republic which had been
an amalgamation of the several separate Boer republics
that had been set up by Voortrekkers who crossed the
Vaal River. Thus, prior to the implementation of the

Act of Union in May, 1910, the term Transvaal was
often used as a geographic synonym for the South African Republic. Many Swazis have spent at least a couple
of years working in the mines or on the farms of the
Transvaal.

TRIUMVIRATE GOVERNMENT see PROVISIONAL GOVERN-
MENT.

TSHANENI. A settlement of about one thousand people in
northeastern Swaziland, it is five miles northwest of
Mhlume and five miles from the border at the town of
Bordergate. Its name means "where the grass is, "
which may help to explain why large numbers of certain
game animals can still be found in the game sanctuary
there. More important in the long run, Tshaneni is the
headquarters of the Swaziland Irrigation Scheme, a
Commonwealth Development Corporation project, and
both citrus fruits and rice are grown in the area for
export to South Africa. The large reservoir, the Sand
River Dam at Tshaneni, has increased by 12, 000 acres
the land under irrigation.

TUBERCULOSIS. For many years this has been one of the
most serious health problems for Swaziland. In 1963
the World Health Organization set up a TB control unit,
headquartered in Manzini, and the disease is now under
control, if not yet eliminated.

TWALA, REGINA D. An early and active member of the
Swaziland Progressive Party (SPP), she was a member
of the executive committee in 1963. She voted to ex-
pel Dr. Ambrose Zwane when he presented a leadership
challenge to J. J. Nquku. She later joined Zwane's
Ngwane National Liberatory Congress, however, and
was one of its unsuccessful candidates for the Legislative Council in 1964.

-U-

UBOMBO RANCHES, LTD. A principal sugar-producing firm
in Swaziland, it is registered there but controlled by
South African and British interests. Conditions for
workers had been comparatively poor and wages low in
1963 when a wing of the SPP led by Dr. Ambrose Zwane
and Mr. Dumisa Dlamini led the workers in making de-

mands. When the demands were rejected and workers
dismissed, a very effective strike of 2, 500 workers at
Ubombo Ranches and several smaller estates eventually
forced the Government to act. The nine-day strike in
March, 1963, was free from violence but its success
perhaps inspired Swaziland's largest strike, at the Havelock Asbestos Mine, in May, 1963.

UKUGIDZA. Communal dancing accompanied by singing and
     hand-clapping. Solos may also be interspersed. The
     dancing is done primarily in place.

UKUQOMA. A custom practiced by Swazi Kings in the past
     that allowed the Ngwenyama the privilege of taking by
     force any unmarried girls he wanted. This was notably
     practiced by Mswati, whose harem was very large.

UMBELUZI RIVER. Variant spelling of Mbuluzi. Draining
     much of north-central Swaziland by means of its two
     main branches, the Black Umbeluzi and the White Um-
     beluzi, it leaves the country at Umbeluzipoort near
     Goba, Mozambique. From there it flows north and east
     a short distance to Delagoa Bay. Historically, the
     Swazi have begun their annual ritual, the Ncwala, only
     after sending designated men with sacred containers to
     carry water from the Umbeluzi (and three other sources)
     back to the royal village.

UMBANDINE. Variant spelling of Mbandzeni (q. v.).

UMBIKI. A newspaper published fortnightly in Siswati by the
     Swaziland Government Information Services.

UMHLABA. Arable lands, and by extension, the people who
     use the land. Sometimes it is used in place of the word
     live in the expression live laka Ngwane (q. v.), with the
     meaning of the expression becoming: the land of the
     place of Ngwane (q. v.).

UMHLANGA. The Reed Dance, an annual colorful ceremony
     held in June or July for a week. Not unlike a girl's
     camp, its goal is to encourage unmarried girls to co-
     operate in a work project under discipline. The maid-
     ens go to the Royal Village (currently Lobamba) from
     whence they leave in groups according to age to collect
     reeds for use in later repairs of the windbreaks around
     the home of the Queen Mother. They return a couple of

days later (they have been escorted by older women)
with a bundle of the longest and strongest reeds they
can find, sometimes fifteen feet long. They spend one
day preparing their hair and costumes for the Reed
Dance itself. The next two afternoons are spent dancing the unique and complex slow-motion dance, the
second day for the King and Queen Mother. This is
followed by singing and finally feasting.

UMLUNGU. The word for a white person or "European"
(q. v.) in the Siswati language.

UMNTFWANA. Variant spelling of Umtwana. Literally
"Child" (of the Nation), it is a title given to the newly
designated heir to the Swazi Kingship following the death
of an Ngwenyama. After a mourning period he lives in
his new capital with his mother, the Nabomntfwana, and
stays in communication with the Queen Regent until he
comes of age. He may neither rule "with power" nor
take the lead in national affairs until he is considered
old enough to marry his first recognized wife. He then
also loses the title Umntfwana and becomes Ngwenyama.

UMNUMZANA. A headman, the ruler of an umuti (q. v.).
While he may divide the umuti (homestead) into subsec-
tions, all are under his control. Ideally he will be
polygamous, but this is not possible most of the time.
The umnumzana usually tries to keep the umuti close to
other paternal kin. Upon his death, the main heir has
the duty to perpetuate his father's umuti.

UMPHAKATSI. The capital, that is to say, the section of
the umuti (homestead) where the "mother" of the headman lives. She is so important to the homestead that
if the real mother dies, a substitute is put in her place.
The indlunkulu (q. v.) is under her supervision. At the
national level, the umphakatsi is at the homestead controlled by the Queen Mother or Ndlovukazi. The annual
Ncwala takes place there.

UMSTAKATSI. Plural: Batsakatsi. An evildoer, especially
a witch or a sorcerer. These operate in the traditional
society as opposites to medicine men (tinyanga) and diviners (tangoma). Whether their evil be physiological
or just psychological in its effects, it is motivated by
fear, jealousy, hatred and similar causes. All death
and misfortune is attributed to batsakatsi. Sometimes,

of course, an umstakatsi will indeed be responsible for death, as in the case of the so-called "ritual murders" (q. v.).

UMTFWANENKOSI. Variant spelling of Mtfanenkosi (q. v.).

UMTILANE RIVER. A lesser tributary of the Little Usutu, it begins ten miles east of Mbabane and flows south through the fertile Umtilane Valley to its meeting point with the Little Usutu west of Matsapa.

UMUNTU (variant: MUNTFU). The word for "a person" in the Siswati language. Stillborn children and a child that dies within a couple of months of birth are not considered to be persons. Likewise the Swazi would not lament a child dying under the age of three months or so, when it would be taken to the cattle kraal for the ukalalatela rite. A child's father should not see it until this time, the time when it is actually considered to be a child.

UMUTI. A homestead or small village, under the control of an umnumzano (headman). These are found scattered throughout Swaziland depending on the availability of good grazing land, proximity of water, and arable land for gardens. The population of an umuti would generally be between seven and twenty-five in number, and usually more than a single biological family. The homestead usually has three key structures: the sibaya, the indlunkulu, and the lilawu. (See entries for each of these.)

UMVIKELI WABANTU NATIONAL MOVEMENT. A small group formed in 1967 just before the elections. It quickly became part of the Swaziland United Front (q. v.) and has continued to cooperate with it to the point of having little identification left other than its name. In mid-1971, Austin W. Nxumalo was identified as Secretary-General and Obed Mabuza as President of both groups, and by the March elections in 1972 there was little evidence of its continued independent existence.

UNALLOTTED LAND CONCESSION. A concession granted to John Thorburn (q. v.) and a Mr. Watkins on July 26, 1889, just a couple of months before King Mbandzeni's death. The concession was for fifty years with a right of renewal at a yearly rent of one hundred Rand. In

exchange they received farming and grazing rights over
the whole of the area of Swaziland south of the Komati
River for which grants had not previously been given.
It is said that this was about sixteen per cent of the
country. This concession was made while Allister Miller was adviser to Mbandzeni. Later, Miller joined
with his father-in-law Thorburn and became manager of
all their land. In the 1920's this concession was challenged in the courts by King Sobhuza, who failed ultimately at the level of the Privy Council in London in
1926.

UNALLOTTED MINERAL CONCESSION. A grant by King
Mbandzeni, in exchange for token annual payments, of
all mineral rights in the entire country which had not
been previously allocated. In addition, mineral rights
that had been held by others but had lapsed would re-
vert, not to the Swazi nation, but to the holder of this
concession. After the British assumed control, however, this concession was expropriated upon payment of
compensation to the holder; thus all lapsed mineral concessions reverted to the Crown.

UNION OF SOUTH AFRICA. Officially launched May 31,
1910, the country now known as the Republic of South
Africa (q. v.) used the term Union in its name because
it was a union of four previously distinct territories,
those now referred to as the Transvaal, the Orange
Free State, the Natal, and the Cape of Good Hope Provinces. The name was changed to the Republic of South
Africa under the Constitution Act of 1961 which wished
to accentuate the country's new condition as a republic,
free from any control by the British monarch.

UNITED KINGDOM, RELATIONS WITH. Throughout the middle part of the nineteenth century the Swazis, seeing the
British as the lesser of evils facing them, sought British protection against the Zulus and the Boers. Despite
the Convention of 1881 that ensured Swazi independence,
the British reversed themselves in the Convention of
1894 that allowed a Boer administration of Swaziland.
The end of the Boer War in 1903, however, gave responsibility for administration to British officials. Despite numerous controversies between the Swazis and
the British, especially over the question of land ownership, British administration of Swaziland through a High
Commissioner and Resident Commissioner continued for

decades.   Very little economic aid was given to Swaziland until after the Pim Report in 1932.   It was another
decade before significant assistance would arrive.   The
British decision to rid itself of colonies in the 1950's
brought major constitutional changes in the 1960's, re-
sulting eventually in independence for Swaziland in 1968.
After independence the Swazis continued participation in
the Commonwealth.   After a couple of years of helping
Swaziland balance its budget, British aid for recurring
expenses was no longer needed.   Capital improvement
aid has continued, however.   Over R12 million was
approved for the period from April, 1970 to April, 1973;
and almost R13 million for the next three years, especially for land purchase and developments.   In addition, the British buy almost £8 million of Swazi products each year, but export less than 10 per cent of
that to Swaziland.   British aid also goes to the Swazi
campus of the University of Botswana, Lesotho and
Swaziland.

UNITED NATIONS DEVELOPMENT PROGRAMME (UNDP).
A major source of aid to Swaziland, which had received
over two million dollars in aid by 1970 and now gets
over a million dollars a year from it.   It has been
active in irrigation and hydroelectric studies of the
major Swazi rivers, and has helped stimulate local industries especially through the Small Enterprises Development Company which it founded.   Swaziland joined
the United Nations shortly after independence.   Use of
R4 million of UNDP funds was approved in July, 1973.

UNITED NATIONS SPECIAL COMMITTEE ON COLONIALISM.
A United Nations committee which, after hearing testimony from political leaders of the High Commission
Territories (from Swaziland, J. J. Nquku), passed a
resolution on June 7, 1962, that recommended immediate action by Great Britain on independence for the
Territories.   It recommended that elections be held on
the basis of direct, universal, adult suffrage.   The
same committee was concerned three years later about
South Africa's increasing involvement in the political
and economic life of the Territories.

UNITED STATES, RELATIONS WITH.   A U. S. consul, Richard St. Francis Xavier Post, arrived in 1965, serving
the three High Commission Territories from Mbabane.
He was suceeded by Christopher Pappas in 1966, who

became chargé d'affaires at independence in 1968. Mr.
Charles Nelson was Ambassador to Botswana, Lesotho
and Swaziland, from 1971 until 1974 but resided in
Botswana. He was succeeded by Mr. David Bolen. In
1968 the United States arranged to send a forty-five
member Peace Corps team, mostly teachers and community action aides, but also including two lawyers and
a radio man. The U. S. has an A. I. D. branch there,
as well as the Office of the Southern African Regional
Activities Coordination. American financial aid has
assisted several projects and both surplus food and
some technical assistance have been provided, and more
of all forms of aid has been promised. Investment is
growing, with Holiday Inns International perhaps the
most obvious American company involved. The first
Swazi ambassador to the United States, Dr. Msindazwe
Sukati, was an important link in the relationship between the two countries.

UNITED SWAZILAND ASSOCIATION (USA). A political association formed by members of the European community
in Swaziland in 1963 as a counter-force to the African
nationalist parties. It would remain politically active
until 1967. While its leading force was Carl Todd and
other members of the European Advisory Council, Willie Meyer was elected its first chairman in 1964 and
Willie Van Rensburg its first secretary. From the beginning it cooperated with Swazi traditionalists, urging
a "50-50" division of legislative seats between those
two groups. Subsequent events forced them to accept
a different arrangement, but they successfully cam-
paigned for the four White seats in the 1964 Legislative
Council, defeating the Swaziland Independent Front.
Close cooperation with traditionalists continued, but soon
the Imbokodvo Party turned away from its previous position of support for the USA. In 1965 Imbokodvo rejected the continuance of reserved seats for Europeans
in future Parliaments. The USA was also unsuccessful
in its fight to extend voting rights of South African citizens in Swaziland past the December 31, 1965 deadline.
The position of the USA that Swazis and Europeans
should have separate representation yet cooperate with
each other reminded many people of South Africa's
Apartheid policy. It was also strongly opposed to all
African nationalist movements, depicting them as Com-
munist-inspired. The USA did not contest the 1967
elections.

UNIVERSITY OF BOTSWANA, LESOTHO AND SWAZILAND
(UBLS). Opened on April 8, 1945, as the University
College of Pius XII, it was run by Catholic missionaries
until it became the University of Basutoland, Bechuanaland and Swaziland under a British Royal Charter in
1963. Change to its present name came after the independence of Lesotho and Botswana in 1966. Located in
Roma, Lesotho, in the Maluti Mountains, it has attracted students from all over Africa and faculty from
around the world. In recent years it has also received
financial aid from the Government of Great Britain,
Canada, and the United States. Having emphasized education to suit the needs of the three African nations,
it has established branches in Botswana and Swaziland.
The latter's branch was temporarily at Luyengo, but a
new campus has been built at Kwaluseni. The University is the principal source of post-secondary education
for Swazis today.

URBAN AREA ADVISORY COMMITTEE. Committees in each
of six urban areas (Mbabane, Manzini, Goedgegun,
Hlatikulu, Pigg's Peak, and Stegi) which functioned under
the chairmanship of the District Commissioners. These
committees of five elected members (Europeans) and
government officials advised the District Commissioner
on the administration and welfare of the urban areas.
This was the extent of urban self-government until the
Town Management Proclamation of the mid-1960's.

USUSHWANE RIVER. Also called the Little Usutu River, it
rises in the Transvaal about 20 miles from Swaziland.
It passes a few miles south of Mbabane, loops north of
Lobamba and south of Matsapa before joining the Great
Usutu River south of Edwaleni. Its waters were the
first used to power the large Edwaleni Power Station ·
which produced the first hydro-electricity for Swaziland
in the mid-1960's.

USUTU FORESTS. Established in the central Highveld by the
Commonwealth Development Corporation which began
planting pines in 1950 on its 100, 000 acres in the area
near the town of Bunya.

USUTU PULP COMPANY. Established in 1959 by the Commonwealth Development Corporation and Courtould's
Ltd. , with the Swazi nation as a preference share-
holder, to exploit the CDC plantation. The mill at

Bunya produces more than 135, 000 metric tons of pulp
a year.   The first Swazi strike centering on trade union
organization occurred at the Pulp Company in 1962.   It
was a short strike but total, and achieved some of its
goals.

USUTU RIVER   see   GREAT USUTU RIVER.   See also
USUSHWANE RIVER (Little Usutu River).

-V-

VAN RENSBURG, WILLIE.   One of the original organizers of
the United Swaziland Association, he also became its
first secretary.   He was a member of the European Advisory Council at this time (1963).

VERMAAK, COENRAAD JOHANNES.   Recipient of the first
concession from the Swazis of which there is written
record.   He was granted the right by King Mswati II
to hunt and farm a 500, 000-acre ranch in southeastern
Swaziland.   He gave kukhonta (q. v.) to Mswati and in
turn was made chief over the area.   He also observed
Zulu impis in the area for Mswati and reported on them.

VERWOERD, DR. HENDRIK FRENSCH.   Prime Minister of
South Africa from 1958 until he was assassinated in
September, 1966.   Dr. Verwoerd offered both the car-
rot and the stick to the three High Commission Territories.   He promised them economic gain and (in September, 1963) quicker progress toward independence
than Great Britain would give if they would link with
South Africa under the Bantustan program (see TOM-
LINSON COMMISSION REPORT).   South Africa would
be their protector.   On the other hand, Dr. Verwoerd
saw to the establishment of rigid border controls to stop
South African refugees from using the Territories as
escape routes, and occasionally threatened to keep mi-
grant workers from the Territories from entering South
Africa.

VILAKAZI, JOSIAH   (variant spelling, JOSIAHA VILAKATI).
Secretary to Queen Mother Gwamile and a member of
the Deputation of 1907 (q. v.) to England.   While of
fairly humble parentage and not from one of the major
clans, he managed to get a good education and to im-
press the Queen Mother.   As a result he raised his

whole clan to greater importance.

"THE VOICE OF THE SWAZI"   see   IZWI LAMA SWAZI

VOLKSRAAD PROCLAMATION.   A proclamation of 1868 by
    the Volksraad (Parliament) of the South African Repub-
    lic which, among other things, declared as theirs a
    one-mile strip of land on each side of the Pongola-
    Maputo River, all the way to Delagoa Bay.   The British
    and Portuguese governments both protested, but the
    Boers and Portuguese signed a treaty showing the Lu-
    bombo Mountains as the border between the Republic
    and Mozambique, thus making Swaziland part of the Re-
    public.   The British would not allow implementation of
    this, but the future goals of the Republic were obvious.

VUVULANE.   A community three miles east of Mhlume in
    northeastern Swaziland.   There are over a hundred
    small farms there operated as part of the Vuvulane Ir-
    rigated Farms settlement scheme operated by the Com-
    monwealth Development Corporation.   Sugar is the prin-
    cipal crop but other cash crops are also grown there.
    In 1971 the settlement scheme sold R350,000 in sugar
    and R97,000 in other crops, double the value of crops
    marketed by Swazis in the rest of the country

-W-

WATERFORD-KAMHLABA SCHOOL.   Opened by a young
    Britisher, Michael Stern, in 1962, it is a private school
    open to boys of any race or religion.   It is a center
    for liberal and progressive education.   At its fifth an-
    niversary celebration, King Sobhuza added "Kamhlaba"
    to the original name, Waterford.   The addition means
    "The World."   Stern has been replaced as headmaster
    by Mr. Athol Jennings.

WATTS, REV. CHRISTOPHER.   An early missionary to Swa-
    ziland.   He came in 1907 and founded the first school
    for European children, in Mbabane, and later built a
    boarding school for Eurafrican children at Mpolonjeni,
    ten miles from Mbabane.   He also wrote a book, Dawn
    in Swaziland, published in 1922.

WAVERLEY.   Also: Red Hill.   A border town in Swaziland
    along the western border with South Africa.   It is on the

edge of the Usutu Forest. The road at the Waverley
border-crossing goes on to Johannesburg.

WELLS, BILL. The first European settler on the site of
    present-day Mbabane. An ex-artilleryman, he was
    called Bombardier Bill. Wells founded an inn and a
    store.

WENTZEL, ROSEMARY. An active member of the South
    African Liberal Party in the 1960's, she fled to Swazi-
    land, fearing arrest under the ninety-day detention pro-
    vision. She was given political asylum and worked as
    a government teacher. On August 10, 1964 she was
    kidnapped from her house and driven across the border.
    There she was released and picked up by South Africa
    security police. Despite widespread publicity, Great
    Britain did not take any action.

THE "WHITE COMMITTEE. " A committee of White conces-
    sion holders set up in 1887 to try to regularize the con-
    fusion among the Europeans in Swaziland. King Mband-
    zeni reluctantly allowed the Whites to meet on May 16,
    1887 and elect twenty-five men as a temporary com-
    mittee. This group organized a second meeting of
    Europeans on July 31, 1887. Five men were chosen to
    represent each of four segments: mineral concession-
    holders, storekeepers and residents, grazing-right
    holders, and the King. Allister Miller was chosen
    secretary and (sources disagree) either C. J. Swears
    or Capt. A. Ewing (q. v.) was selected chairman. The
    Committee, also called the Swaziland Government Com-
    mittee, was given a Charter of Rights by the King and
    allowed to deal with all conflicts between the Whites
    and provide them with a degree of self-government.
    However, all decisions of the Committee could be vetoed
    by Mbandzeni. Nevertheless, it was not successful in
    pleasing all the Europeans, and the Boers of the South
    African Republic especially failed to accept it. Finally,
    the committee, on July 29, 1889, voted to dissolve it-
    self and recommended that Swaziland be governed by the
    South African Republic. This led the British and Boers
    to appoint a Joint Commission (q. v.) to look into Swa-
    ziland's internal affairs.

WHITE UMBELUZI RIVER. The southern one of the two
    main branches of the Umbeluzi River. It rises about
    seven miles north of Matsapa in central Swaziland, and

flows northeast where it is joined by the Msulatane.
They both join the Black Umbeluzi fifteen miles west
of the Mozambique border.

WHITSON REPORT.   The report delivered to Her Majesty's
Commissioner in March, 1964 by Mr. H. A. Whitson
after he conducted a commission of inquiry into the
wage and employment situation in Swaziland.   The inquiry was motivated by the strikes and labor disturbances of 1962 and 1963.   The Report recommended immediate action on both wages and working conditions,
but recommended that no general minimum wage be set.
Wage councils were recommended for certain industries
and it stressed the desirability of the formation of
trade-unions.

WILKINSON, BISHOP THOMAS.   The first Anglican Bishop
of Zululand, he visited the Swazi Ndlovukazi Thandile in
1871.   He was finally allowed by the Swazis to form
two missions, one near the present road from Ermelo
to Swaziland, the other near Piet Retief.

WILLIAM PITCHER COLLEGE.   The government's teacher
training college, providing free education to those selected for admission.   Called the Swaziland Teacher
Training College until 1963, it was renamed in memory
of a former Director of Education.   It is now affiliated
with the University of Botswana, Lesotho and Swaziland,
and its graduates are awarded a University Diploma.

WINN, E. G.   A South African citizen but an active member
of the United Swaziland Association, he successfully ran
for election to the Legislative Council in 1964 on the
USA ticket.   In 1960, he had participated by British in-
vitation in Swaziland constitutional talks.   In 1966 he
was again appointed to the constitutional committee, this
time as a representative of the USA in the Legislative
Council.

WINTON, SIR FRANCIS DE.   Chairman of the Joint Commission (q. v.) set up by Great Britain and the South African
Republic in 1889 to investigate Swaziland internal affairs
with the intention of reconciling demands of the White
settlers with Swazi interests.   Sir Francis, the principal British representative, seemed particularly convinced that the concessions by the Swazi King were le-
gitimate, and that the concession holders were not mere

"adventurers. " He was also struck by the extent of
control by the Transvaal Government through concessions from Mbandzeni.   (See PROVISIONAL GOVERN-
MENT.)

WITWATERSRAND UNIVERSITY.   Founded in Johannesburg in
1922, it has been one of the most liberal universities
politically and in the realm of ideas in all of South
Africa.   Dr. Ambrose Zwane and Dr. Allen Nxumalo
are just two of the Swazis who received some of their
education at "The Wit. "

WOLSELEY, SIR GARNET. An administrator and a military
reformer, he was given leadership positions in Canada,
West Africa, Natal (1875) and Cyprus, before returning
to South Africa in 1879.   Ending the Zulu War, he became Governor of Natal.   He sent troops against the
Bapedi and solicited the aid of Swazi troops against
Sekhukhune.   The valor and strength of the Swazis in
capturing Sekhukhune persuaded Wolseley to give most
of the captured cattle to King Mbandzeni.   Wolseley had
also promised that, if the battle was successful, the
British would insure the independence of the Swazis
forever.   The Swazis reminded the British of this periodically in the twentieth century.   As Administrator of
the Transvaal, Wolseley also set up the commission
which set the boundaries between Transvaal and Swazi
territory.

WOOD, SIR H. EVELYN.   British soldier born February 9,
1838, in Essex.   He served in Africa in Ashanti and in
the Zulu War, as well as in the Boer War from 1897
to 1901.   Wood fought Sekhukhune and the Bapedi from
1877 to 1881 and, under Wolseley, secured the aid of
the Swazis in 1879.   In early September, 1881, Wood,
as Deputy High Commissioner, went to Swaziland to
thank the Swazis, to explain the (Pretoria) Convention
of 1881, and to assure King Mbandzeni of the friendship
of the British Government and the guarantee of Swazi
independence.   Wood (called Lukhuni by the Swazis) died
on December 21, 1919.

WYLDSDALE.   An area in the extreme northwestern part of
Swaziland that had been the site of the old Wyldsdale
Gold Mine.   Re-examination in recent years indicated
that the mine could be reopened.

-Z-

ZIDZE   see   ZWIDE

ZIHLATHI, NDLOVUKAZI.   A cousin of King Sobhuza II and
    one of his senior wives until the death of Ndlovukazi
    Nukwase in 1956.   Zihlathi was then chosen to be Ndlo-
    vukazi, being also of the Ndwandwe clan, as were her
    two predecessors.

ZIONISM.   The largest religious denomination in Swaziland
    aside from those Swazis holding traditional beliefs.   Of
    73,000 Christian adults in 1962, 29,000 were Zionists.
    Claiming prophetic gifts and divinatory powers, the
    leaders of this Church have provided a link between
    traditional acceptance of healers and Christianity.   There
    are at least ten main branches of Zionism in Swaziland.
    The Church originated in Zion City, Illinois.

ZOMBODZE.   Variant spelling of Zombode.   The name of the
    tribal capital founded by King Ngwane III in the mid-
    eighteenth century.   The Ncwala ceremony was held
    there during his reign.   King Bhunu's capital was also
    called Zombodze and is located about five miles due
    east of the present capital at Lobamba.   As a recent
    capital it continues to have some ceremonial and admin-
    istrative significance.   It is also the site of a national
    school.

ZOMBODZE NATIONAL SCHOOL (variant: ZOMBODE
    SCHOOL).   A school built near the former capital at
    Zombodze on the initiative of Queen Regent Labotsibeni.
    It was for the purpose of educating the future king,
    Sobhuza II, away from the denominational conflicts of
    mission schools.   In part, the Swazi National Fund was
    created to collect money for it.   Eventually the young
    Sobhuza did receive his primary education there, as
    have many young Swazis since him.

ZULU.   Nguni peoples who are southern neighbors of the
    Swazis.   The languages and customs of the Zulus and
    Swazis have much in common.   While the two peoples
    did not live in perfect peace, the Swazis stayed out of the
    way of the Zulus for the most part and were not as
    affected by them as other southern African peoples were.
    Swazi relations with Kings Chaka and Dingane were not
    generally hostile.   The 1850's, however, saw a series

of Zulu raids encouraged by their chief Mpande, with
the worst being the Battle of Lubuya. Swazi King
Mswati persuaded Sir Theophilus Shepstone to intervene,
however, and the Zulu raids stopped.

ZULWINI (variant: EZULWINI). A village founded by King
Sobhuza I somewhere in the area between the Mbabane
and Lushushwana Rivers. The senior indvuna at the
time was Nyezi Nkambule.

ZWANE, DR. AMBROSE PHESHEYA. Perhaps the most pub-
licized Swazi politician of the last fifteen years, although not the most successful by usual standards.
Struggling against the forces of traditionalism, he has
made significant inroads. Born in 1922 in Manzini, son
of a noted Swazi counsellor, Amos Mdolomba Zwane
(q. v.), he was educated in Swazi mission schools and a
high school in Zululand. He studied medicine at Fort
Hare College for one year, and then went to Witwatersrand University to complete his studies. He became
the first Swazi doctor when he graduated in 1951. After
an internship in Zululand he was a Swaziland Government Medical Officer for seven years before resigning
in 1960 to enter politics. On July 30, 1960, he became
Secretary-General of J. J. Nquku's Swaziland Progressive Party. Appointed to the Constitutional Committee
in 1960 by the Ngwenyama, one of three members of the
SPP appointed, he came into conflict there with the traditionalists. When Nquku was expelled from the committee, Dr. Zwane and Obed Mabuza resigned. An
active speaker and traveller to Pan-African meetings,
Zwane came into personal conflict, finally, with Nquku,
and the SPP split. A special conference on February
24, 1962 chose Zwane as President (but Nquku continued
as President of his part of the SPP). In April, 1963,
he renamed his party the Ngwane National Liberatory
Congress (NNLC). The NNLC gained recognition when
Zwane and his Secretary-General, Clement Dumisa
Dlamini, actively took the side of the workers in the
1963 strikes that hit Swaziland. They were especially
active at the Ubombo Ranches and the Usutu Pulp Mill.
The party's platform was independence now!, one man-
one vote, minimal role for chiefs, African Socialism,
and Pan-African Unity. Despite visits to both Moscow
and Peking, Zwane (a Roman Catholic) denies that he
could ever be a Communist. Conflict with traditionalists continued as Zwane was not allowed to participate

in the 1963 Constitutional talks.   A series of legal problems and court cases distracted Dr. Zwane in the
period preceding the 1964 elections.   NNLC candidates
did better than parties other than Imbokodvo but were
still beaten by more than four to one in each constituency.   Zwane received 2, 438 votes.   The growing
strength of Imbokodvo and defections from the NNLC
(especially Dumisa Dlamini in 1966) hindered Zwane's
political efforts for several years.   His main issue was
opposition to the electoral system that required three-
man constituencies.   Feeble attempts to unite the various opposition parties failed, as did Dr. Zwane and the
NNLC candidates in the 1967 elections.   His total of
3, 035 votes was more than doubled by his Imbokodvo
opposition.   In February, 1968, Dr. Zwane and his
Secretary-General, K. T. Samketi, gained considerable
attention in London when they delayed the final Independence talks at Marlborough House by blocking the
steps with their prostrate bodies.   Police carried them
away. ·Since Independence, Dr. Zwane has met with
both success and failure.   A group led by Samketi broke
away from the NNLC in 1971 but had minimal electoral
success.   The 1972 elections, on the other hand, resulted in Dr. Zwane and two other NNLC members
winning seats in Parliament from the Mpumalanga constituency, receiving over 4, 500 votes, thus defeating
the Imbokodvo candidates by less than one hundred votes.
When seated in Parliament, however, Dr. Zwane's
vocal opposition aroused government anger and retalia-
tion.   His election victory was the indirect cause of the
scrapping of Parliament and the Independence Constitution.   Dr. Zwane was under several periods of detention
in 1973 and 1974, accused by the government of holding
illegal political meetings.

ZWANE, AMOS MDOLOMBA.   A counselor to the young King
Sobhuza II and a member of the Swazi delegation led by
Sobhuza that arrived in England in January, 1923 to
protest the earlier partition of the land of the Swazis.
His son, Dr. Ambrose P. Zwane (q. v.), became a ma-
jor political party leader in Swaziland.

ZWANE, MSHUDULWANE.   Indvuna lenkulu (great councillor)
of the royal capital at Lobamba in the 1930's.

ZWANE, SANDLANE (variant spellings: SANDLANA, SAND-
HLAND).   An important warrior and official, serving

several kings from Mswati to Mbandzeni. He led an
army during the reign of King Mswati when it became
necessary to intervene in a succession crisis involving
Soshangane (q. v.) in 1845.   Zwane was senior indvuna
at the royal village of Ludzidzini, residence of the
Queen Mother. In a special ceremony in June, 1875,
he installed the youth Mbandzeni after the death of King
Ludvonga II and served as his advisor along with Thandile (q. v.) during the next few extremely important
years for Swaziland.   Zwane signed as a witness most
of the land and mineral concessions of this time.   He
argued before the "White Committee" (q. v.), however,
that Swazi grazing rights persisted, thereby acknowl-
edging that all concessions were "limited" ones.   Zwane
was considered to be Prime Minister by some of the
whites, and appeared to be well-liked by most people.
A fair judge in the Swazi courts, he had a remarkable
memory for past cases as well as current facts.   One
writer called him "the grand old man of Swaziland. "
This popularity eventually did him in, however, as
Mbandzeni seemed to be jealous.   Other Swazis convinced the young King that Zwane was supporting a rival
for the throne, the King's half-brother, Kopolo.   When
the King became ill, he instructed Tikhuba Magongo
(q. v.) to seek out the reason.   Zwane was "smelled
out" and eventually killed in 1888.

ZWANE, TIMOTHY.   Permanent Secretary of Swaziland's
    important Ministry of Industry, Mines, and Tourism.
    While a student at Pius XII College in Basutoland in
    1960, he formed and became president of The Swaziland
    Student Union (q. v.).   This organization of secondary
    and college students took a stand on constitutional is-
    sues that was very close to that of the Swaziland Pro-
    gressive Party.   Not related to Dr. Ambrose Zwane,
    he nevertheless participated in some of the demonstra-
    tions in Mbabane.   He later got a degree from the
    American University in Washington; eventually, he re-
    turned to Swaziland and entered government service.
    In July, 1973 he was given additional duties as Ambas-
    sador to the European Economic Community, stationed
    in Belgium.

ZWIDE (also: ZIDZE).   The chief of the Ndwandwe people
    in the early nineteenth century.   Strong militarily,
    Zwide was able to challenge King Sobhuza I in a dispute
    over maize fields near the Pongola River.   Sobhuza,

threatened by Zwide with invasion, backed off. Nevertheless, Sobhuza's settlement and also his residence at Shiselweni were attacked and burned by Zwide and his men. Zwide later agreed to Sobhuza's request for one of his daughters for his bride and to be mother of his heir. The choice was Thandile, later as Ndlovukazi to be called Lazidze. Zwide said that the marriage would not prevent him from attacking Sobhuza in the future, if he wished. A year later, however, Zwide was attacked and killed by the Zulu king Chaka.

BIBLIOGRAPHY

BIBLIOGRAPHY: TABLE OF CONTENTS

INTRODUCTION

Apart from official government publications, one does not find a great abundance of books dealing solely with Swaziland. As one of Africa's smaller units, it has never attracted the attention that countries like Nigeria, Ghana, Kenya, the Congo (now Zaïre) and the Republic of South Africa have attracted. A few of the better books are shared with the other former High Commission Territories, Botswana and Lesotho. Of course, there are a number of works dealing with Southern Africa in general or parts of South Africa that include Swaziland to one or another degree.

Nevertheless, if the average reader wishes guidance to the principal works on Swaziland, the following recommendations can be made. Daily life in Swaziland before extensive European contact has been described in detail by Hilda Kuper in The Swazi: A South African Kingdom, and by Brian Marwick in The Swazi. The best general history of Swaziland up to independence in 1968 is J. S. Matsebula's A History of Swaziland. A general history and evaluation of the administration of the country while under British rule can be found in Lord Hailey's Native Administration in the British African Territories. Part V. The High Commission Territories. More modern political activities up to the mid-1960's are covered in R. P. Stevens' Lesotho, Botswana, and Swaziland, and Jack Halpern's South Africa's Hostages. These last three deal with all three High Commission Territories. The best work being done in recent years on Swaziland is the product of Christian Potholm, a young American scholar. His work, Swaziland, The Dynamics of Political Modernization, concentrates on Swaziland from post-World War II to 1972. The area of economics is well handled by T. J. D. Fair, G. Murdoch, and H. M. Jones in Development in Swaziland. International relations in southern Africa in general is covered well by Ronald Hyam in The Failure of South African Expansion, 1908-1948, Lord Hailey in The Republic of South Africa and the High Commission Territories, and Kenneth Grundy in Confrontation and Accomodation in Southern Africa: The Limits of Independence. Two very general books along

198

the travel guidebook or general information line are A Hand-
book to the Kingdom of Swaziland, published by the Swaziland
Government Information Service, and Bruce Andrews' The
Guide to Swaziland. Bibliographies of interest are John B.
Webster and Paulus Mohome, A Bibliography of Swaziland,
J. W. Arnheim's Swaziland: a Bibliography, and the exten-
sive bibliography at the end of the Potholm book cited above.
It is hoped, however, that the bibliography that follows this
introduction will be considered more complete than any here-
tofore assembled.

Aside from the above books, a brief word about articles is in order. An adequate and highly pictorial article
by Volkmar Wentzel can be found in National Geographic,
August, 1969. Additionally, any of the articles by Potholm,
especially those in Africa Report and the Journal of Modern
African Studies can be recommended. A recent article on
the current constitutional transition by Harry Mashabela in
Africa Report is also good. There are few newspaper
sources available, but The Times of Swaziland is in English
and fairly reliable in its reporting. Its letters to the editor
have frequently allowed the opposition to have a forum it
would not otherwise have.

1. GENERAL

Travel and Description

Alston, Madeline. From the Heart of the Veld. London:
J. Lane, 1916.

_____. "A Vacation in Swaziland," African Monthly, Vol.
4 (September 1908): pp. 327-337.

Bulpin, Thomas Victor. Lost Trails on the Low Veld. Cape
Town: H. B. Timmins; London: Hodder and Stough-
ton, 1950.

_____. Storm over the Transvaal. Capetown: Standard
Press, 1955.

_____. The White Whirlwind. Johannesburg: H. F. G.
Witherby, 1938.

Cooke, J. "Mountains of North Swaziland," South African
Mountain Club, No. 31 (1928): pp. 7-34.

Creswicke, Louis. South Africa and the Transvaal. Edin-
     burgh: T. C. and E. C. Jack, 1900.

Fife, D. "Tour of Swaziland," Lantern 2 (October 1952): pp.
     157-159.

Filmer, Harry J. and Jameson, Patricia. Usutu! A Story
     about the Early Days of Swaziland. Johannesburg:
     Central News Agency, 1960.

Griffithes, T. P. From Bedford Row To Swazieland. Lon-
     don: Bradbury, Agnew, 1890.

Hendy, H. R. Swaziland: The Tourist's Paradise. Durban:
     John Ramsey, 1953.

Herd, Norman. "This is Swaziland," Swaziland Recorder,
     No. 1 (January-March 1961): pp. 7-10.

Lee, A. W. Bishop. Once Dark Country. London: S. P. C. K.,
     1949.

Miller, Allister Mitchell (A. M.). Swaziland. Mendelson, 1900.

_____. Swaziland: The California of South Africa. Johan-
     nesburg: Argus Publishing Company, 1970.

_____. Swaziland: The Land of Green Pastures and Run-
     ning Streams. Johannesburg: 1936.

Nelson, Ivar. "Swaziland," in Philip M. Allen and Aaron
     Segal (eds.) The Traveler's Africa. New York: Hop-
     kinson and Blake, 1973.

O'Neil, Owen Rowe. Adventures in Swaziland. The Adven-
     tures of a South African Boer. New York: Century, 1921.

Schoeman, Pieter Johannes. Mboza die Swazi, en ander
     verhale. Bloemfontein: Nasionale Pers, bpk., 1939.

Scutt, Joan Frances. African Hands. London: Edinburgh
     House Press, 1961.

_____. This is Our Life in Swaziland. London: Edin-
     burgh House Press, 1962.

Spurdens, Constance. Sunshine in Swaziland. Reminiscences

of Africa. Saltburn, England: J. Parks, 1930.

Watt, C. J. "Swaziland, " Travel in Africa, 1 (March 1952):
    pp. 25-26.

Wentzel, Volkmar. "Swaziland Tries Independence, " National
    Geographic, Vol. 136, No. 2 (August, 1969): pp. 266-
    293.

General Information

Agar-Hamilton, J. A. I. "The South African Protectorates,"
    Journal of the African Society, Vol. 29 (1929-1930):
    pp. 12-26.

Ashton, H. "The High Commission Territories, " Race Rela-
    tions Handbook. London: Oxford University Press,
    1949.

Barker, Dudley. Swaziland. London: Her Majesty's Station-
    ery Office, 1965.

Challis, Rev. W. A. "Swaziland from Within, " The East and
    West, Vol. VI No. 23 (July, 1908): p. 312.

Coertze, P. J. "Volkerkundige Studies in Swaziland, "
    Tydskrif van Wetenskap en Kuns (Bloemfontein), Vol.
    9 (1930-1931): pp. 10-20.

Coryndon, R. T. "Swaziland, " Journal of the African Soci-
    ety, Vol. 14 (1915): pp. 250-265.

Gordon, W. R. "Swaziland, " Contemporary 177 (February,
    1950): pp. 91-94.

Gray, Alan. "Three 'Islands' in South Africa, " New Com-
    monwealth (London), Vol. 39, No. 7 (July 1961): pp.
    431-435.

Greaves, Lionel Bruce. The High Commission Territories.
    London: Edinburgh House Press, 1953.

_____ . The High Commission Territories. London:
    British Information Service, 1963.

Hailey, Lord. An African Survey. (Revised 1956) London:

Oxford University Press, 1957.

Hancock, W. K. A Survey of British Commonwealth Affairs. London: Oxford University Press, 1963.

Hendy, H. R. Swaziland, South Africa. Mbabane: Swaziland Chamber of Commerce and Industries, 1953.

Houlton, John. "The High Commission Territories in South Africa, " Geographical Magazine, 26 (August 1953): pp. 175-181.

Lystad, Robert A. "Research Opportunities in the Social Sciences and Humanities in Sudan, Ethiopia, South Africa, Lesotho, and Swaziland, " African Studies Bulletin, Vol. 12, No. 2 (September 1969): pp. 111-129.

Miller, Allister Mitchell (A. M.). "Swaziland, " Transactions of the Royal Colonial Institute, Vol. 31 (1899-1900): pp. 274-304.

_____. Swaziland. London: Weightman and Company, 1934.

Munger, Edwin S. "Swaziland: The Tribe and the Country, " American Universities Field Staff Reports Service, Vol. 10, No. 2 (1962).

"1965 Swaziland, das kleinste aber reichste Territorium Afrikas, " Aussenhandeldienst (Frankfurt/M): 14. Jahrg. , Nr. 22 (August 1965): ss. 2-5.

Nxumalo, Simon. "Swaziland, " Optima, (September 1969): pp. 149-156.

Orchard, Ronald. The High Commission Territories of South Africa. London: World Dominion Press, 1951.

Pott, Douglas. "The Story of the Swaziland Protectorate, " Race Relations Journal (Johannesburg): Vol. 18, (1951): pp. 125-165.

_____. Swaziland: A General Survey (revised). Johannesburg: South African Institute of Race Relations, 1955.

Rawlins, R. "Swaziland, " Corona, Vol. 17, No. 2 (February 1955): pp. 63-66.

Schoeman, Pieter Johannes. "Volkekundige Navorsing onder
    die Swazis, " Annale van die Universiteit van Stellen-
    bosch (Cape Town): Vol. 9, No. 3 (April 1931): p. 23.

"Swaziland-1968. " Internationales Afrikaforum (München):
    Jahr. 4, Nr. 11 (November 1968): ss. 612-614.

"Swaziland, " Libertas, Vol. 6, No. 1 (December 1945): pp.
    36-37.

"Swaziland: Poor, Little, and Rich, " Africa Confidential,
    No. 21 (October 25, 1968): pp. 6-8.

"Swaziland: a symposium, " Africa Institute Bulletin 6 (8)
    (September 1968), pp. 227-276.

Guides and Annual Reports

Andrews, Bruce. The Guide to Swaziland. Johannesburg
    and Mbabane: Winchester Press, 1970.

British Information Service. The High Commission Terri-
    tories. London: Central Office of Information, 1963.

Great Britain, Government of. Colonial Office. Swaziland.
    London: Her Majesty's Stationery Office, 1946, 1947,
    1948, 1949, 1950, 1951, 1952, 1953.

_____ . Swaziland. Her Majesty's Stationery Office, 1954,
    1955, 1956, 1957, 1961, 1962, 1963, 1964, 1965,
    1966, 1967, 1968.

Gunther, J. Inside Africa. London: Hamish Hamilton, Ltd. ,
    1965.

A Handbook to the Kingdom of Swaziland. Swaziland Govern-
    ment Information Services, Flamingo Paper Ltd. , 1968.

South Africa, Government of. Official Yearbook of the Union
    and of Basutoland, Bechuanaland Protectorate, and
    Swaziland. Pretoria: Office of Census and Statistics,
    1919-1934.

Statistical Abstracts

Jones, H. M.   Report on the 1966 Swaziland Population Census. Mbabane: Government Printer, 1968.

Swaziland, Government of.   Census of Swaziland, 1956. Mbabane: Government Printer, 1958.

Bibliographies

Arnheim, Johanna.   Swaziland: A Bibliography (reprint of 1950 Edition).   Cape Town: School of Librarianship, 1963.

Balima, Mildred (compiler).   Botswana, Lesotho, and Swaziland: A Guide to Official Publications 1868-1968. Washington: Library of Congress (U. S. Government Printing Office), 1971.

Dale, Richard.   "Southern Africa: Research Frontiers in Political Science, " in Christian Potholm and Richard Dale (eds.), Southern Africa in Perspective.   New York: The Free Press, 1972.

Garson, Noel George.   "The Swaziland Question and a Road to the Sea 1887-1895. "   Archives Yearbook for South African History, 1957: Part 2, pp. 263-434.

Gusinde, Martin.   Von Gelben und schwarzen Buschmannern: eine untergehende Altkultur in Suden Afrikas (English Summary).   Graz: Akad. Druk-u. Verlagsanstalt, 1966.

Holleman, J F. , (ed.).   Experiment in Swaziland: Report of the Swaziland Sample Survey, 1960.   Cape Town: Oxford University Press, 1964.

Musiker, Ruben.   Guide to South African Reference Books. Cape Town: A. A. Balkema, 1965.

Myburgh, A. C.   The Tribes of Barberton District.   Pretoria: Government Printer, 1949.

Potholm, Christian P.   Swaziland: The Dynamics of Political Modernization.   Berkeley: University of California Press, 1972.

Wallace, Charles Stewart.   Swaziland, A Bibliography.   Uni-

versity of the Witwatersrand, Department of Bibliography, Librarianship and Typography, 1967.

Webster, John B. and Paulus Mohome. A Bibliography of
Swaziland. (Occasional Bibliography No. 10). Syra-
cuse University Maxwell School of Citizenship and
Public Affairs, Program of Eastern African Studies,
Bibliographic Section, 1968.

2. CULTURAL

Archeology

Hamilton, C. N. G. "Ancient Workings in Swaziland, "
South African Archeological Bulletin, Vol. 16, No. 64
(December 1961): pp. 128-133.

Masson, J. R. "Rock-Paintings in Swaziland, " South African
Archeological Bulletin, Vol. 16, No. 64 (December
1961): pp. 128-133.

Fine Arts

African Music Society. "The Music of the Swazis, " African
Music Society Newsletter (Johannesburg), Vol. 1. No.
5 (June 1952): p. 14.

Harding, J. R. "A Note on the Conus Shell Disc Ornament
in Swaziland, " Man, Vol. 64, No. 222 (November-
December 1964): pp. 185-186.

Huskisson, Yvonne. A Survey of Musical Practices of a
Swazi Tribe. Pretoria: National Council for Social
Research, 1960.

Literature

Kuper, Hilda. Bite of Hunger. New York: Harcourt, Brace,
and World, 1965.

_____. A Witch in My Heart. London: Oxford University
Press, 1970.

Miller, Allister Mitchell. Mamisa: The Swazi Warrior.

Pietermaritzburg: Shuter and Shooter, 1933, 1952, 1953, 1954, 1955; edition in Siswati: 1960.

Savory, Phyllis. Swazi Fireside Folktales. Cape Town: Howard Timmins, 1973.

Linguistics

Lanham, L. W. "The Proliferation and Extension of Bantu Phonemic Systems Influenced by Bushman and Hottentot," Proceedings, Ninth Annual Congress of Linguistics, 1962, Cambridge, Mass.: pp. 382-391.

Lanham, L. W., and D. P. Hallowes. "Linguistic Relationships and Contracts Expressed in the Vocabulary of the Eastern Bushman," African Studies, Vol. 15, No. 1 (1956): pp. 45-48.

Letele, G. L. "A Preliminary Study of the Lexicological Influence of the Nguni Languages on Southern Sotho." Communications from the School of African Studies, Univ. of Cape Town, Series 2, No. 12, March 1945.

Louw, J. A. "The Development of the Bantu Languages in South Africa," Africa Institute Bulletin, Vol. 3, No. 5 (June 1963): pp. 133-141.

_____. "The Nomenclature of Cattle in South Eastern Bantu Languages," Communications of the University of South Africa, C2, (1957).

Van Warmelo, N. J. "Kinship Terminology of the South African Bantu," Union of South Africa, Department of Native Affairs. Ethnological Publications, No. 2.

_____. "Language Map of South Africa," Union of South Africa. Department of Native Affairs. Ethnological Publications, No. 27.

Werner, A. "Note on Clicks in the Bantu Languages," Journal of African Society, Vol. 2 (1902-1903): pp. 416-421; editorial note, pp. 422-424; and Vol. 4 (1904-1905): pp. 142-143.

Ziervogel, D. A Grammar of Swazi (SiSwati). Johannesburg: Witwatersrand University Press, 1952.

_____ . Swazi-gebruike anaaf geboorte tot Huwelik (Texte
met vertaling en koort grammatiese inleiding).   Pretoria University: Department of Bantu Studies. 1944.

_____ . Swazi Texts with an English Translation, Notes,
and a Glossary of Swazi Terms. Pretoria: J. L.
Van Schaik, 1957.

3. SCIENTIFIC

Geography

Best, Alan C. G.   The Swaziland Railway: A Study in Polit-
ico-Economic Geography.   East Lansing, Michigan:
Michigan State University, African Studies Center, 1966.

Brooks, Charles. "On the Banks of the Great Usutu River,"
Swaziland Reporter, No. 2 (March-June 1961): p. 19.

Daniel, John Benjamin McIntyre.   The Geography of the Rural
Economy of Swaziland.   Durban: Institute for Social
Research, University of Natal, 1962.

DeBlij, Harm Jan.   "The Concept of the Physiographic Province Applied to Swaziland, " Tydskrif vir aardryks-
kunde-Journal of Geography, Vol. 1, No. 7 (September 1960): pp. 7-20.

_____ . A Geography of Southern Africa.   Chicago: Rand
McNally, 1964.

_____ . "A Note on the Relationship Between the Swaziland Low Veld and Adjoining Areas, " Transactions
and Proceedings of the Geological Society, South Africa.
Vol. 63, (1960): pp. 175-187.

Doveton, Dorothy M.   "The Economic Geography of Swaziland, " The Geographical Journal (London): Vol. 88
(1936): pp. 322-331.

_____ . The Human Geography of Swaziland.   London:
George Philip and Son, 1937.

Nquku, J. J.   Geography of Swaziland.   Bremersdorp, Swaziland: Servite Fathers, 1936.

A Soil and Irrigability Survey of the Lower Usutu Basin
    (South) in Swaziland Low Veld. London: H. M. S. O.,
    1965. (Department of Technical Co-operation Over-
    seas Research Publication No. 3.)

Geology

Allsopp, H. L., H. R. Roberts, G. D. L. Schreiner and
    D. R. Hunter. "Rb-Sr Age measurements on Various
    Swaziland Granites. " Journal Geophysical Research,
    Vol. 67, No. 13 (1962).

Bursill, C., J. F. M. Luyt, and J. G. Urie. "The Bomvu
    Ridge Iron Ore Deposit, " Transactions of Geological
    Society of South Africa, 1964.

Clark, W. M. "Swaziland Mineral Deposits, " South African
    Mine Engineers Journal, No. 74 (November 15, 1963):
    p. 323.

Dart, R. A. ."The Multimillenial Prehistory of Ochre Min-
    ing, " Nsda 9 (5) (1968): pp. 7-13.

Dart, R. A. and P. B. Beaumont. "Ratification and Retro-
    cession of Earlier Swaziland Iron Ore Mining Radio
    Carbon Datings, " South African Journal of Science 64
    (6) (juin 1968): pp. 241-246.

Davies, D. N. "The Intrusion of the Jamestown Igneous
    Complex in Swaziland, " Compte Rendu XXth Interna-
    tional Geological Congress. Mexico City: 1956.

_____. "The Sedimentation Features of the Karroo Sys-
    tem in Swaziland, " Proceedings of CCTA Southern
    Regional Committee on Geology. Pretoria: 1961.

_____. "The Tin Deposits of Swaziland, " Transactions
    of Geological Society of South Africa, 1964.

Davies, D. N. and D. R. Hunter. "The Gold 'Deposits of
    the Barberton Mountainland in Swaziland, " Transac-
    tions of Geological Society of South Africa, 1964.

Davies, D. N. and J. G. Urie. The Bomvu Ridge Hematite
    Deposits. Mbabane: Government Printer, 1956.

Herd, Norman. "Modern Techniques Revive Hope in New Gold Deposits, " Swaziland Reporter, No. 10 (March-June 1963): pp. 15-19.

_____. "Swaziland's Mineral Projects Must Be Regarded as Bright, " South African Mining Engineering Journal 74 (February 8, 1963): pp. 307-308.

Holz, P. "Swaziland Iron Projects Develop, " Mining Magazine, Vol. 108 (May 1963): pp. 268-270.

Hunter, D. R. "Geology, Petrology and Classification of the Swaziland Granites and Gnoisses, " Transactions of the Geological Society of South Africa (Johannesburg). Vol. 40, (1957): pp. 85-125.

_____. The Mineral Resources of Swaziland. Mbabane: High Commission Printing and Publishing Co. , 1962. (Geological Survey and Mines Department, Swaziland, Bulletin No. 3.)

_____. "Occurrence of Chrysotile Asbestos Usushwana Valley, Mbabane District Swaziland, " Geological Magazine, Vol. 19 (July 1953): pp. 241-247.

_____. "The Petrochemistry of Some Swaziland Granites, " Compte Rendu XXth International Geological Congress. Mexico City: 1956.

_____. "The Swaziland Geological Survey and Mineral Exploration, " Commission de coopération technique en Afrique au sud du Sahara. Comité regional du sud pour la geologie. London: Publication No. 80, pp. 39-45.

Hunter, D. R. , and J. G. Urie. "The Origin of Kaolin Deposits, Mahlangatsha Mountains, Swaziland, " Economic Geology, (1966): pp. 1104-1114.

_____ and _____. "Some Problems of Stormberg Volcanicity, " Proceedings of CCTA Southern Regional Committee on Geology. Leopoldville: 1958.

"Iron Ore: New Sources, New Patterns, " Economist, Vol. 213 (November 14, 1964): p. 742.

Jones, T. Rupert. "The Great Glacial Moraine of Permian

Age in South Africa, " Natural Science, Vol. 14
    (1899): pp. 199-202.

_____ . "Notes on the Geology of West Swaziland, South
    Africa, " Geological Magazine, Vol. 6 (1899): pp. 105-
    111.

Lenz, C. J. "The Sub-Karroo and Post Cretaceous Surfaces
    of Eastern Swaziland, " Compte Rendu XXth Interna-
    tional Geological Congress. Mexico City: 1956.

Mehliss, A. T. M. "Barytes in Swaziland, " S. A. Mining
    and Engineering Journal Vol. LVII, Part 1, No. 2786
    (1945).

"Prospects for Swaziland's Minerals, " Mining Journal, Vol.
    261 (August 1963): p. 131.

Scott, Peter, "Mineral Development in Swaziland, " Economic
    Geography, Vol. 26, No. 3 (July 1950): pp. 196-213.

Spargo, P. E. "The Thermal Springs of the Pigg's Peak
    District, Swaziland, " South African Journal of Sci-
    ence, Vol. 61, No. 4 (April 1965): pp. 179-182.

"Swaziland Mineral Resources: Possibilities in the Future, "
    South African Mining Engineering Journal, 57 (1)
    (March 23, 1946): pp. 71-73.

"Swaziland's Minerals: Another Change, " Africa 1966, No.
    19, (September 23, 1966): pp. 4-5.

Thain, G. M. "Focus on Mineral Wealth in Recent Geo-
    graphical Surveys, " Swaziland Recorder, No. 6
    (March-June 1962): p. 31.

_____ . "Kaolin, " Swaziland Recorder, No. 7 (July-
    September 1962): p. 19.

_____ . "Swaziland Minerals, " Swaziland Recorder, No.
    18 (March-June 1965): p. 21.

Thompson, A. C. "Mhlume, " South African Mining Engi-
    neering Journal 53 (May 1962): pp. 28-29.

Way, H. R. J. "The Archean of Swaziland, " Compte Rendu
    XIXth International Geological Congress. Algiers: 1952.

_____. "Major Swaziland Structures, " East-Central and Southern Regional Committees for Geology, CCTA. Tananarive: 1957.

_____. Mineral Ownership as Affecting Mineral Development of Swaziland. Mbabane: Government Printer, 1955.

_____. "Radiometric Survey as an Aid to the Geological Mapping of the Ancient Systems of Swaziland, " Southern Regional Committee for Geology, CCTA. Salisbury: 1955.

Wellington, J. H. "Notes on the Physiography of Swaziland and Adjoining Areas, " South African Geographical Journal (Johannesburg): Vol. 38 (1956): pp. 30-36.

Medicine

Keen, P. "Infantile Mortality in Swaziland. " Race Relations, Vol. 9, No. 2 (1942): pp. 77-82.

Mastbaum, O. "Past and present position of malaria in Swaziland, " Journal of Tropical Medicine & Hygiene (London) 60, 5 (May 1957).

Natural Science and Zoology

Alston, M. "Birds in Swaziland, " National Review, Vol. 89 (1927): pp. 600-607.

Davy, J. Burtt. "Addition and Correction to the Recorded Flora of the Transvaal in Swaziland, " South African Association for the Advancement of Science, Vol. 9 (1913): pp. 343-356.

Reilly, T. E. "Native Reserve in Swaziland, " African Wildlife 14 (June 1960): pp. 113-115.

"Swaziland's New Forests, " Times British Colonies Review, (Spring 1953), p. 12.

"Wood for the Trees, " Economist, Vol. 206 (January 26, 1963): pp. 300+.

Technology

Hawkins, L. A. W. "Important Ore Line Will Be Ready for Traffic, " Railway Engineering 8 (1964): pp. 26-27.

_____. "Major Bridges on the Swaziland Railway, " Railway Gazette, Vol. 119 (11 October 1963): pp. 402-405.

_____. "Planning Standardization and Mechanization, " South African Mining Engineering Journal 75 (November 13, 1964): pp. 1366-1368.

_____. "Rich Iron Ore Deposits Give Swaziland Its Long-Awaited Railroad, " Optim 14, No. 2 (June 1964): pp. 84-87.

"More Electric Power in Swaziland, " African World, (June 1967): p. 7.

Warden, W. "Steel for the Swaziland Railroad, " Iscar News 29 (July 1964): pp. 6-10.

4. SOCIAL

Anthropology: General Ethnology

Beemer [Kuper], Hilda. The Bantu Tribes of South Africa. Vol. III, Section IV. Cambridge, 1941.

Coetzee, J. H. "The Southern Bantu, " Bantu, Vol. 12 (December 1965): pp. 448-449.

Cronin, A. M. D. "The Swazi, " The Bantu Tribes of South Africa, Vol. viii, Sec. 4. Cambridge University Press, 1941.

Gusinde, Martin. Von Gelben und schwarzen Buschmannern: eine untergehende Altkultur im Suden Afrikas (English summary). Graz: Akad. Druk-u. Verlagsanstalt, 1966.

"Homeland of the Swazi, " Ba-Ntu, Vol. 7, No. 4 (1960): pp. 240-248.

Kuper, Hilda. An African Aristocracy: Rank Among the

Swazis. London: Oxford University Press, 1947.

_____. "The Development of a Primitive Nation," Bantu Studies, Vol. 15, No. 4 (December 1941): pp. 339-368.

_____. The Swazi. London: International African Institute, 1952.

_____. The Swazi, a South African Kingdom. New York: Holt, Rinehart, and Winston, 1963.

_____. "The Swazis of Swaziland," in J. L. Gibbs (ed.), Peoples of Africa. New York: Holt, Rinehart, & Winston, 1965, pp. 479-511.

Marwick, Brian. Abantu Bakwa Ngwane. Cape Town: University of Cape Town Press, 1939.

_____. The Swazi: An Ethnographic Account of the Natives of Swaziland Protectorate. Cambridge University Press, 1940.

Myburgh, A. C. The Tribes of Barberton District. Government Printer, 1949.

Report of the South African Native Commission, 1903-1905, Vol. V.

Schapera, I., (ed.). The Bantu-Speaking Tribes of South Africa. London: Routledge, 1937.

_____. Government and Politics in Tribal Societies. London: C. A. Watts, and Company, 1956.

Van Warmelo, N. J. "Early Bantu Ethnography from a Philological Point of View." Africa, Vol. 3, No. 1 (January 1930), pp. 31-47.

Anthropology: Royalty and Royal Ceremonies

Akeley, Mary L. Jobe. "The Swazi Queen at Home: Intimate Observations on Love, Life and Death in South Africa's Timeless Swaziland," Natural History (New York). Vol. 62, pp. 21-32.

Beidelman, T. O. "Swazi Royal Ritual," Africa (London).
     Vol. 36, No. 4 (October 1966): pp. 373-405.

_____. "Swazi Royal Ritual," Reprinted in Africa and
     Change, Turnbull, Colin M. (ed.). Alfred A. Knopf,
     1973.

Carter, G. M. "Sacred Fertility Festival," Africa Special
     Report, Vol. II, No. 4 (April, 1957), p. 5.

Cook, P. A. W. "The First-fruits Ceremony," Bantu Stud-
     ies, Vol. I (1930).

_____. "The Inqwala Ceremony of the Swazis," Bantu
     Studies (Johannesburg), Vol. 4, No. 3 (1930): pp. 205-
     210.

Kuper, Hilda. "Celebration of Growth and Kingship: Inqwala
     in Swaziland," African Arts/Arts d'Afrique, Vol. 1,
     No. 3 (Spring 1968): pp. 56-59, 90.

_____. "A Ritual of Kingship Among the Swazi," Africa,
     Vol. 14, No. 5 (January 1944): pp. 230-257.

Richards, Audrey I. "African Kings and Their Royal Rela-
     tives," Journal of the Royal Anthropological Institute,
     Vol. 91, No. 2, pp. 135-150.

Rubin, N. N. "The Swazi Law of Succession: A Restate-
     ment," Journal of African Law, Vol. 9, No. 2 (Sum-
     mer 1965): pp. 90-113.

Schoeman, P. J. "Die Swazis se jaarliks seremonie van die
     eerst vrugte," Annals of University of Stellenbosch,
     15, Sect. B., No. 3 (1937).

"A Swazi National Festival: Feast of the First Fruits and Its
     Significance," African World, (December 1952): pp.
     11-12.

Twala, Regina G. "Umhlanga (Reed) Ceremony of the Swazi
     Maiden," African Studies, 11 (3 September, 1952):
     pp. 91-104.

Venter, W. A. "Die Familietwis in die Swazi- Koningshuis:
     Was Buitestaanders Asndadig?" Historia, Vol. 10,
     No. 2 (June 1965): pp. 130-133.

Watt, C. J.   "Swaziland National Festival, "   African World,
     (December 1952): pp. 11-12.

Anthropology: Military Organization

Beemer, [Kuper] Hilda.   "The Development of the Military
     Organization in Swaziland, "   Africa,   Vol. 10, No. 1
     (January 1937): pp. 55-74; Vol. 10, No. 2 (April
     1937): pp. 176-205.

"Military Organization in Swaziland, "   Nature (London), Vol.
     139, No. 3525 (22 May 1937): p. 888.

Anthropology: Marriage

Engelbrecht, J. A.   "Swazi Customs Relating to Marriage, "
     Annals of University of Stellenbosch, Vol. 8, Section
     6, No. 2, (1930): Cape Town: Nasionale Pers. Bkp.

Kuper, Hilda.   "The Marriage of a Swazi Princess, " Africa,
     Vol. 15, No. 3 (July 1945): pp. 145-155.

Matsebula, J. S. M.   "A Traditional Swazi Wedding, " Swazi-
     land Teachers' Journal, 55 (September, 1967): pp. 42-
     44.

Mohlomi, G.   "Royal Swazi Wedding, " Zonk 15 (September
     1963): pp. 15-17.

Anthropology: Diet

Beemer [Kuper], Hilda.   "Notes on the Diet of the Swazi in
     the Protectorate, " Bantu Studies, Vol. 13, No. 3,
     (1939): pp. 199-236.

Jones, Sonya M.   A Study of Swazi Nutrition: Report of the
     Swaziland Nutrition Survey 1961-62 for the Swaziland
     Administration.   Durban: Institute for Social Research,
     University of Natal, 1963.

Velcich, G.   "Bantu Know Secrets of Cassava, " Ba-Ntu,
     Vol. 10, No. 9, pp. 492-497.

Anthropology: Occult Practice

Butler, P. "Ritual Murder, " Outspan, No. 51 (April 4, 1952): pp. 38-41.

Robertson, T. C. "Swaziland Magic, " Libertas 4, No. 12 (November 1944): pp. 18-37.

"Witchcraft in Swaziland, " Nature, Vol. 145 (April 27, 1940): p. 664.

Anthropology: Miscellaneous

Dumbrell, H. J. E. "Pyre Burning in Swaziland, " African Studies, Vol. 11, No. 4 (December 1952): pp. 190-191.

Kuper, Hilda. "Kinship Among the Swazis, " in Radcliffe Brown, A. R. and D. Forde, (eds), African Systems of Kinship and Marriage. London: Oxford University Press, 1950.

Schoeman, P. J. "The Swazi Rain Ceremony, " Bantu Studies (Johannesburg), Vol. 9, (1935): pp. 169-175.

Twala, R. G. "Beads as Regulating the Social Life of the Zulu and the Swazi, " African Studies 10 (1951): pp. 113-123.

Demography and Population

Holleman, J. F. , editor. Experiment in Swaziland: Report of the Swaziland Sample Survey, 1960. Cape Town: Oxford University Press, 1964.

Kuczynski, R. R. Demographic Survey of the British Colonial Empire, Vol. II. London: Oxford University Press, 1949.

Education

Arnold, L. M. "The Swaziland English Scheme, Playing to Learn, " Swaziland Teachers Journal, (September 1966).

Broderick, Rev. G. E.   The Handymen Class at the Swazi
      National School, Matsapa.   1934.

"Education in Swaziland, " Commonwealth Survey, Education
      and Culture, (4 July 1952): pp. 39-41.

"Education in Swaziland, 1952, " Commonwealth Survey, (24
      April 1953).

Engelbrecht, J. A.   Swazi Texts with Notes.   Cape Town:
      Nasionale Pers, 1930.

Matsebula, J. S. M.   Education Administration in Swaziland
      and United Kingdom.   London University, 1965.

Morgan, D.   Some Views on the Present and Future Educa-
      tional Programme in the High Commission Territories,
      1962. cyclostyled.

Rose, Brian.   "Educational Policy and Problems in the
      Former High Commission Territories of Africa, "
      Comparative Education 1, 2 (March, 1965).

Stevens, R. P.   "Southern Africa's Multiracial University, "
      Africa Report 9, No. 3 (March 1964): pp. 16-18.

White, A.   "Swazi National Schools, " Overseas Education,
      Vol. 30, No. 2 (July 1958): pp. 62-63.

Religion

Du Plessis, J.   A History of Christian Missions in South
      Africa.   Longman, Green, & Co. Ltd. , 1911.

Hullweck, Karl.   "Der Weg ist jetzt offen!" Bilder aus der
      Mission im ungebrochen Heidentum (Swaziland, Sud-
      afrika) Berlin: Buchhandlung der Berliner evangeli-
      schen Missionsgesellschaft, 1936.   (Neue Mission-
      schriften, Nr. 83).

Kuper, Hilda.   "The Swazi Reaction to Missions, " African
      Studies, Vol. 5, No. 3 (September 1946): pp. 177-188.

Mears, Gordon.   Methodism in Swaziland.   Rondebosch:
      Methodist Missionary Department, 1955.

Nilsen, Marie and Paul H. Sheetz. Malla Moe. Chicago:
    Moody Press, 1956.

Roman Catholic Mission, Swaziland. 50 Years of Missionary
    Work, 1914-1964. Report, 1964.

Scutt, Joan Frances. The Drums are Beating. London: H. E.
    Walter, 1951.

Watts, C. C. Dawn in Swaziland. Westminster, London:
    Society for the Propagation of the Gospel in Foreign
    Parts, 1922.

Ziervogel, D. "A Swazi Translation of 1846" (A Wesleyan
    Methodist Catechism), African Studies, IX, 4, (De-
    cember 1950): pp. 167-184.

Sociology

Gamede, A. "Erziehungsprobleme in Swaziland, " Afrika
    Heute, (15 August, 1968): pp. 213-215.

Sherwood, E. T. Swazi Personality and the Assimilation of
    Western Culture. Chicago: Photoduplication Dept. ,
    University of Chicago Library, 1961.

Van den Berghe, Pierre L. "Institutionalized License and
    Normative Stability, " Cahiers d' Etudes Africaines,
    Vol. 3, No. 11 (1963): pp. 413-423.

Race Relations

Africa Bureau, London. Apartheid Challenge to British
    Policy in Swaziland. London: 1964. (Copy located
    at Northwestern University, Evanston, Illinois).

Betts, T. F. "Swaziland: Economics of Racial Integration,"
    Venture (London), 14 (January, 1962): pp. 6-7.

Kuper, Hilda. The Uniform of Colour; a Study of White-
    Black relationships in Swaziland. Johannesburg: Wit-
    watersrand University Press, 1947.

"Must Swaziland Be Racialist?" Africa 1962, No. 9 (May 4,
    1962): p. 4.

Niven, D. J. "Nonracial State Is Theme of Planners, "
Swaziland Recorder, No. 3 (July-September 1961):
p. 25.

"Non- or Multi-Racialism in Swaziland?" Africa 1961, No.
19 (September 22, 1961): pp. 6-8.

5. HISTORIC

Pre-Colonial

Becker, Peter. Rule of Fear: The Life and Times of Dingane, King of the Zulu. London: Longmans, 1964.

Bryant, A. T. The History of the Zulu and Neighboring
Tribes. Cape Town: C. Struik, 1964. First pub-
lished in Izindaba Zabantu by the Brothers of the
Marianhill Monastery in 1911 and 1913.

Cook, P. A. W. "History and Izibongo of the Swazi Chiefs,"
Bantu Studies (Johannesburg), Vol. 5, No. 2, (1931):
pp. 181-201.

Gabel, C. "Lochinvar Mound: A Later Stone Age Camp-site
in the Kafue Basin, " South African Archeological
Bulletin, B., Vol. 18, No. 63 (April 1963): pp. 24-
26.

Kuper, Hilda. An African Aristocracy: Rank Among the
Swazis. London: Oxford University Press, 1947.

Malan, B. D. "The Middle Stone Age in the Eastern Transvaal and Swaziland, " South African Journal of Science, Vol. 47, No. 5 (December 1950): pp. 146-150.

Matsebula, J. S. M. Izakhiwo Zama Swazi. Johannesburg:
Afrikaanse Pers Boekhandel, 1952.

Van Warmelo, N. J., editor. History of Matiwane and the
Amangwane Tribe as Told by Msebenzi to his Kinsman
Albert Hlongwane. Union of South Africa Department
of Native Affairs, Ethnological Publication 7.

Contact with Europeans

Agar-Hamilton, J. A. I.   The Native Policy of the Voortrek-
    kers.   Cape Town: Maskew Miller, 1928.

Barnes, Leonard. The New Boer War. London: Hogarth, 1932.

Bartlett, Sir Ellis Ashmead. The Appeal of the Swazi People.
    London: Simpkin, Marshall, Hamilton, Kent, & Co. , 1894.
    This and the following citation are two different
    editions of the same work.

_____. British Natives and Boers in the Transvaal:
    Appeal of the Swazis.   London: McCorquodale & Co.,
    1894.

Bryant, Rev. A. T.   Olden Times in Zululand and Natal.
    London: 1929.

Coope, W. J.   Swaziland as Imperial Factor.   James Barker
    & Co., 1853.

Coryndon, R. T.   Some Account of George Grey and his
    Work in Africa.   London: Chiswick Press, 1914.

Davis, Alexander.   Umbandine, A Romance of Swaziland.
    London: Unwin, 1898.

"Elias N'Kosi Reminiscences, "   Ba-Ntu, Vol. 10, No. 8
    (1963): pp. 432-433.

Forbes, David. My Life in South Africa.   London: Witherby,
    1938.

Galbraith, John S.   Reluctant Empire: British Policy on the
    South African Frontier, 1834-1854.   Berkeley and Los
    Angeles: University of California Press, 1963.

Garson, Noel George.   "The Swaziland Question and a Road
    to the Sea, 1887-1895, " Archives Yearbook for South
    African History, Part 2 (1957): pp. 263-434.

Harvey, Pirie J. H.   Swaziland and the New Republic.   Jo-
    hannesburg: The Philatelic Federation of South Africa.

Leyds, W. J.   The Transvaal Surrounded.   Unwin, 1919.

Long, W. H.   Peace and War in the Transvaal.   London:
    Low, Marston, Searle, and Rivington, 1882.

Marais, J. S.   The Fall of Kruger's Republic.   Oxford: 1961.

Matsebula, James S. M. A.   A History of Swaziland.   Cape
    Town: Longman Southern Africa Ltd., 1972.

Miller, Allister Mitchell.   The South East Coast of Africa
    and Its Development.   St. Albans: Cambridge Press, 1923.

_____ .   Swazieland and The Swazieland Corporation.   Lon-
    don: 1900.

Omer-Cooper, J. D.   The Zulu Aftermath.   Evanston:
    Northwestern University Press, 1966.

"Paulus Mopeli, vriend van die vrystaat, "   Ba-Ntu, Vol. 9,
    No. 6 (1962): pp. 381-385.

Pratt, E. A.   Leading Points in South African History, 1486-
    to March 30, 1900.   John Murray, 1900.

Raddatz, H.   The Transvaal and the Swaziland Gold Fields.
    Cape Town: Saul Solomon, 1886.

Robinson, H. C. R.   "Swaziland Question, "   Fortnightly Re-
    view, (February 1890): pp. 283-291.

Scutt, J. F.   The Story of Swaziland.   Mbabane: Swaziland
    Printing and Publishing Co., 1966.

Stevenson-Hamilton, J.   The Lowveld.   London: 1929.

Thompson, Leonard Monteath.   The Unification of South
    Africa.   Oxford: Clarendon Press, 1960.

Walker, Eric A.   A History of Southern Africa.   London:
    Longmans, Green, 1957; revised 1965.

Wilson, William.   England and the Transvaal.   London:
    Grosvenor Press, 1899.

Colonial

Booth, Alan R.   "Lord Selbourne and the British Protecto-
    rates 1908-1910, "   Journal of African History, X
    (1969): pp. 133-148.

"Claim of the Native," Spectator, Vol. 153 (August 17, 1934): p. 212.

Davidson, B. "Country of King Sobhuza," New Statesman, Vol. 46 (September 19, 1953) and (October 3, 1953): pp. 308+, 367-368.

Hailey, Lord. Native Administration in the British African Territories. Part V. The High Commission Territories: Basutoland, The Bechuanaland Protectorate, and Swaziland. London: Her Majesty's Stationery Office, 1953.

Harris, Sir John Hobbis. South Africa: From the Cape to the Zambesi. London: Anti-Slavery and Aborigines Protection Society, 1938. (A series of articles contributed to the Manchester Guardian and reproduced in pamphlet form by permission of the editor.).

Hodgson, Margaret L. Indirect Rule in Southern Africa. Alice, South Africa: Lovedale Press, 1931.

Johnson, Kathryn M. Stealing a Nation. Chicago: Pyramid Publishing Co., 1939.

Kuper, Hilda. "The Colonial Situation in Southern Africa," Journal of Modern African Studies, II (1964), pp. 149-164.

_____. The Uniform of Colour: a Study of White-Black relationships in Swaziland. Johannesburg: Witwatersrand University Press, 1947.

MacMillan, W. M. "The Protectorates," in Cambridge History of the British Empire, Vol. 8, Cambridge University Press, 1963, pp. 671-675.

Penn-Smith, F. "Old Queen," New Statesman and Nation, Vol. 6 (July 15, 1933): pp. 73-74.

Pim, Sir Alan. "British Protectorates and Territories. An Address Delivered at a Meeting of the Royal Empire Society," United Empire, Vol. 25, No. 5 (May 1934): pp. 266-279.

_____. "Questions of the South African Protectorates," International Affairs 13, No. 3 (September 1934): pp. 668-688.

Pirie, J. H. H.   "Swaziland Postal History and Stamps, "
South African Philatelist 29 (August 1953): pp. 24-26.

"Reform in the Protectorates, " The Round Table, XXV, pp.
746-753.

Rhodes-Wood, E. H.   A War History of the Royal Pioneer
Corps, 1939-1945. Gales & Polden, 1960.

Spence, J. E.   "British Policy towards the High Commission
Territories, " Journal of Modern African Studies, II
(2) (1964): p. 240.

Incorporation or Independence?

Africa Bureau, London. Apartheid Challenge to British
Policy in Swaziland. London: Africa Bureau, 1964.
(Copy located at Northwestern University, Evanston,
Illinois).

Arden-Clarke, Sir Charles.   "The Problem of the High Commission Territories, " Optima 8, No. 4 (December
1958): pp. 163-170.

Baring, E.   "Problems of the High Commission Territories,"
International Affairs 28 (April 1952): pp. 184-189.

Butler, Jeffrey.   "South Africa and the High Commission
Territories: The Ganyile Case, 1961, " in Gwendolen
M. Carter, (ed.), Politics in Africa: 7 Cases. New
York: Harcourt, Brace, & World, 1966, pp. 245-283.

Clark, W. M.   "Problems of the Protectorates, " Spectator,
183 (November 25, 1949): p. 731.

Cockram, Ben.   Problems of Southern Africa. Johannesburg:
South African Institute of International Affairs, 1963.

_____.   "The Protectorates: An International Problem, "
Optima (Johannesburg), Vol. 13, No. 4 (December
1963): pp. 177-183.

Davey, H. W.   "South African Territories, " Contemporary
Review, Vol. 185 (January 1954): pp. 16-19.

Davis, John A. and James K. Baker, (eds.). Southern

Africa in Transition. New York: Praeger, 1966.

"Dr. Verwoerd's British Colonies," *Economist*, Vol. 216 (August 7, 1965): p. 29.

Doxey, G. V. *The High Commission Territories and the Republic of South Africa.* Chatham House Memoranda London: Distributed for the Royal Institute of International Affairs by the Oxford University Press, 1963.

_____. *South Africa, Negotiations Regarding the Transfer to the Union of South Africa of the Government of Basutoland, the Bechuanaland Protectorate, and Swaziland, 1910-1939.* Pretoria: Government Printer, 1953.

Dundas, Sir Charles and Dr. Hugh Ashton. *Problem Territories of Southern Africa: Basutoland, Bechuanaland Protectorate, and Swaziland.* Johannesburg: South African Institute of International Affairs, 1952.

Edwards, Isobel. *Protectorates or Native Reserves? A Political and Constitutional Survey of the High Commission Territories in South Africa--Basutoland. Bechuanaland and Swaziland.* London: Africa Bureau, 1956.

Evans, I. L. *Policy in Southern Africa.* Cambridge: Cambridge University Press, 1934.

Fitzgerald, R. C. "South Africa and the High Commission Territories," *World Affairs* 4, No. 3 (July 1950): pp. 306-320.

Great Britain, Government of. *Basutoland, the Bechuanaland Protectorate, and Swaziland: History of Discussions with the Union of South Africa, 1919-1939.* London: Her Majesty's Stationery Office, 1952.

Hailey, Lord. *The Republic of South Africa and the High Commission Territories.* London: Oxford University Press, 1963.

Halpern, Jack. "South Africa: Enclaves of Trouble," *Nation,* Vol. 197 (July 27, 1963): pp. 49-52.

Hyam, Ronald. *The Failure of South African Expansion, 1908-1948.* New York: Africana Pub. Corp., 1972.

Maud, Sir John. "The Challenge of the High Commission
     Territories, " African Affairs, 63 (April 1964): pp. 94-
     103.

Mohen, J. T.   The Commonwealth Without South Africa.
     Toronto: Canadian Institute of International Affairs,
     1961.

Norton, George.   Should South Africa Expand?   London: Union
     of Democratic Control, 1951.

Perham, Margery and Lionel Curtis.   The Protectorates of
     South Africa: The Question of Their Transfer to the
     Union.   London: Oxford University Press, 1935.

"The Protectorates and the Union, "   The Round Table, XXV,
     No. 96 (1934): pp. 785-802.

Roberts, Margaret.   "High Commission Territories: In Pawn
     to Apartheid?", Africa Today, X, 9 (Nov.1963): pp. 12-15.

South Africa, Government of.   High Commission Territories
     and the Union of South Africa.   London: Royal Insti-
     tute of International Affairs, 1956.

_____.   Negotiations Regarding the Transfer to the Union
     of South Africa of the Government of Basutoland, the
     Bechuanaland Protectorate, and Swaziland, 1910-1939.
     Pretoria: Government Printer, 1953.

"The South African Protectorates, "   The Round Table XXV,
     No. 98 (1935): pp. 318-323.

Stevens, Richard P.   "The History of the Anglo-South African
     Conflict over the Proposed Incorporation of the High
     Commission Territories, " in Christian Potholm and
     Richard Dale, (eds.), Southern Africa in Perspective,
     New York: The Free Press, 1972.

Thompson, A. C.   "The Republic and the High Commission
     Territories, " Swaziland Recorder, No. 1 (January-
     March 1961): p. 11.

Verwoerd, Dr. H. F.   I. Crisis in World Conscience.   II.
     The Road to Freedom for Basutoland, Bechuanaland,
     and Swaziland.   Fact Paper No. 107.   Pretoria, South
     Africa: Department of Information, 1964.

"Verwoerd's Tame Lion?" Economist, Vol. 211 (April 25, 1964): p. 371.

"Verwoerd's Victory, " New Statesman, Vol. 68 (July 17, 1964): p. 84.

Young, B. S. "High Commission Territories of Southern Africa, " Focus 14 (December 1963): pp. 1-6.

Decolonization

Baring, Evelyn. "The Emergence of Swaziland, " Optima (June 1962): pp. 104-109.

Barnes, John A. Politics in a Changing Society. London: Oxford University Press, for the Rhodes-Livingston Institute, 1954.

Boermer, G. von. "London entlässt Swaziland aus dem Protektorat, " Aussenpolitik 18 (3) (March 1967): pp. 166-170.

Brooks, Charles. "Paramount Chief Speaks of Swaziland's Future, " Swaziland Recorder, No. 4 (September-December 1961): p. 21.

Clark, W. M. "Swaziland Split Personality, " South African Financial Mail, No. 10 (November 1, 1963): pp. 466-468.

_____. "United Kingdom Government Prepares Final Analysis of Necessities, " Swaziland Recorder, No. 10 (March-June 1963): pp. 11-19.

"Constitutional Advance in Swaziland, " Commonwealth Survey, Vol. 12, No. 23 (November 11, 1966): pp. 1130-1136.

"False Start In Swaziland, " Africa 1963, No. 12 (June 14, 1963): 8.

Franzelli, P. G. "1968-Buon Viaggio, Swaziland!" Nigrisia, (Verona) Anno 86; N. 9 (September 1968): pp. 4-8, 5111.

Gluckman, Max. Rituals of Rebellion. (Frazer Lecture). Manchester: Manchester University Press, 1952.

Great Britain. Government of. The Swaziland Order of
     Council, 1963. London: Her Majesty's Stationery
     Office, 1963.

Grotpeter, John J. and Warren Weinstein. An Alternative
     Model for Political Change in Pre-independence Africa.
     Based on: Ruanda-Urundi and the High Commission
     Territories. Presented at the Fourteenth Annual Meet-
     ing of the African Studies Association, 1971. Avail-
     able: African Studies Association.

_____. The Pattern of African Decolonization: A New In-
     terpretation. Syracuse: Syracuse University, 1973.

Halpern, Jack. South Africa's Hostages: Basutoland, Bechu-
     analand, and Swaziland. Baltimore: Penguin Books,
     1965.

Herd, Norman. "Carl Todd Looks at Swaziland, " Swaziland
     Recorder, No. 16 (September-December 1964): pp. 11-
     15.

_____. "Swaziland's Advance, " Swaziland Recorder, No.
     8 (September-December 1962): pp. 19-21.

Hodgson, M. L. "Britain as Trustee in Southern Africa, "
     Political Quarterly, No. 3 (July 1932): pp. 398-408.

Jowitt, H. "The Protectorate of Southern Africa, " Year-
     book of Education 1954, pp. 144-154.

Khale, J. E. "Swazis on the Move, " Our Africa No. 2
     (July 1960): pp. 5-7.

Lashinger, M. "Roads to Independence: the Case of Swazi-
     land, " World Today (London), Vol. 21, No. 11 (No-
     vember 1965): pp. 486-494.

"Das letste britische Hoheitsgebiet auf dem afrikanischen
     Kontinent wird unabhängig, " Afrika heute 22, 15 (No-
     vember, 1967): pp. 325-326.

Maud, Sir John. "My Hope for Swaziland, " Swaziland Re-
     corder, No. 10 (March-June 1963): pp. 11-13.

Mohlomi, G. "Swaziland: Panic or Progress, " South Afri-
     can Financial Mail, No. 8 (March 1963): pp. 11-13.

Mollatt, E. B.   "Chief Knew His Onions, "   Outspan 15 (July
    1, 1955): pp. 34-35.

_____   "Swaziland Means Business," Outspan 15 (June
    1955): pp. 23-25.

"1967--Swasiland auf dem Wege zur Unabhängigkeit, " Die
    Aussenwirtschaft (Köln), 11. Jahrgang, Nr. 23,
    (8. 6.1967): 556-557.

Progress in Swaziland 1965. Commonwealth Survey (London),
    Vol. 11, No. 7 (30 March 1965): pp. 304-307.

"Power for Swaziland, " New Commonwealth, Vol. 41 (Octo-
    ber 1963): pp. 653-654.

Reilly, T. E.   "Protectorate with a Future, " South African
    Financial Mail 7 (November 2, 1962): pp. 73-75.

Rubin, L. , and R. P. Stevens.   "The High Commission Ter-
    ritories: What Now?" Africa Report 9, No. 4 (April
    1964): pp. 9-17.

Rose, Brian.   "Swaziland: A Contemporary Survey, " African
    World, (May 1965): pp. 4-7.

Roucek, Joseph S.   "Swaziland: Bright Future, " New Africa,
    Vol. 9 (May-June 1967): pp. 13-17.

Scutt, J. F.   "Independent Swaziland, " African World,
    (October 1968): pp. 4-6.

Smit, P. G. M. E. , A. J. van Wyk Leistner and E. J. van
    der Merwe. Swaziland on the Eve of Independence.
    (Occasional Papers of the Africa Institute of South
    Africa No. 4.) Pretoria: Africa Institute of South
    Africa, 1968.

Stevens, Richard P.   Lesotho, Botswana, and Swaziland: The
    Former High Commission Territories in Southern
    Africa. New York: Frederick A. Praeger, 1968.

"Le Swaziland indépendant devient le Ngwane, " Afrique Con-
    temporaine, No. 7 (38-39) (juil. -août-sept. -oct. 1968):
    pp. 23-24.

Swaziland--"Long Live the King, " Africa 1966, No. 11 (June
    3, 1966): pp. 5-7.

"Swaziland: No Break with Paternalism, " Africa 1964, No. 12 (June 12, 1964): pp. 4-5.

"Swaziland: No Change for the Last Lap, " Africa Confidential, No. 24 (December 8, 1967): pp. 3-5.

"Swaziland Shelter," Economist, Vol. 201 (Oct. 28, 1961): p. 354.

"The Union Jack Comes Down At Last, " African Development, Vol. 2, No. 4 (1968): p. 3.

White, E. "Last Steps Toward Independence, " African Affairs 64, No. 257 (October, 1965): pp. 261-270.

6.   POLITICAL

Constitution

Clark, W. M. "Views on the Constitution of Swaziland, " Swaziland Recorder, No. 14 (March-June 1964): pp. 11-19.

Cowen, D. V. Report on Constitutional Reform. Cape Town: Lincey and Watson, 1961.

_____. Swaziland: Report on Constitutional Reform Made on Behalf of the Swaziland Progressive Party, and the Eurafrican (Coloured) Welfare Association. 1961.

Herd, Norman. "Public Discussion of New Constitution, " Swaziland Recorder, No. 5 (January-March 1962): pp. 15-16.

Mashabela, Harry. "Swaziland: A Royal Coup, " Africa Report, Vol. 18, No. 3 (May-June 1973): p. 12.

Stevens, Richard P. "A Constitution Imposed, " Africa Report, (April 1964): p. 3.

Swaziland, Government of. Proposals for a Swaziland Constitution. Mbabane: Government Printer, 1962.

"Swaziland's Constitution, " Africa 1963, No. 5 (March 1, 1963): pp. 5-7.

"Swaziland's Constitution: Part II, " Africa 1963, No. 7 (March 29, 1963): p. 3.

"Tradition Means the King," Africa Report, Vol. 18, No. 4
(July-August 1973): pp. 26-27.

Welch, Claude E. "Constitutional Confusion in Swaziland,"
Africa Report, (April 1963): pp. 7-9.

Government

Dening, B. H. "Local Government Trends in Swaziland,"
Journal of Administration Overseas, 8 (3) (July, 1969):
pp. 197-207.

McCartney, W. J. "The Parliament of Botswana, Lesotho,
and Swaziland," Parliamentarian, 50 (2) (April 1969):
pp. 92-101.

Marwick, A. G. The Attitude of the Swazi Towards Government and Its Causes. Mbabane: September 1955.

Nxumalo, Simon. Profiles of Parliamentarians in The Kingdom of Swaziland. Mbabane: Swaziland Printing and
Publishing Co., 1968.

Potholm, C. P. Monarchical Response to Modernity: The
Case of the Ngwenyama of Swaziland. Paper prepared
for delivery at the Fourteenth Annual Meeting of the
African Studies Association Denver, 1971. Available:
African Studies Association.

_____. "The Ngwenyama of Swaziland: The Dynamics of
Political Adaptation," in Rene Lemarchand, (ed.),
Kingship in Africa. London: Frank Cass, 1973.

_____. Remembrance of Things Past?: The Process of
Institutional Change in Swaziland. Prepared for pre-
sentation at African Studies Association Convention,
November, 1972. Available: African Studies Association.

Ramage, Sir Richard. Report on the Structure of the Public
Services in Basutoland, Bechuanaland, and Swaziland,
1961. Cape Town: High Commissioner's Office, 1962.

Stevens, Richard P. Prospects for Self-Government in the
Former High Commission Territories. Unpublished
Monograph.

Law

Juta, H. C.   Revised Edition of the Laws of Swaziland in Force on the First Day of April, 1949.   3 vols. London: C. F. Roworth, 1951.

Rubin, N. N.   "Swaziland Legislation: the Marriage Proclamation, 1964, " Journal of African Law, Vol. 9, No. 1 (1965): pp. 60-64.

Thompson, A. C.   The Laws of Swaziland.   4 vols. Mbabane, Swaziland: 1960.

Politics and Political Parties

"Disputes in Swaziland, " Africa Institute Bulletin, Vol. 6 (April, 1968): pp. 79, 82-85.

"Dr. Zwane's London Visit, " Africa 1962, No. 17 (August 24, 1962): pp. 5-6.

Grotpeter, John Joseph.   Political Leadership and Political Development in the High Commission Territories.   St. Louis: Washington University, unpublished Ph. D. dissertation, 1965.

Halpern, Jack.   South Africa's Hostages: Basutoland, Bechuanaland, and Swaziland.   Baltimore: Penguin Books, 1965.

Huteau, J.   "Partis nationalistes noirs en Afrique méridionale britannique, " Mois en Afrique, Vol. 7 (July 1966): pp. 115-134.

"Lion Beats Reindeer, " Africa 1964, No. 3 (Feb. 7, 1964): pp. 5-7.

Martin, A.   "Constitutional Aftermath, " Swaziland Recorder, No. 16 (September-December 1964): pp. 29-30.

Ndwandwe [Nxumalo], Sishayi Simon, (ed.).   Politics in Swaziland, 1960 to 1968.   (African Studies Programme, Occasional Papers No. 5.) Johannesburg: University of Witwatersrand, 1968.

"Political Developments in Swaziland, " International Bulletin, Vol. 2, No. 4 (1964): pp. 119-133.

"Politics and the Havelock Strike, " Africa 1963, No. 13
    (June 28, 1963): pp. 5-6.

Potholm, C. P.   "Changing Political Configurations in Swazi-
    land, " Journal of Modern African Studies, Vol. 4
    (November 1966): pp. 313-322.

_____.   "Swaziland in Transition to Independence, " Africa
    Report, Vol. 12, No. 6 (June 1967): pp. 49-54.

_____.   Swaziland: The Dynamics of Political Moderniza-
    tion.   Berkeley: University of California Press, 1972.

"Recent Political Development in Swaziland, " International
    Bulletin, Vol. 1, No. 8 (1963): pp. 218-222.

Segal, Ronald.   African Profiles.   Baltimore: Penguin Books,
    1962.

_____.   Political Africa.   New York: Praeger, 1961.

Stevens, Richard P.   Lesotho, Botswana, and Swaziland: The
    Former High Commission Territories in Southern
    Africa.   New York: Frederick A. Praeger, 1968.

_____.   "Report from Swaziland, " Africa Report, Vol. 8
    (October 1963): p. 8.

_____.   "Swaziland Political Development, " Journal of
    Modern African Studies, Vol. 1, No. 3 (September
    1963): pp. 327-350.

"Swaziland: élections et autonomie. "   Afrique contemporaine
    6 (31) (mai-juin 67): pp. 23-24.

Swaziland Democratic Party.   Totalitarianism Opposed.
    Mbabane: High Commission Printing and Publishing
    Company, 1962.

"The Trouble in Swaziland, " Voice of Africa (Accra, Ghana),
    Vol. 3, No. 11 (November, 1963).

van Wyk, A. J.   Swaziland: A Political Study.   (Communica-
    tions of the Africa Institute No. 9) Pretoria: Africa
    Institute of Southern Africa, 1969.

Zwane, Timothy.   "The Struggle for Power in Swaziland, "
    Africa Today, (May 1964): pp. 4-6.

Foreign Affairs

Bowman, Larry W.   "The Subordinate State System of South-
    ern Africa, " International Studies Quarterly, Vol. 12,
    No. 3 (September, 1968): pp. 231-261. Paper de-
    livered at the African Studies Convention meeting, No-
    vember, 1967.

Gross, Ernst A.   "The Coalescing Problem of Southern
    Africa, " Foreign Affairs 46, No. 4 (July 1968): pp.
    743-757.

Grundy, Kenneth.   Confrontation and Accommodation in South-
    ern Africa: The Limits of Independence.   Berkeley,
    California: University of California Press, 1973.

Hance, William A., (ed.).   Southern Africa and the United
    States.   New York and London: Columbia University
    Press, 1968.

Howe, Russell Warren.   "War In Southern Africa, " Foreign
    Affairs, 48, No. 1 (October, 1969): pp. 150-165.

Nielson, Waldemar A.   African Battleline.   New York: Harper
    & Row, 1965.

Potholm, C. P.   "The Protectorates, the O. A. U. and South
    Africa" International Journal, Vol. XXII, No. 1
    (Winter, 1966-67): pp. 68-72.

_____. "Swaziland, " in Christian Potholm and Richard
    Dale, (eds.), Southern Africa in Perspective. New
    York: The Free Press, 1972.

_____. Transaction Flows and Policy Formation: The
    Limits of Choice for Swaziland in the Southern African
    Complex.   Presented at the Thirteenth Annual Meeting
    of the African Studies Association, Boston, 1970.
    Available: African Studies Association.

_____ and Richard Dale, (eds.).   Southern Africa in Per-
    spective.   New York: The Free Press, 1972.

Rhodie, Eschel M.   "Southern Africa: Towards a New Com-
    monwealth?" in Christian Potholm and Richard Dale,
    (eds.), Southern Africa in Perspective.   New York:
    The Free Press, 1972.

Rubin, Leslie. "South Africa and Her Immediate Neighbors,"
    African Forum, Vol. 2, No. 2 (Fall 1966): pp. 78-84.

Schmidt, Charles F. South Africa and the Former High Com-
    mission Territories: Political Independence in an In-
    teracting Space Economy. Carbondale: Southern Illi-
    nois University, unpublished M. A. thesis, 1969.

Sparks, Alistair. "A Time for Detente? South Africa: A
    View from Within, " Africa Report, Vol. 12, No. 3
    (March 1967): p. 40.

Spence, J. E. "The Implications of the Rhodesia Issue for
    the Former High Commission Territories, " Journal
    of Commonwealth Political Studies, VII, No. 2 (July
    1963): pp. 104-111.

Vandenbosch, Amry. South Africa and the World: The
    Foreign Policy of Apartheid. Lexington: University
    Press of Kentucky, 1970.

See also citations in the history section under the heading
"Incorporation or Independence" and in the economic section
under the heading "Southern African Customs Union. "

7. ECONOMIC

Agriculture: Crops

"Cotton Growing in Swaziland, " Bulletin of the Imperial In-
    stitute, Vol. 24 (1923): pp. 468-474.

Herd, Norman. "Maize for Swazi Famine Relief, " Swazi-
    land Recorder, No. 6 (March-June 1962): p. 33.

Velcich, G. "Bantu Know Secrets of Cassava, " Ba-Ntu,
    Vol. 10, No. 9, pp. 492-497.

Wood, R. C. "Cotton in Swaziland, " Empire Cotton Grow-
    ing Review, Vol. 4 (1927): pp. 13-19.

_____. "A Report on Experimental Working on Cotton in
    Swaziland Season, 1925-1926, " Empire Cotton Grow-
    ing Review, Vol. 4 (1927): pp. 64-78.

_____. "Report on the Work of the Cotton Experiment

Station, Bremersdorp, for the Season, 1926-1927,"
Empire Cotton Growing Corporation Reports, (1928):
pp. 83-104.

_____. "Report on the Work of Cotton Experiments Station
Bremersdorp, for the Season, 1927-1928," _Empire
Cotton Growing Corporation Report,_ (1928): pp. 83-104.

Agriculture: Land Tenure

Hughes, A. J. B.   "Reflections on Traditional and Individual
Land Tenure in Swaziland," _Journal of Local Administration Overseas,_ Vol. 3, No. 1 (January 1964): pp.
3-13.

_____. "Some Swazi Views on Land Tenure," _Africa_
(London), Vol. 32, No. 3 (July 1962): pp. 253-278.

_____. "Some Swazi Views on Land Tenure," Reprinted
in _Africa and Change,_ Turnbull, Colin M., (ed.).
Alfred A. Knopf, 1973.

_____. _Swazi Land Tenure._ Durban: Institute for Social
Research, University of Natal, 1964.

"Land for Settlement in Swaziland," _Anti-Slavery Reporter,_
(July 1943).

Mitchell, N. P.   _Land Problems and Policies in the African
Mandates of the British Commonwealth._   Baton Rouge:
Louisiana State University Press, 1931.

"Native Land Settlement in Swaziland," _Commonwealth Survey,_
(May 14, 1954): pp. 60-62.

Scott, Peter.   "Land Policy and the Native Population of
Swaziland," _The Geographical Journal,_ Vol. 117,
Part 4 (December 1951): pp. 435-447.

Agriculture: Miscellaneous

Ashburner, W. F.   "Massive Scheme Brings Fertility to
Swaziland," _Farmer's Weekly,_ No. 103 (May 30,
1962): p. 18.

Batson, E. Swaziland Agricultural Survey. Cape Town:
    School of Social Studies, University of Cape Town, 1953.

Best, Alan C. G. "Development of Commercial Agriculture
    in Swaziland, 1943-1963, " Papers of the Michigan
    Academy of Science, Arts, and Letters. Vol. 52
    (1967): pp. 269-287.

Daniel, John Benjamin McIntyre. The Geography of the
    Rural Economy of Swaziland. Durban: Institute for
    Social Research, University of Natal, 1962.

_____. "Some Governmental Measures to Improve African
    Agriculture in Swaziland, " Geographical Journal,
    (London), Vol. 132, Part 4 (December 1966): pp. 506-515.

_____. "Swaziland: Some Problems of An African Rural
    Economy in a Developing Country, " South African Geo-
    graphical Journal, Vol. 48 (December 1966): pp. 90-100.

Erleigh, N. S. "Swaziland as Sheep Country, " Sun and Agri-
    cultural Journal of South Africa, (1928): pp. 262-264.

"1969--Swaziland, " Bulletin Agricole du Rwanda, Kigali, 2e
    annee, n. 1 (janvier 1969): pp. 39-43.

Murdoch, G. "Soil Survey and Soil Classification in Swazi-
    land, " African Soils, Vol. 9, No. 1 (January-April
    1964): pp. 117-123.

Raitt, I. "Operation 'Green Belt' in Swaziland, " Journal of
    the Royal United Service Institution, Vol. 109 (Febru-
    ary 1964): pp. 40-44.

A Soil and Irrigability Survey of the Lower Usutu Basin
    (South) in Swaziland Low Veld. London: H. M. S. O.,
    (Department of Technical Co-operation Overseas Re-
    search Publication No. 3.)

"Swaziland Today, " Sun and Agricultural Journal of South
    Africa, (February 1923): pp. 45-49.

"A Tour of Swaziland, " Sun and Agricultural Journal of South
    Africa, (1927): pp. 755-765.

Watt, C. J. "Conditions in Swaziland, " Farmer's Weekly,
    79 (August 2, 1950): pp. 29-31.

Commerce and Trade

Gross, S. I. "Basutoland, Bechuanaland Protectorate, Swa-
        ziland, " Board of Trade Journal 183 (September 28,
        1962): pp. 641-646.

Herd, Norman. "Foreign Trade of the Union of South Africa
        (including South West Africa, Basutoland, Swaziland
        and the Bechuanaland Protectorate), " Trade Review 4
        (March 1960): p. 11.

Neumark, S. D. Economic Influences on the South African
        Frontier. Stanford: Stanford University Press, 1957.

Nxumalo, Sishayi S. "International Trade and Investment:
        the Case of Swaziland" in J. Barratt, et al. (eds.).
        Accelerated Development in Southern Africa. New
        York: St. Martin's Press, 1974.

"Opening up Swaziland, " New Statesman, Vol. 60 (Decem-
        ber 17, 1960): p. 954.

Robson, Peter. "Economic Integration in Southern Africa, "
        Journal of Modern African Studies, Vol. 5, No. 4
        (December, 1967): pp. 469-490.

Sanger, Clyde. "Ancient or Modern Goods in Swazi Show-
        Window? Choice for London Conference, " Guardian,
        28 (January 1963): p. 17.

Smit, P. , and E. J. van der Merwe. "Economic Co-opera-
        tion in Southern Africa, " Journal of Geography,
        (Stellenbosch): 3, No. 3 (September 1968): pp. 279-94.

Swaziland Annual and Trade Index, 1966-1967. Johannesburg:
        Norton, Glyn, and Associates, Ltd. , 1967.

Southern African Customs Union

Standard Bank Organization. "Southern African Customs
        Union, " Standard Bank Review (London), (July 1970):
        pp. 7-10.

Swaziland, Government of. Customs Union Agreement Be-
        tween the Government of Swaziland, Botswana, Lesotho,
        & South Africa. Mbabane: Swaziland Government Ga-
        zette, 1969.

Turner, Biff. "A Fresh Start for The Southern African Customs Union, " African Affairs, LXX, No. 280 (1971): pp. 269-276.

Development

Clark, W. M. "Marshall Clark Looks at Swaziland's Economic Future, " Swaziland Recorder, No. 9 (January-March 1963): pp. 15-17.

Fair, T. J. D. , and L. P. Green. "Preparing for Swaziland's Future Growth, " Optima 10, No. 4, (December 1960): pp. 194-206.

Fair, T. J. D. , G. Murdoch, and H. M. Jones. Development in Swaziland: A Regional Analysis. Johannesburg: Witwatersrand University Press, 1969.

Galbraith, John S. "Economic Development in the High Commission Territories, " New Commonwealth, Vol. 33 (January 7, 1957).

Great Britain. The Development of the Swaziland Economy. London: H. M. S. O. , 1965.

Green, L. P. , and T. J. D. Fair. Development in Africa. Johannesburg: Witwatersrand University Press, 1962.

Lea, John P. "Underlying Determinants of Housing Location: A Case Study from Swaziland, " Journal of Modern African Studies, 11, 2 (1973), pp. 211-225.

Leistner, G. M. E. , and P. Smit. Swaziland: Resources and Development. (Communication of the Africa Institute No. 8) Pretoria: African Institute of South Africa, 1969.

Liversage, V. Swaziland Development. 1947? Mimeographed.

Mollatt, E. B. "Swaziland's Development, " South African Mining Engineering Journal 70 (March 20, 1954): pp. 589-591.

Smit, P. "1968--Swaziland: Resources and Development, " Bulletin of the Africa Institute (Pretoria), Vol. VI,

No. 8 (September 1968): pp. 227-243.

_____. "Swaziland: Resources and Development, " Swazi-
land on the Eve of Independence.   Pretoria: Africa
Institute of South Africa, 1969, pp. 15-31.

Smith, E.   "1968--An Exercise in Rural Development Planning in Swaziland, " Journal of Administration Overseas (London), Vol. VII, No. 2 (April 1968): pp. 367-
377.

Sneesby, G. W.   "Economic Development in Swaziland, "
Geography 53 (2) (April 1968): pp. 186-189.

Swaziland, Government of.   Post Independence Development
Plan. Mbabane: Government Printer, 1969.

Finance and General Economy

Barclays Bank.   Basutoland, Bechuanaland, and Swaziland.
London: Barclays Bank D. C. O. , 1962.

Carter, W. M.   "Colonial Development Corporation's Swaziland Investment, " Swaziland Recorder, No. 7 (July-
September 1962): p. 138.

Clark, W. M.   "Swazi Economy, " South Africa Financial
Mail, (July 17, 1964): pp. 140-143.

"Financial and Economic Situation of Swaziland, " Report of
the Commission appointed by the Secretary of State for
Dominion Affairs, Cmd. 4114 (January 1932).

Great Britain, Government of.   Commonwealth Relations
Office. Basutoland, Bechuanaland Protectorate, and
Swaziland: Report of an Economic Survey Mission.
London: Her Majesty's Stationery Office, 1960.

Gregory, T. E.   Ernest Oppenheimer and the Economic Development of Southern Africa. Cape Town: Oxford
University Press, 1962.

Howick, Lord.   "The Emergence of Swaziland (Personal
Reminiscences of the Economic Advance of the Territory), " Optima (June 1962): pp. 104-109.

Leistner, G. M. E. "1968--Economic Problems and Prospect, " Bulletin of the Africa Institute (Pretoria), Vol.
VI, No. 8 (September 1968): pp. 244-259.

Manzini Indaba Society. Progress and Prosperity: How Can
They Be Endured in Swaziland? Manzini: 1962.

Miller, I. "Partnership with Private Enterprise, " Swaziland Recorder, No. 14 (March-June 1964): pp. 23-25.

"1964--Development Projects in Swaziland, World Bank Helps
Finance Economic Transformation, " African World
(London), (September 1964): pp. 4-5.

"Prosperous Hostage: In the Short Term Swaziland May Find
Itself Fairly Well Managed under the King's Men; But
What about the Longer Term?" Financial Mail (South
Africa), Vol. 24.

Spence, J. E. "The High Commission Territories with Special Reference to Swaziland, " Chapter 8 in Problems
of Smaller Territories, Burton Benedict, (ed.).   University of London, Published for the Institute of Commonwealth Studies, The Athlone Press, 1967.

Thompson, A. C. "Swaziland's First Building Society, "
Swaziland Recorder, No. 5 (January-March 1962): p.
25.

Industry: Mining

Anglo-American Corporation of South Africa Partners in Pro-
gress: The Opening of Swaziland's Railway and Iron
Ore Mine. Johannesburg: Public Relations Dept. ,
Anglo-American Corp. of South Africa, 1964.

"Coal Working in Swaziland, " Colliery Guardian, Vol. 211,
19 (November 1965): pp. 662-663.

"Developing Swaziland's Iron Ore Deposits, " Standard Bank
Review (July 1966): pp. 18-20.

Stone, G. Mining Laws of the British Empire and Foreign
Countries, Vol. 3: South Africa, Part II, Swaziland,
1923.

Thain, G. M. "Swaziland Has Scope for a Small Mines Industry," Swaziland Recorder, No. 5 (January-March
1962): p. 21.

See also numerous references to ore deposits in Geology and
Transportation Sections of this bibliography.

Industry: Other

Aldred, F. C. "Swaziland's Pulp Industry," Paper Technology, Vol. 6 (June 1965): p. 180.

Harrington, L. "Afforestation Brings Wealth to Swaziland,"
Canadian Geographical Journal, Vol. 58 (June 1959):
pp. 180-181.

Industrial Opportunities in Swaziland. Published by Swaziland
Ministry of Commerce, Industry, and Mines.

"More Electric Power in Swaziland," African World, (June
1967): p. 7.

"Pulp for Swaziland," Economist, Vol. 192 (July 11, 1959):
p. 112.

Smith, D. "Railroad Key to Many New Industries," Swaziland Recorder, No. 16 (September-December 1964):
pp. 15-19.

"Swaziland's New Forests," Times British Colonies Review,
(Spring, 1953): p. 12.

Labor

International Labour Office. Expanded Programme of Technical Assistance: Report to the Government of Swaziland on Manpower Assessment. Geneva: ILO, 1965.

_____. Expanded Programme of Technical Assistance: Re-
port to the Government of Swaziland on the Development of Vocational Training. Geneva: ILO, 1966.

"Labour Problems of Basutoland, Bechuanaland, and Swaziland," International Labour Review, (March 1934).

Moses, Macdonald. "Havelock Mine Report: Coming Clash
    in Swaziland, " Newscheck (Johannesburg) (October 11,
    1963): p. 24.

Transport: Railway

Best, Alan C. G. The Swaziland Railway: A Study in Poli-
    tico-Economic Geography. East Lansing, Michigan:
    Michigan State University, African Studies Center, 1966.

"Commonwealth Railway Development, " Railway Gazette,
    Vol. 120, 17 (January 1964): pp. 78-79.

Hawkins, L. A. W. "Excellent Progress with Railway, "
    Swaziland Recorder, No. 13 (January-March 1964):
    p. 9-13.

_____. "Important Ore Line Will Be Ready for Traffic, "
    Railway Engineering 8 (1964): pp. 26-27.

_____. "Major Bridges on the Swaziland Railway, " Rail-
    way Gazette, Vol. 119 (11 October 1963): pp. 402-405.

_____. "Rich Iron Ore Deposits Give Swaziland Its Long-
    Awaited Railroad, " Optima, 14, No. 2 (June, 1964):
    pp. 84-87.

Herd, Norman. "Green Lights on the Swaziland Railroad, "
    Industrial Review of Africa, 12, No. 10 (May, 1961):
    p. 8.

_____. "Track Beds Being Prepared, " Swaziland Re-
    corder, No. 12 (September-December 1964): pp. 11-15.

Kruger, C. M. "Contract to Supply Rails, " Swaziland Re-
    corder, No. 6 (March-June 1962): p. 27.

Reilly, T. E. "Swaziland's Mine Railway Project, " South
    African Mining Engineering Journal 72 (September
    1961): pp. 685-687.

"Swaziland Railway Progress, " Railway Gazette, Vol. 120,
    6 (March 1964): pp. 203-205.

Thain, G. M. "Swaziland Railroad, " Swaziland Recorder,
    No. 2 (March-June 1961): p. 13.

Thompson, A. C. "Railway Comes to Swaziland," Swaziland Recorder, No. 3 (July-September 1961): pp. 8-9.

_____. "Tracking the Railroad," Swaziland Recorder, No. 5 (January-March 1962): p. 19.

Warden, W. "New Ore Line," Railway Engineering 8 (November-December 1964): pp. 23-57.

Whittington, G. "The Swaziland Railway," Tijdschrift voor economische en sociale geografie, Vol. 57, No. 2 (March-April 1966): pp. 68-73.

Transport: Other

Hawkins, L. A. W. "Swaziland and Its Ocean Outlet," African Roads 21, No. 4 (April 1964): pp. 12-13.

Varcoe, J. R. "The Development of Roads in Swaziland," Road International, No. 55 (December 1964): pp. 22-27.

APPENDIX A

A Chronology of Some Important Dates for Swaziland
(Adapted in Part from J. S. Matsebula's
A History of Swaziland.)

1550   The Bembo-Nguni settle below Lubombo.

1750   Ngwane III enters Southern Swaziland.

1780   Death of Ngwane III.

1815   Death of Ndvungunye.

1816   Sobhuza I succeeds Ndvungunye.

1836   Death of Sobhuza I.

1840   Mswati II installed.

1843   Mswati builds northern military outposts.

1846   The Swazis meet the Boers in the north.

1847   Wesleyan missionaries arrive in Swaziland.

1856   Mswati sends his impi to aid Mawewe.

1860   First personal concession granted to Coenraad Vermaak.

        Berlin Lutheran missionaries visit Mswati at Hhohho.

1866   First attempt to survey the boundary between the Transvaal and Swaziland.

1868   Death of Mswati II.

1869   Transvaal-Portuguese boundary treaty.

1871   Anglican mission work started at Ndlotane.

1872   Death of Ludvonga II.

1874   Gold discovered in the De Kaap valley.

1875   Installation of Mbandzeni.

1877   Mbandzeni gives permission to Boers to settle at Ndlotane.

1879   Swazi impi assists British troops against the Pedi.

Gold discovered at Phophonyane.

1880   The Royal Commission demarcates the Transvaal-Swaziland boundary.

1881   Convention of Pretoria signed.

Sir Evelyn Wood visits Swaziland.

1884   Convention of London.

Discovery of gold at Piggs Peak.

1886   A group of Boers at Ndlotane declare "Little Free State. "

Mbandzeni appoints Shepstone.

1887   Mbandzeni's famous address to a meeting of concessionaires at Mbekelweni.

Election of the "White Committee. "

Berlin Missionary Society sends African evangelists to start mission work in Swaziland.

1888   Mbandzeni gives Royal Charter to the "White Committee. "

Mixed commission surveys Swaziland-Portuguese boundary.

First police force set up.

Death of Sandlane Zwane.

1889   Dismissal of Shepstone and appointment of Miller as King's Adviser.

De Winton Commission appointed and arrives in Swaziland.

Provisional Government set up.

Dismissal of Miller and reappointment of Shepstone.

Death of Mbandzeni.

1890   South African General Mission arrives in Swaziland.

Provisional Government offices moved from Mbekelweni to Bremersdorp.

Appointment of Bhunu as king.

First Convention of Swaziland.

1891   High Court inquires into validity of contested concessions.

1893   Loch and Kruger meet at Colesberg.

Second Convention of Swaziland.

1894   Bhunu is installed.

Dismissal of Shepstone and appointment of Hulett.

Third Convention of Swaziland.

Longcanga deputation to England.

1895   Transvaal Volksraad approves Third Convention of Swaziland.

Britain annexes Ngwavuma area territories.

South African Republic assumes administration of Swaziland.

1896   Hut tax imposed for the first time.

1897   Telegraph office opened at Embabaan (Mbabane).

Swaziland-Portuguese boundary continued northwards.

1898   Mbhabha episode.

Bhunu's flight, and his later return and trial.

Protocol added to the third convention of Swaziland.

1899   Bhunu visits Pretoria.

Sobhuza II born.

Anglo-Boer War begins.

Death of Bhunu.

Labotsibeni becomes Regent.

1902   Bremersdorp burnt down.

Anglo-Boer War ends.

British administration in Swaziland begins.

1903   The Order-in-Council changes status of Swaziland.

1905   Lord Selborne suceeds Milner.

Administration of Swaziland separated from that of Transvaal.

Tax registers introduced.

Announcement of Partition Proclamation.

Appointment of first Resident Commissioner.

1907   Malunge deputation to England.

1908   Delimitation of the country completed.

1909   Lord Selborne's second visit to Swaziland.

1910   The formation of the Union of South Africa.

1911   The Swazi National Fund started.

1913   Prince Malunge and a group of Swazi chiefs meet Lord Selborne at Barberton.

1915   Death of Prince Malunge.

1916   Sobhuza II goes to Lovedale.

Mandanda Mtsetfwa becomes Ndvunankhulu.

1917   Lord Buxton visits Swaziland.

1918   Sobhuza II returns from Lovedale.

Asbestos discovered at Dudusi, near Bulembu.

1921   Sobhuza II installed.

European Advisory Council formed.

1922   Sobhuza II deputation to England.

1924   Sobhuza II vs. A. M. Miller case begins.

1925   Death of Labotsibeni.

1926   Privy Council decides on case Sobhuza II vs. Allister M. Miller.

1928   First South African Railway bus service introduced into Swaziland.

Havelock Mine opened.

1929   Swaziland Progressive Association is formed.

1931   Office of the High Commissioner separated from that of the Governor-General of the Union of South Africa.

Matsapha High School opened.

1933   Alan W. Pim visits Swaziland.

1938   Death of Ndlovukazi Lomawa.

Formation of a joint advisory committee to study the question of the transfer of the three High Commission Territories to the Union of South Africa.

1940   Land settlement scheme introduced.

1941   Swazi impi recruited for active service in Second World War.

1944   Lifa Fund started.

Forestry started in Swaziland.

Swazi National Treasury started.

1946   Swazi impi officially welcomed home from war.

1947   King George VI visits Swaziland.

1953   King Sobhuza II goes to London for coronation of Queen Elizabeth II of Great Britain.

1954   Tinkhundla centres established.

1956   Swazi nation petitions the Queen of England concerning land and mineral rights.

Death of Ndlovukazi Nukwase.

1959   Secretary of State replies to the Swazi petition.

1960   European Advisory Council presents memorandum to Resident Commissioner on Multiracial Legislative Council.

King Sobhuza II initiates constitutional talks.

Swaziland Progressive Party formed, first political party.

Constitutional Committee formed.

1961   Decimal coinage introduced.

Constitutional Adviser arrives in Swaziland.

1962   Railway line construction begins.

The Proposal for Swaziland Constitution released.

1963   First Constitutional Conference in London.

Strikes provoke British to send troops to Swaziland.

1964   Imbokodvo party formed.

Elections for the Legislative Council.

Official opening of Swaziland Legislative Council.

1966   Last British troops leave Swaziland.

1967   Elections for the House of Assembly.

Swaziland becomes a Protected Kingdom.

1968   Independence Constitution Conference in London.

Land Question Conference in London.

Swaziland regains her independence on September 6.

Graded tax introduced.

1969   Government launches 5-year Development Plan.

Foot and mouth disease outbreak near Eastern border.

Government implements plans for localization.

1970   Numerous economic breakthroughs in trade and development projects.

1971   First major cabinet shuffle.

Land Speculation Control Act passed by Parliament.

1972   Parliamentary elections held; Imbokodvo Party wins, but Dr. Zwane's NNLC wins three seats.

Swazis compete in the Olympic games.

The Ngwenya case prompts new Immigration and Citizenship measures.

1973   Swazi Nation given 40 per cent ownership of Havelock mine.

Courts rule against Government and Immigration Act in Ngwenya Case.

King Sobhuza declares present Constitution unsuitable and voids it.

King Sobhuza revives the emabutfo as his private armed force.

1974   Royal Constitutional Commission concludes its study for a new constitution.

A Swazi currency, the Emalangeni is introduced to replace the Rand in Swaziland.

APPENDIX B

KINGS OF SWAZILAND

*Dlamini I (died c. 1530)

Mswati I

Ngwane II

Dlamini II

Nkosi II

Mavuso I

Ludvonga I

Dlamini III

Ngwane III (died c. 1780)

Ndvungunye (died c. 1815)

Sobhuza I (died 1836)

Mswati II (1821?-1868)

Ludvonga II (died 1872)

Dlamini IV (Mbandzeni) (1855-1889)

Ngwane V (Bhunu) (1876-1899)

Sobhuza II (1899-   )

*There were Bembo-Nguni leaders who preceded Dlamini I. Their names and order of succession are in doubt, but J. S. M. Matsebula lists the following: Mkhulunkhosi, Qomizitha, Sukuta, Madlasomo, Ndlovu, Ngwekati, Mawawa, Sidwabasiluthuli, Gebase, Kunene, Nkabingwe, Madlabane, Hhili, Dulunga, Dondobala, Sihuba, Mlangeni, Msimude, Mbhoholo, Sikhulumaloyi, Langa, Samuketi, Nkomo, Khabako, and Ngwane I.

APPENDIX C

ABBREVIATIONS AND ACRONYMS

AME	African Methodist Episocopal Church
ANC	African National Congress
CDC	Colonial or Commonwealth Development Corp-oration
E	The Emalangeni, the principal Swazi monetary unit.
EAC	European Advisory Council
Legco	Legislative Council
MNC	Mbandzeni National Convention
NNLC	Ngwane National Liberatory Congress
OAU	Organization of African Unity
PAC	Pan-Africanist Congress
R	The Rand, a monetary unit
REAC	Reconstituted European Advisory Council
SACUC	Swaziland Agricultural College and University Centre
SDP	Swaziland Democratic Party
SIF	Swaziland Independent Front
SNC	Swazi National Council
SPA	Swaziland Progressive Association
SPP	Swaziland Progressive Party
UBLS	University of Botswana, Lesotho, and Swaziland
UNDP	United Nations Development Program
USA	United Swaziland Association

251